THE
ULTIMATE
JOB SEARCH

Intelligent Strategies
to Get the Right Job *FAST*

Richard H. Beatty

JIST
Works
America's Career Publisher

The Ultimate Job Search

© 2006 by Richard H. Beatty

Published by JIST Works, an imprint of JIST Publishing, Inc.
8902 Otis Avenue
Indianapolis, IN 46216-1033
Phone: 1-800-648-JIST   Fax: 1-800-JIST-FAX   E-mail: info@jist.com

Visit our Web site at **www.jist.com** for information on JIST, free job search tips, book chapters, and ordering instructions for our many products! For free information on 14,000 job titles, visit **www.careeroink.com**.

See the back of this book for additional JIST titles and ordering information. Quantity discounts are available for JIST books. Have future editions of JIST books automatically delivered to you on publication through our convenient standing order program. Please call our Sales Department at 1-800-648-5478 for a free catalog and more information.

Trade Product Manager: Lori Cates Hand
Production Editor: Jill Mazurczyk
Interior Designer: designLab
Page Layout: Marie Kristine Parial-Leonardo, Toi Davis
Proofreader: Linda Quigley
Indexer: Kelly Henthorne

Printed in the United States of America
10 09 08 07 06   9 8 7 6 5 4 3 2 1

Library of Congress Cataloging-in-Publication Data

Beatty, Richard H., 1939-
    The ultimate job search : intelligent strategies to get the right job fast / Richard H. Beatty.
        p. cm.
    Includes bibliographical references and index.
    ISBN-13: 978-1-59357-324-9 (alk. paper)
    ISBN-10: 1-59357-324-3 (alk. paper)
  1. Job hunting. 2. Résumés (Employment). 3. Employment interviewing. I. Title.
    HF5382.7.B446 2006
    650.14--dc22

                        2006012461

ISBN-13: 978-1-59357-324-9

ISBN-10: 1-59357-324-3

About This Book

The world of job search has changed dramatically in recent years, and requires an entirely new approach. Through the use of automation, combined with the awesome power of the Internet, job seekers, if knowledgeable, can now find more jobs, better jobs, and find them faster and easier than ever before.

Along with this change comes new challenges, especially for those unfamiliar with the new way of doing things. Such is the case with modern-day job search. Survival and success in the job market now demand new and creative approaches to meet the competition head-on.

The Ultimate Job Search is written for the experienced and novice job seeker alike. As the title suggests, it provides the job seeker with a complete, proven plan for running an effective job search in today's ever-changing job market—a plan that takes full advantage of the latest technology and techniques for winning exciting job offers and cutting precious time off your job search.

This book goes well beyond the typical job search guide. It includes powerful, cutting-edge job search methods and helps you focus on landing a job that will yield short- and long-term career satisfaction. Also included is a fail-safe, proven formula to ensure both job and career success.

This book will show you the way to a better job and richer career—one that can be exciting, fun, and invigorating—the ultimate goal of every job seeker. And, now you can do it in record time!

About the Author

Richard H. Beatty is a leading career author and internationally known consultant with considerable hands-on experience in human resources and staffing. His 14 career books—including *The Interview Kit, The Perfect Cover Letter, The Resume Kit, The Five-Minute Interview, 175 High-Impact Resumes,* and *175 High-Impact Cover Letters*—have sold more than 1 million copies worldwide. He is the founder and Chairman of Brandywine Consulting Group, Inc., which has provided training and support to thousands of individuals, at all organizational levels, who have undergone career transition as a result of corporate downsizing. His clients have included such well-known companies as Procter & Gamble, E.I. DuPont, Scott Paper Company, Caterpillar Corporation, General Electric, Armstrong World Industries, and numerous others.

Mr. Beatty's earlier background includes experience in the executive search field, where he served as Vice President of MSL International, an executive search firm with offices throughout the world. Here he represented corporate clients in the identification, evaluation, and recruitment of key managers and executives for assignments in a wide range of occupations and industries.

Prior to his executive search career, Mr. Beatty was employed as a human resources executive with the Scott Paper Company, a Fortune 100 company, where he worked as Corporate Staff Human Resources Manager and Manager of Technical Employment. In this capacity, he was responsible for all technical hiring for the corporate staff of four operating divisions and 13 manufacturing facilities.

Acknowledgments

My thanks to the many friends, professional colleagues, and career experts who, over the years, have significantly contributed to my knowledge of the career, staffing, and job search fields. All have contributed in some small way to the writing of this book.

In particular, I would like to single out and thank Lan Spilman, former boss and Director of Staffing of Scott Paper Company, who first introduced me to the world of corporate recruiting and staffing; Ginger Moore, former boss and current Director of Staffing—Global Outsourcing for Unisys Corporation, ever willing to lend a friendly, helping hand; Michael English, human resources consultant, staffing expert, and long-time friend; Karen Livingston and Marian Gigliotti, former employees and career transition experts in their own right; Jim Lemke, recent Vice President of Staffing Systems for Wachovia Bank and world-class corporate staffing and systems expert; Dave McCarthy, former boss and Vice President of Spencer Stuart and The Hay Group; Nick Burkholder, founder and trustee of Staffing.Org, former Johnson & Johnson corporate staffing executive, and noted employment expert and author; Mark Mehler, co-author of *CareerXroads* and a world-class expert on Internet recruiting and job search; Joyce Lain Kennedy, noted syndicated career columnist and acclaimed author; and numerous others, far too numerous to mention here.

Thank you all for your help and support along the way!

Dedication

This book is dedicated to those who have made my life so rich and so very worth living—my lovely wife, Carolyn; my fine sons, Chris and Scott; and my very close friends, Janet and Jeff.

May others be as fortunate as I am and come to realize the true value and enduring nature of love and close friendship.

CONTENTS

CONTENTS

CHAPTER 1

The Ultimate Job Search: Things to Know Before You Start

If you haven't been in the job market lately, chances are you have a lot to learn. Things are changing rapidly—almost daily. What worked well as recently as three or six months ago might be obsolete today. And, what works well today is liable to change tomorrow! Moreover, competition for jobs has moved to an entirely new level. Highly competitive, computer-savvy job seekers have flocked to the Internet and flooded the market with their resumes (now in the millions).

Job search isn't local anymore; it's global. The right job posting on the right Internet site can instantly generate an avalanche of resumes cascading through an employer's electronic floodgates. Employers are reeling from the effect, struggling to efficiently process thousands upon thousands of resumes and relying on less-than-perfect digitized keyword scanning to identify the resume of that one ideal candidate.

Such is the current state of job search. This is the job market in which you must compete. You just can't jump in blindly and hope for the best. So, what can you do? How can you win in this tumultuous, ever-changing environment? There are good answers! This chapter gives an overview of the effective strategy I recommend in this book—a strategy that's been proven to reduce the time it takes to find a job by as much as 50 percent.

The Top Five Strategic Mistakes Job Seekers Make

You can no longer leave your job search to chance. You must formulate an intelligently planned and well executed strategy that uses the best methods and techniques to capitalize on the most productive job sources—those that produce the most jobs. Your strategy must maximize the use of technology to conduct searches faster and with greater efficiency than ever before. In today's technology-driven job market, you must not only be good; you must also be quick in responding to job postings. Competition demands it!

Stripped down to its basics, intelligent job search requires three things:

- Knowledge of top job sources
- Knowing how to best use them
- Using technology to speed the process

Over the years, as a career consultant and former Fortune 100 staffing executive, I have seen many job seekers unknowingly waste considerable time using the wrong employment sources and using them ineffectively. What you don't know can really hurt you! If you're uninformed, you can expend enormous energy, work really hard at your job search, and end up with little or nothing to show for your efforts. I have observed hundreds of job seekers struggling with the job search process and repeating the same strategic mistakes others have made for years, time after time.

The Biggest Mistakes Job Seekers Make

- Using the wrong sources (those that are least productive)
- Using sources ineffectively (not knowing when and how best to use them)
- Depending too much on a single source
- Failing to use technology effectively (doing things manually)
- Lack of a strategic, integrated market approach

Using the Wrong Sources

Job seekers are often one- or two-dimensional. They are familiar with only one or two employment sources, and tend to stick with what has worked for them in the past. Unfortunately, the field has changed dramatically; so the sources and methods that worked well three to five years ago are far less effective today. You need to understand which employment sources produce the most jobs *today*, and how best to capitalize on these sources.

Using Sources Ineffectively

Poor or inefficient use of employment sources can also drain away valuable time and try your patience. For example, I have witnessed job seekers spend days calling employment agencies to see whether they have an appropriate opportunity. This is a tremendous waste of time. I have nothing against employment agencies, but they account for only 12 percent of hiring results. Further, many will avoid taking your call because they already know the probabilities are extremely low that a person calling will just happen to have the right credentials for one of their current assignments.

As you will later see, there are far more efficient ways to exploit employment agencies and search firms, which will take only a fraction of your time and produce substantially greater results.

I have also seen job seekers waste huge amounts of time by mailing their resumes to company staffing departments. Studies show that this technique accounts for only about 3 percent of a company's hires, and it can also cost several hundred dollars to do so. So this is not something you will want to waste time on.

Depending Too Much on a Single Source

Over-reliance on a single job source is also a fatal mistake. For example, if you are relying on reading the classified section of your local newspaper and not using the Internet, you are missing out on 33 percent of the market. Additionally, if you are not using networking, you are missing out on another 25 percent of the market. So, in total, by sticking with only one or two newspapers, you have effectively screened yourself out of an estimated 58 percent of the job market. Not only that, but newspapers produce only about 7 percent of hiring results. At this rate, your job search could take quite some time.

Failing to Use Technology Effectively

And then there is the Internet. I have witnessed many a job seeker waste hour upon hour reading through job listing after job listing on Monster.com or CareerBuilder and other career and job board sites. Although the Internet accounts for an estimated 33 percent of all hiring, Monster and CareerBuilder combined account for only about 17 percent of all Internet hiring. Because Internet hiring accounts for about 33 percent of all hiring, this means that Monster and CareerBuilder account for only about 5.6 percent of the job market. Do you really want to spend the majority of your job search time working with two sources that account for only about 5.6 percent of the total hires? I don't think so!

As you will learn from this book, there is newer technology today (for example, job aggregators) that allow you to use only three sites to search practically the entire Internet (including Monster and CareerBuilder), with more than 16 million job listings, and bring back only those jobs that meet your job criteria. This process, which I tentatively refer to as "Quick Search" (see figure 1.1), is fully automated and costs nothing to use.

> **Note:** To find out more about my recommended strategy for using the Internet and the "Quick Search" process to find a job, see chapter 5, "Internet Job Search."

Lack of a Strategic Plan

A serious mistake made by many job seekers is to approach the job search process in a piecemeal manner, without having a well-thought-out plan and sticking to it. In such cases, they jump from job source to job source on a scattershot basis, without giving much thought to putting together an integrated, step-by-step plan designed to capitalize on the most productive employment sources and optimize use of their time to produce the greatest results in the shortest possible time frame.

When your search is poorly planned, the time it takes to find a job can easily be doubled or tripled, causing considerable frustration and loss of confidence in your marketability. More importantly, it can severely limit your job choices and compel you to accept the first offer that comes along, despite the fact that the position falls considerably short of your ideal criteria.

This book presents an effective job search strategy. It is, of itself, a proven, logical, step-by-step job search process designed to cut considerable time off your job search and greatly increase the odds of being able to choose from multiple career options at the end of the process. By following each chapter in sequence, you will automatically be putting in place a well-thought-out, integrated strategy designed to help you reach your job search goals quickly and efficiently.

At the center of effective job search strategy is knowing which employment sources to use, when to use them, and how best to capitalize on them. This book answers these questions. Lack of such knowledge can waste considerable time and cause much stress and heartburn in the process. So, what is the answer? How do you know what sources to use and how best to use them? Read on!

The Top Job Sources

Intelligent job search starts with knowing which employment sources work best and produce the most jobs. Knowing this can save you considerable time and help you find more job opportunities sooner.

Table 1.1 ranks the most productive job sources in order of their effectiveness. The percentages shown in this summary are based on a comparison of the results of several well-known studies used to measure employment source effectiveness. Many of these studies are specifically referenced throughout the book.

Table 1.1: Top Job Sources

Rank	Source	Percent of Jobs
1	Internet	33
2	Networking/employee referral	25
3	Search firms/employment agencies	12
4	Classified ads	7
5	Direct mail/targeted mailing	3
	All other*	20
Total:		**100**

*Includes a wide variety of sources, such as college recruiting, job fairs, walk-ins, billboard ads, direct mailing (to candidates), direct sourcing, and so on.

Take a moment to briefly study the top job source summary in table 1.1. As you can see from the data, in recent years the Internet has advanced significantly as a source of jobs and now accounts for approximately 33 percent of all jobs found. Not surprisingly, networking/employee referral continues to be a major factor, and is now believed to account for about 25 percent of all hiring. Search firms and employment agencies, on the other hand, rank fourth and produce about 10 percent of job placements. And finally, newspaper classified ads are thought to account for about 7 percent of hiring, with direct resume mailing resulting in only about 3 percent of hires.

You will note that the "all other" category, although producing approximately 20 percent of the jobs, is greatly fractured and spread among a number of different sources. So it is difficult, and probably not very efficient or cost-effective, to attempt to build a job search strategy focused on this "all other" category. My recommendation is—forget it!

Now, step back from this data for a moment and take a broader, strategic look. From a strategy standpoint, what does this data tell you about job search efficiency? Which sources do you need to use, and where do you need to be spending your time? I think the evidence speaks for itself.

Using the Right Sources the Right Way

Hopefully, by now, I have made my point. If you are intent on running an efficient and cost-effective job search, you need to focus on the right employment sources, but you also need to use these sources in the most efficient way.

In this chapter, I have already helped you to identify the most productive employment sources. Table 1.1 shows what they are. Now, the next objective is to learn how to effectively use these sources so that you don't waste time but still get the full benefit from what each has to offer.

As you will learn from this book, with the aid of technology, you will be able to optimize your time and simultaneously use most of these sources quite efficiently and effectively. The "Quick Search" process shown in figure 1.1 is just one example. As you will find, there are many more ways to exploit these top job sources, save considerable time, and greatly increase the number of career opportunities and job offers made available to you.

As you review the chapter titles in this book, you will find that I have dedicated a full chapter to each of the "Five Top Employment Sources." Each chapter doesn't just contain a description of the job source, but also provides specific "how-to" directions and advice that will fully equip you to effectively exploit its potential to generate jobs. I have also included comprehensive advice on how to use the right combination of employment source and technology to save you considerable time and multiply your job search results.

Quick Search

(More Than 16 Million Job Listings)

Automated Search of
More Than 16 Million Job Listings

Search Category	Job Listings
"Big Three" Job Boards	4.6+ million jobs
• Monster	
• CareerBuilder	
• Yahoo! HotJobs	
Internet Job Aggregators	9.4 million jobs
• Indeed	
• Simply Hired	
• Jobster	
Internet Classifieds Search	2.4 million jobs
• Adicio	
Total Job Listings	**16.4** million jobs

Figure 1.1: The "Quick Search" process.

You also will note that there is a logical flow to the sequence in which these chapters are presented. The book is basically presented as a step-by-step process, covering the full job search process—from defining your ultimate job, to preparing a resume, to using the "Five Top Job Sources," to developing strategies for winning the interview, to effective negotiation strategies and techniques, through making sure you accept the "right" job—the one that is best for you and will ensure both career success and personal happiness. This book provides all of the key steps and requisite "how-to" advice needed to implement a highly organized, efficient, and results-focused job search campaign.

The Ultimate Job Search

This book will provide you with all of the steps and know-how needed to conduct the "ultimate job search" and land your ideal job. It is based on proven, time-tested methods and techniques that have worked successfully for literally thousands of corporate job seekers who have passed though my company's career transition programs over the years. Moreover, we have fully adapted the latest technology to greatly speed the process and generate a much greater number of job opportunities from which you can choose.

By starting with a huge critical mass of job opportunities, and using sound methods and technology, the process described in this book will help you find more jobs, better and faster, than ever before.

Chapter Summary

The biggest mistakes to avoid when conducting an efficient job search are

- Using the wrong (least productive) job sources
- Using job sources ineffectively
- Relying too much on a single job source
- Failing to use technology to save time and effort
- Lack of a well-planned, integrated job-search strategy

The keys to conducting the Ultimate Job Search are

- Focusing on the most productive job sources
- Knowing how to capitalize on each job source
- Using the right combination of sources
- Effectively using technology to significantly cut job search time and produce more job opportunities faster
- Having a well-planned, integrated job search strategy that keeps you focused and efficient

This book shows you the most productive job sources and how to effectively exploit each to its fullest. Following each chapter in sequence will enable you to plan and execute a highly effective, integrated job search strategy that thousands of job seekers have successfully used to find better jobs faster.

CHAPTER 2

The Ultimate Job: Will You Know It When You See It?

Would you know the ultimate job if you saw it? How would you know it? What criteria could you use to measure it? What factors should influence and guide your decision? How do you know whether you would be happy in that job?

Is your ultimate job a position with stimulating and varied assignments, or one with lots of repetition and a predictable work schedule? Is it one requiring continuous action with little letup, or is it one that allows you to sit back and really think things through? Is it a job with a boss who hands you the reins, or one who provides detailed instructions and keeps a close eye? Is it a position requiring work with a close-knit team, or working alone to solve complex problems using your creativity and cerebral skills? Is it a job that fully utilizes your expressiveness and verbal skills, or one that capitalizes on your exceptional arithmetic competency?

Just what is it that makes a job exciting and rewarding for you? What would it take to make you feel you can't wait to get to the office in the morning? What will you need to make it difficult to leave at day's end? What is truly the ultimate job for you, and how will you know it when you see it? Do you really know, or are you just going by "gut feel"?

Recent studies suggest that many job seekers have never really thought their way through these basic questions. For example, an October 2005 survey of more than 1,000 U.S. workers, conducted by Yahoo! HotJobs, reported that 40 percent were dissatisfied and planning to make a career move in the next 12 months. A CareerBuilder survey of 1,900 workers, conducted two years earlier, found identical results. So, it appears that many people make employment decisions that prove less than satisfactory, and sooner or later feel a need to move on.

But, will they repeat the same mistake? What have they learned, and what will they do differently? Do they really understand what will make them happy, or will they once again join the 40 percent of the population who are discontent and unhappy with their work lives?

This chapter is intended to assist those of you who want meaningful answers to these questions. You will come away with a better understanding of yourself as well as the job- and work-related characteristics that are so important to both your success and your happiness. It does not offer "pie in the sky" solutions, a bunch of meaningless and abstract career concepts, or half-baked theories on career planning. Instead, it is well grounded in some practical, fundamental self-analysis, based on your own real-life experiences. I think you will find the results insightful and meaningful, and you will come away with a much clearer understanding of the type of job and work environment that are so important to your success and overall feelings of well-being.

For the remaining 60 percent of the population, who already have the answers, let me suggest that you skip this chapter and move on to the next. You are among the lucky ones who have a clear understanding of yourself and what is needed to ensure your success and career satisfaction. So, if you fit this fortunate category, please feel free to move on.

A New Beginning

You should view the start of a new job search as a beginning, the opening of a new door in the next chapter of your life. It offers you one of those rare lifetime opportunities to put a number of things right in your life. It offers you the chance to find employment that is professionally rewarding and personally satisfying, a work environment in which you will flourish and find a sense of peace and contentment.

Job seekers too often plunge headlong into a new job search full of positive anticipation but give little or no thought to their end goal or objective. As a result, three to six months into the new assignment they realize the job is not what they had expected, and begin to entertain thoughts of moving on.

Why not take the time to get it right, right from the beginning? Why not take the time to understand the fundamentals, the basic building blocks of good career planning? With a little work and practical introspection, you can get a much clearer vision and better understanding of the factors that are essential to job success and career satisfaction. Knowing these parameters, and how to measure them, can provide you with a powerful tool that gives you a sense of control over your destiny, and a higher level of confidence in your next job and career choice.

The following practical assessment exercises will help you get a handle on the "ultimate job" and how to know it when you see it. They will provide you with good insight on the various factors that influence job satisfaction and, specifically, how these apply to you. These exercises examine work from the standpoint of the work itself as well as the environment in which that work is performed. If you work at it, you will come away from these exercises with a far better understanding of yourself as well as the type of work and work environment you need in order to feel stimulated, motivated, and excited.

This should give you what you need to make sure the next job you land will be one that is both personally rewarding and personally satisfying.

The "Critical Three"

In 1978, William Crockett of National Training Laboratories developed a concept known as "Managing the Critical Three." This has proven an invaluable, easy-to-understand tool for job seekers to use in ferreting out the components of a job that are important to successful performance and satisfaction.

According to Crockett, all jobs can be divided into three core parts, known as the *Critical Three*. These core parts are

- Task management
- Self-management
- Interpersonal relationships

Each of these core job parts, with a little guidance, can be described in terms of identifiable activities as well as attributes. And all three of these job parts are interdependent (dependent on one another) because of the way in which work is actually performed in the job environment.

Thus, in order for you to construct your own self-profile and measure how well it aligns (or doesn't align) with a given job opportunity, you must first understand not only the *job tasks* you will need to perform, but also the *organizational climate,* or work environment, in which you will need to perform this work as well.

The entire process, however, must start with understanding yourself. It is this self-profile that will enable you to make an informed decision about a specific job opportunity based on the factors that are important to your own personal success.

In this and the following sections of this chapter, you will be guided through a series of exercises that will help you learn important things about yourself. Certain of these things you will already understand, others will come into clearer focus, and a few will be completely new discoveries.

As a supplement to these exercises, you are encouraged to make use of an additional resource. David Kiersey and Marilyn Bates' book, *Please Understand Me* (Promethean Books, 1978), provides a comprehensive but easily understood explanation of personality types, career choices, relationship patterns, and thinking styles based on the widely used and highly respected Myers-Briggs Type Indicator (MBTI). A particularly helpful part of this book is a version of the MBTI that you can complete and score on your own prior to reading the rest of the book.

Developing Your "Critical Three" Profile (Exercises 1, 2, and 3)

Begin this exercise by taking three sheets of clean paper. Label each sheet of paper separately as follows:

- **Sheet 1:** Job-Task Preferences
- **Sheet 2:** Self-Management Preferences
- **Sheet 3:** Interpersonal Relationship Preferences

As you complete Exercises 1, 2, and 3 on the next three pages, record the words you have selected, while doing each exercise, on the sheet of paper with the same heading.

As you complete these three exercises, it is very important to remember that there aren't any "right" or "wrong" answers. As you read down through the pairings in each list, therefore, be as spontaneous as possible. Choose the first word or phrase that "jumps out" as your true preference.

When completing these exercises, do not overanalyze or overevaluate. It would also be wise to adhere to that old adage, "To thine own self be true." These exercises are intended to help you, not anyone else. So, you will want to be completely candid and honest with your responses, being certain that you end up with an accurate profile that will help you to make an informed and intelligent employment decision.

Once you have completed the three excises and recorded the results on the sheets of paper you have prepared for this purpose, take a look at the list of preferences you have developed. Note, in particular, any similarities or recurring themes that appear in more than one of these lists. To make these stand out, you can use a highlighter to mark these predominant themes. In doing so, you will begin to see the early identification of some "personal preference patterns" for the types of work and work environments that you find motivational or satisfying.

As you will see later in this chapter, the results of these three exercises will be incorporated into an "ultimate job profile," which will help you better understand and measure the suitability of various employment opportunities throughout the course of your job search.

But, before you get too far ahead of yourself, you need to collect some more data about yourself so that you can complete the overall picture and better understand and measure the factors that are most important to your job and career happiness.

Exercise 1: Job Task Preferences

Directions: This a "forced-choice comparison." Circle only one item from each pair that best represents your preference. Don't overanalyze; circle the first item that "jumps out" as what you prefer. Then record the words you have circled on the sheet you have labeled as "Sheet 1—Job Task Preferences."

Statement	Choices (Circle One Preference)		
I prefer to work with	information	hands-on problem solving	helping people
I prefer	analyzing data to make decisions	using my instincts to solve problems	
I prefer working with	detail	general trends	
I prefer dealing with	today's challenges	long-term issues	
I prefer	complex tasks	simple tasks	
I prefer	predictable work	work full of surprises	
I prefer to	rely on procedures and precedents	break new ground	
I prefer to	maintain tradition	implement change	
I prefer to	improve what exists	search for new opportunities	
I prefer to	play a supporting role	be at the point of action	

Exercise 2: Self-Management Preferences

Directions: This a "forced-choice comparison." Circle only one item from each pair that best represents your preference. Don't overanalyze; circle the first item that "jumps out" as what you prefer. Then record the words you have circled on the sheet you have labeled as "Sheet 2—Self-Management Preferences."

Statement	Choices (Circle One Preference)	
I prefer to	work in privacy	interact with others
I prefer to	plan out my day	respond to a variety of unscheduled requests
I prefer to	exercise independent judgment when making decisions	rely on policies and procedures when making decisions
I prefer to be	an individual contributor	a member of a team
I prefer to	receive personal recognition	let the achievement speak for itself

I prefer to draw energy from	my work	relationships with those around me
I prefer to	lead	follow
I prefer to learn from	doing	reading; observing
I prefer to be known for	my knowledge	my interpersonal skills
I prefer to	do it myself	enable others to do it

Exercise 3: Interpersonal Relationship Preferences

Directions: This a "forced-choice comparison." Circle only one item from each pair that best represents your preference. Don't overanalyze; circle the first item that "jumps out" as what you prefer. Then record the words you have circled on the sheet you have labeled as "Sheet 3—Interpersonal Relationship Preferences."

Statement	Choices (Circle One Preference)	
I prefer to	deal with conflict	keep the peace
I prefer to work	one on one	in a group with people
I prefer to	be actively involved with conflict resolution	let others work it out
I prefer to	use authority to get things done	negotiate to reach a compromise solution
I prefer to be seen as	a boss	a friend
When in a group, I prefer to	focus on the task	focus on the interaction of people
When in a group, I prefer to be	the idea person	the director; the arbitrator
I prefer personal differences	to be resolved	I can live with the differences
I prefer to	talk to others	listen to others
I prefer to connect with others	through ideas	through feelings

Refining Your Ultimate Job Profile

Up to this point, you have been using William Crockett's concept of the "Critical Three" as the basis for developing your ideal job profile. This approach, although certainly useful, has a tendency to focus more on the present and future dimensions of your job-task preferences, self-management preferences, and interpersonal relationship preferences. An equally important dimension to consider, however, is your past experience. What has your past experience told you about yourself and these preferences?

Past experiences have, in many ways, shaped who you are today and helped you to formulate your likes, dislikes, and preferences. There is a lot you can learn about yourself from examining these past experiences. Doing so will help you gain further insight into what it is, from both a job and work-environment standpoint, that impacts or drives your motivation and enjoyment.

This section of the chapter, therefore, will focus your attention on past experience to learn more about yourself, and to provide the basis for further refinement of your ultimate job profile. Specifically, you will be using the following exercises to accomplish this:

- Motivational Mapping (exercises 4 and 5)
- Career Mapping (exercise 6)
- Best Boss Profiling (exercise 7)

As you complete each of these exercises, you will want to review the resulting information, not only for its own unique value, but also as an important component of the ultimate job profile you are beginning to develop. It is one more piece of the important picture you have begun painting.

Motivational Mapping: What Factors Affect Your Work Motivation?

In the following two exercises (exercises 4 and 5), you will take a walk back through your past work experience to discover certain factors that have contributed to your level of satisfaction or dissatisfaction (that is, your motivational level) throughout your working lifetime. When completing these exercises, you can think back on different types of jobs you have held—full-time, part-time, or volunteer work—any work experience you feel would be helpful to you in making your next career choice.

You will be completing two separate exercises to help you define and clarify those jobs and work-environment factors that most influence your motivation and, therefore, your levels of satisfaction. In exercise 4, you will be examining the factors and circumstances that influence your satisfaction levels with regard to your need for impact, influence, and control. Exercise 5 then explores job satisfaction from the standpoint of the factors and circumstances that cause you to feel a sense of "belonging" or "fitting in." Both of these dimensions are important contributors to your feelings of motivation and job satisfaction.

Personal Impact (Exercise 4)

When completing exercise 4, think about the degree of *individual impact* you felt that you had on the events around you while you were in the job. As you rate your level of satisfaction for each position you have held, consider such factors as

- your ability to exercise personal initiative
- your ability to be self-reliant
- your ability to make decisions
- your ability to influence and impact others
- your ability to influence and/or control events

Exercise 4: Motivational Mapping—"My Impact"

Directions: Starting with your most recent job, list each job you have held, going back in time. Then, for each of these positions, put an X in the box that best describes your feelings of personal impact (your feelings of influence and control) while in the job. How satisfied were you with your sense of influence and control?

Job and Company	Feelings of Personal Impact (Influence and Control)				
	Very Dissatisfied	Somewhat Dissatisfied	Neutral	Somewhat Satisfied	Very Satisfied

Once you have completed this exercise, put a double + sign next to the jobs that you rated as very satisfying and a single + sign next to those you rated as somewhat satisfying. Then put a double – sign next to the positions you rated as very dissatisfying and a single – sign next to the positions you rated as somewhat dissatisfying.

Now, step back and look at the positions you marked with the double + sign and then ask yourself the following questions:

- What did these positions have in common?
- What caused me to feel such a high level of satisfaction?
- What was present that caused me to feel that way?

- Which factors *most* influenced my positive feelings?
- Which factors *somewhat* contributed to my feelings?

Make sure to take some notes as you go along. Try to be as specific as possible, and avoid broad generalities.

When answering these questions regarding your ability to have personal impact, you may want to consider such factors as the ones in the following table. These categories are intended only to stimulate your thinking. There are many other factors to consider, so don't be limited by this list. Try to think at a deeper level to get at the actual causes of your high satisfaction level.

Personal Impact (Categories to Consider)

Job content
Work environment
Freedom to act
Your boss's management style
Intellectual challenge
Etc., etc., etc.

Often, it is quite useful to look at the opposite end of the spectrum—those positions you rated as very dissatisfying (the ones you have marked with the double –). This will help you to better understand what you need to avoid in that next job opportunity.

To examine this "very dissatisfying" category, try answering the following questions, and take some notes while you are in the process.

- What did these positions have in common?
- What caused me to feel so dissatisfied?
- What factors *most* influenced my feelings of dissatisfaction?
- What factors *somewhat* influenced my negative feelings?

Now go back and further refine and fine-tune your original list of those key factors that have most influenced and accounted for your positive feelings. What new things have you learned about yourself? What type of job and work environment do you need in order to feel satisfied that you have meaningful impact, influence, and control? What factors need to be present to ensure a high level of satisfaction and contentment? Now, divide these factors into the "Critical Three" (job task preference, self-management, and interpersonal relationship preference) and add them to the three sheets you prepared earlier, under the same three headings. On each of these sheets, list these new factors under the new subheading of *Motivational Factors—Personal Impact*.

Fitting In (Exercise 5)

When completing exercise 5, you will look at your sense of "belonging" or "fitting in." This exercise will help you to identify and understand the factors that are important to making you feel "comfortable" and "at home" in a given job and work environment.

Therefore, when rating your level of satisfaction or dissatisfaction, you will want to consider such factors as these:

- your general level of comfort
- your feelings of acceptance by the group
- the degree to which you felt you could be open with others
- your ability to resolve conflict constructively
- the degree to which you felt others listened to your opinions
- the degree to which others showed they cared about you

Exercise 5: Motivational Mapping—"Fitting In"

Directions: Starting with your most recent job, list each job you have held, going back in time. Then, for each of these positions, put an X in the box that best describes how comfortable you felt—how well you felt you "belonged" or "fit in." How satisfied were you with your sense of belonging or fitting in?

Job and Company	Feelings of Personal Impact (Influence and Control)				
	Very Dissatisfied	Somewhat Dissatisfied	Neutral	Somewhat Satisfied	Very Satisfied

Once you have completed this exercise, place a double + sign next to the positions you rated as very satisfying, and a single + sign next to those you rated as somewhat satisfying. Then mark the positions you have rated as very dissatisfying with a double – sign, and those you rated somewhat dissatisfying with a single –.

Now, step back and look at the positions you marked with the double + sign and ask yourself the following questions:

- What did these positions have in common?
- What caused me to feel such a high level of satisfaction?
- What was present that caused me to feel that way?
- Which factors *most* influenced my positive feelings?
- Which factors *somewhat* contributed to my feelings?

Make sure to take some notes as you go along. Try to be as specific as possible, and avoid broad generalities.

When answering these questions, consider such factors as the ones in the following table. These categories are intended only to stimulate your thinking. There are many other factors to consider, so don't be limited by this list. Try to think at a deeper level to get at the actual causes of your high satisfaction level.

Belonging/Fitting In (Categories to Consider)

Job content
Work environment
Freedom to act
Your boss's management style
Intellectual challenge
Etc., etc., etc.

As previously stated, it is often quite useful to look at the opposite end of the spectrum—the positions you rated as very dissatisfying (the ones you marked with the double −). This will help you to better understand what you need to avoid in that next job opportunity.

To examine this "very dissatisfying" category, try answering the following questions, and take some notes while you are in the process.

- What did these positions have in common?
- What caused me to feel so dissatisfied?
- What factors *most* influenced my feelings of dissatisfaction?
- What factors *somewhat* influenced my negative feelings?

Now go back and further refine and fine-tune your original list of the key factors that have most influenced and accounted for your positive feelings. Again, what new things have you learned about yourself? What type of job and work environment do you need in order to feel satisfied that you "belong" and "fit in"? What factors need to be present to ensure a high level of satisfaction and contentment? Now, divide these factors into the "Critical Three" (job task preference, self-management, and interpersonal relationship preference) and add them to the three sheets you prepared earlier, under the same three headings. On each of these sheets, list these new factors under the new subheading of *Motivational Factors—Sense of Belonging/Fitting In.*

Career Mapping (Exercise 6)

You have just used your past experience and the motivational mapping exercise to discover more about what motivates and demotivates you. You will now use a *career-mapping* exercise as the basis for gaining some insight about the kind of work environments that have allowed you to be more productive (in other words, to get the most from your skills and abilities).

From this exercise, you will discover some additional things about yourself that should prove helpful in determining the kind of work environment in which you best fit, and in which your career will flourish.

Exercise 6 is the career-mapping exercise. Once again, starting with your most recent job, list the various jobs you have held, going back in time. Now let your mind wander back to each of the positions you have held with each past employer. Then, in the columns provided, list the five "Best Aspects" and the five "Worst Aspects" of each of these positions.

Exercise 6: Career Mapping—Your Ideal Work Environment		
Job and Company	**Best Aspects**	**Worst Aspects**

(continued)

(continued)

Job and Company	Best Aspects	Worst Aspects

As you complete this exercise, think about the quality of your experience in the various work settings or environments in which you have worked. Think about how you felt and how you responded in that environment. How conducive was this environment to your overall motivation and productivity? What were the best aspects of the work culture, and what were the worst aspects? Some general aspects of the work environment to consider include those in the following table.

Work Environment (Categories to Consider)

Management practices (Close supervision? Broad direction? Fair treatment? Professional recognition? Personal recognition? Performance feedback?)

Freedom to act (Carte blanche? Direction only? Broad guidelines? Well-defined policies and procedures? Specific instructions?)

Quality of work environment (Was it fun? Serious? Formal? Informal? Highly structured? Unstructured? Clear goals? Right tools? Appropriate resources? Good support systems?)

Organizational culture (Good values and beliefs? Desired/rewarded behaviors? Goal- and results-focused? Employee focused? Caring? Learning/development focused?)

Physical environment (Physical surroundings? Bright? Pleasant? Well equipped? Well stocked? Efficient workstation layout?)

Social Environment (Relationship between co-workers? Open? Friendly? Supportive?)

As with motivational mapping, draw on whatever work experiences you have had (for example, full-time, part-time, volunteer activities) that will be helpful in gaining a clearer understanding of the organizational characteristics that are important to your personal job satisfaction and productivity.

Once you have completed this activity, scan down the lists you developed, looking for patterns. With a highlighter, mark any reoccurring themes (positive and negative) that you observe. Note the frequency with which these common themes occur.

Themes that are frequently repeated suggest that they have some relevance or importance to you as compared to other themes that appear only once or twice.

By observing the frequency of theme occurrence, a definite pattern is likely to emerge that can serve to provide you with a great deal of insight concerning the work environment factors that are important to your personal satisfaction and successful job performance. Compile these themes on a list called *Ideal Work Environment* and add them to your ultimate job profile.

Profiling the "Best Boss" (Exercise 7)

The final exercise in developing your ultimate job profile is known as Best Boss Profiling. The relationship with your boss is not only a critical factor in any job, it is also one of the most important role models you will have in your career. This is especially true when people find themselves in a management role and seek a frame of reference to shape their own managerial style. How you felt about a particular boss can provide some very helpful clues about the management traits and characteristics that are important to you for your personal success and happiness.

To get the maximum value from this exercise, take your time with it. An effective relationship with a boss is more than "good chemistry." It requires many factors, such as understanding, communications, personal coaching, training, feedback, work knowledge, similarity of thinking styles, common values and beliefs, and ability to successfully work through disagreements—just to mention a few.

Start exercise 7 by thinking about the various bosses you have had so far in your career. If this is your first effort at seeking full-time employment, think about any bosses you have had in part-time jobs and volunteer work, or coaches and community leaders with whom you have worked. Also try to envision the kind of boss you would want to work for in your first job.

Now, having thought about these bosses, identify that one "best" boss—the one you most admired and for whom you most enjoyed working. Then complete this exercise using the following instructions:

- Write a list of 10 phrases that best describe your best boss.
- What are the traits that made this person your best boss?
- Why are these traits important to you?
- How did these traits benefit you?
- How did you respond when your boss exhibited these traits?
- Why do you think you responded positively to them?

When responding to the preceding questions and recording your observations, think about the following factors:

- How that boss affected your work effort
- The way these traits affected how you managed yourself
- How these traits impacted your interpersonal skills and behavior

When you're finished with this exercise, add this list of traits to your ultimate job profile under the subheading of *Best Boss Profile*.

Exercise 7: "Best Boss" Profile
Best Boss—Descriptive Phrases and Traits

_____

_____

_____

_____

_____

_____

Importance of Traits to Me

_____

_____

_____

_____

_____

How I Responded and Why

_____

_____

_____

_____

_____

_____

Finalizing Your Ultimate Job Profile

You now have all of the important elements for finalizing your ultimate job profile. These include the following:

- Job Task Management Preferences
- Self-Management Preferences
- Interpersonal Relationship Preferences

- Motivational Factors—Personal Impact
- Motivational Factors—Belonging/Fitting In
- Ideal Work Environment
- Best Boss Traits and Characteristics

It's now a matter of pulling it together into a single, usable format that is convenient for you to continuously refer to throughout each of the stages of your job-hunting campaign. Use the following worksheet to record all of the preferences you discovered in this chapter. An example of a completed ultimate job profile is included at the end of this section for your reference.

Your Ultimate Job Profile
Job Task Management

Job Task Preferences (Exercise 1)

Prefer

-
-
-
-
-
-
-
-
-
-

Motivational Factors (Exercises 4 and 5)

Am motivated by

-
-
-
-
-
-
-
-

(continued)

(continued)

Self-Management

Self-Management Preferences (Exercise 2)

Prefer:

-
-
-
-
-
-
-
-
-
-

Motivational Factors (Exercises 4 and 5)

Am motivated by:

-
-
-
-
-
-
-
-

Interpersonal Relationship Management

Interpersonal Relationship Preferences (Exercise 3)

Prefer:

-
-
-
-
-
-
-
-

- ■
- ■

Motivational Factors (Exercises 4 and 5)

Am motivated by:

- ■
- ■
- ■
- ■
- ■
- ■
- ■
- ■

Ideal Work Environment (Exercise 6)

- ■
- ■
- ■
- ■
- ■
- ■
- ■
- ■
- ■
- ■
- ■
- ■
- ■
- ■

Best Boss Profile (Exercise 7)

- ■
- ■

(continued)

(continued)

Best Boss Profile (Exercise 7)

-
-
-
-
-
-
-
-
-
-

Here is an example of a completed profile:

Example: Ultimate Job Profile
Job Task Management

Job Task Preferences (Exercise 1)

Prefer

- To work with hands-on problem solving
- Using instincts to make decisions
- Working with general trends
- Dealing with today's challenges
- Complex tasks
- Work that is full of surprises
- To break new ground
- To implement change
- To search for new opportunities
- To be at the point of action

Motivational Factors (Exercises 4 and 5)

Am motivated by

- Work offering a variety of problems
- Work having tangible/practical value
- Opportunity for major business impact
- Freedom to make decisions and act
- Work that requires creative thinking
- Position as key decision-maker
- Opportunity for broad, strategic involvement
- Directing and motivating others

Self-Management

Self-Management Preferences (Exercise 2)

Prefer:

- To work with others
- To respond to a variety of requests
- To exercise independent judgment
- To be a member of a team
- To let achievement be the recognition
- To draw energy from others around me
- To lead
- To learn from doing
- To be known for interpersonal skills
- To enable others to do it

Motivational Factors (Exercises 4 and 5)

Am motivated by:

- Opportunity to operate under broad direction
- A boss who encourages taking reasonable risks
- High performance expectations (quality)
- Freedom to make own decisions
- Broad strategic goals vs. detailed plans
- Opportunity to be a key decision-maker
- Recognition for results/ accomplishments
- Being part of a key management team

Interpersonal Relationship Management

Interpersonal Relationship Preferences (Exercise 3)

Prefer:

- To deal with conflict
- To work with people in a group
- To be involved with conflict resolution
- To use negotiations to reach compromise solutions
- To be seen as a friend
- To focus on the interaction of people
- To be the director
- To resolve personal conflict with others
- To talk
- To connect with others through ideas

Motivational Factors (Exercises 4 and 5)

Am motivated by:

- Working in a team environment
- Open environment encouraging new ideas
- Commitment to high quality/ professionalism
- Results-focused vs. politically focused
- Organization that values people vs. things
- Boss who sees role as coach/teacher
- A nonpolitical culture
- High performance expectation (broad goals)

Ideal Work Environment (Exercise 6)

- Encourages/rewards team efforts and results
- Nonpolitical (focus on results, not connections)
- Management provides broad goals
- Top management does not micro-manage
- Opportunity for broad strategic involvement
- Freedom to make decisions and act on them
- Values creativity and new ideas
- Committed to continuous improvement
- Demands performance excellence
- Values knowledge but rewards results
- Encourages reasonable risk-taking
- Values honesty and high integrity
- Committed to internal promotion
- Keen sense of competitiveness
- Sense of pride/high morale
- Commitment to developing its employees

Best Boss Profile (Exercise 7)

- Organized, systematic, logical
- Demanding but fair
- Leads by example
- High performance expectations and standards
- Open, honest, has integrity
- Encourages creativity and new ideas
- Encouraging and supportive
- Recognizes and rewards contributions/results
- Encourages employees to stretch and grow
- Delegates—not afraid to hand you the reins
- Holds employees accountable (goals/results)
- Good sense of humor/fun to be with

Final Thoughts

I feel certain that, if you have worked hard at constructing your ultimate job profile, you have learned a great deal about yourself and the type of position you will want to find. You are no longer "flying blind," but have some clear, measurable criteria by which you can gauge each job opportunity and make the "right" decision for you.

Keep this profile handy, as a reference, while going through each step of your job campaign. Use it as you write and develop your resume, and define your job objective. Keep it handy as you enter search criteria into the search engines of job boards and career Web sites. Use it to screen job opportunities and leads as you go along. Review it carefully before going for a job interview. And, most importantly, use it as your guidepost when making that all-important employment decision, to be sure that you are selecting the "right" job for you. Your job satisfaction, happiness, and career success depend on it!

Later in this book, particularly as you look at the topics of interviewing and final job selection, it will become obvious just how valuable this "ultimate job profile" will be.

Chapter Summary

Finding the Ultimate Job is not a decision that you should leave to chance. Certain aspects of a job and work environment are absolutely essential to both job success and career happiness. Chief among these are the following:

- **Job task preferences:** the type of work you find most satisfying and motivating

- **Self-management preferences:** the nature of the work environment and how it impacts your motivation and job satisfaction

- **Interpersonal relationship preferences:** the nature of working relationships—how you prefer to work with and relate to others in the work environment

- **Personal impact:** the opportunity for you to have a sense of meaningful influence or control over decisions and how work is performed

- **Compatibility/"fitting in":** those aspects of the work environment that give you a level of comfort—a sense of belonging and "fitting in"

- **Boss profile:** the traits and characteristics of a good boss —one who motivates and stimulates you to perform at a high level

You will need a clear understanding of these job dimensions and your personal preferences if you want to be successful in selecting that Ultimate Job that will reward you with personal satisfaction, career success, and happiness.

CHAPTER 3

Resume Power: Getting the Most from Your Resume

Your resume is a main focal point for much of your job search. In many ways, the success of your job campaign is dependent on its impact and effectiveness. Writing your resume is not something you will want to leave to chance.

Whether you are e-mailing it to a hundred search firms, responding to a want ad in the *Wall Street Journal*, posting it on an Internet job board, e-mailing it to an employer, using it as a networking tool, or simply handing it to a hiring manager at the time of a job interview—your resume is the key marketing tool by which you are marketing yourself. So, it needs to be good.

A successful job search demands an outstanding resume. If your resume is boring or run-of-the-mill, it will be quickly buried in the masses, and your job candidacy will likely never see the light of day. On the other hand, if it is well designed and carefully written, your resume will immediately seize the reader's attention, stimulate interest, and present a compelling case for the employer to meet you and, later, to extend an offer of employment.

A Snowflake in a Blizzard

The need for an outstanding resume was recently driven home to me during a conversation with a close friend who has been in the executive search business for a number of years. At the time we had been discussing job search on the Internet and the importance of a good resume when attempting to compete in this environment. The following is the analogy he used as a way of visualizing the level of resume competition when using this medium:

> *Imagine you are standing outside in a blizzard, during white-out conditions, and are looking up at the sky. There are millions upon millions of wind-driven snowflakes coming down in sheets of*

white. Now, imagine these are resumes, and yours is only one of them.
This is what it is like for your resume to compete on the Internet.

To me, this was a great way to visualize the intensity of this competition, and to make a strong point about the need for a solid resume. Unfortunately, this visual is closer to reality than you might initially think! Consider the following: A few years back, when employers simply ran a single classified ad in the employment section of a single newspaper, such as the *Cleveland Plain Dealer* or the *Philadelphia Inquirer*, they might have received a hundred resumes or so. Now, posting the identical ad on an Internet job board or two, at a fraction of the cost, can easily generate several thousand resume responses. Think how this alone reduces your chances of getting that job.

The Internet allows the employer to instantly reach a huge global audience. There are no more geographical boundaries. A single ad can literally reach millions. Moreover, employers may choose to supplement their Web advertisement by simultaneously searching one or two of the huge online resume databases (some of which contain more than a million resumes), looking for "just the right candidate." Your resume is now among a cast of millions—that single snowflake in a blizzard of white.

In order to put this into more tangible perspective, consider the following. At the time of this writing, the popular Internet job board Yahoo! HotJobs boasted more than 20 million registered job seekers (most of whom had posted resumes on the site). Many of these people could be searching for the same or similar job as you. Moreover, CareerBuilder, the second largest job board, states that "millions of unique visitors" visit its Web site monthly, many of whom have posted their resumes for viewing by employers. Now, consider that, beyond Yahoo! HotJobs and CareerBuilder, there are an estimated 40,000 job and career sites on the Internet, and you begin to get some idea of the magnitude of the challenge you face.

Considering the extent of today's competition and the huge numbers involved, resume writing is not a process you can afford to leave to chance. Designing the right resume can make all the difference in the world. It will determine whether your candidacy rises to the top or sinks to the bottom of the stack.

Today's Resume—A World of Change

How long ago did you write your last resume? Was it three years ago? Five years ago? Perhaps 10 or more? If so, you are likely in for a few surprises! While you were sleeping, the world has changed! The digital world of the Internet, coupled with extensive use of "talent management software" by employers to screen resumes, has greatly changed the world of resume design. So, if it's been a while since your last resume, you might want to throw away that old, standby resume book and start anew. You have a lot of new things to learn.

Diverse Viewpoints—Who Is Right?

When it comes to resume writing, perhaps one of the more difficult challenges facing you is getting sound, professional advice on resume design from those who "really know." Who are these experts? It seems these days, everyone has an opinion on resumes. Just ask!

Couple this need for sound resume advice with the need for solid writing skills and, for some job seekers, you have a recipe for "anxiety attack." For even the best of writers, the task of writing one's own resume can be a challenge. And, for those who don't have the best writing skills, the very thought of writing a resume is enough to send chills up the spine and cause dry palms to sweat!

What should I put in it? What should I leave out? How long should it be? Should it be electronic or paper-based? How should it be worded? Should I e-mail it to the employer or send it by snail mail? These are but a few of the many questions likely rattling around in your head.

To make matters worse, there is a huge diversity of opinion out there. Just go onto the Internet and have a look. There are thousands of pages on the subject of resume writing, and almost as many views on the "right way" and the "wrong way" to do it. What to believe? Who to believe? Where to start?

This chapter provides well-researched answers to these and other questions concerning resume writing. It is based not solely on my own experience as a seasoned career consultant and former Fortune 100 staffing manager, but also on the results of a large survey of employment professionals. These observations and recommendations are further refined through individual discussions with some of America's top corporate staffing and employment managers.

Who else could be more authoritative on this topic? These human resource and staffing executives are the same professionals who screen each candidate's resume and determine who gets interviewed and who gets screened out. They certainly know the topic well. They read resumes by the thousands—and yours will be one of them!

So let's blow away the myths and the fog and see what these experts have to say.

The SHRM Survey

A few years ago, the Society for Human Resource Management (SHRM) conducted a survey of some 582 human resource and staffing professionals on the subject of resumes and cover letters. Here are some key observations from this study:

- Seventy-four percent (74%) prefer the "reverse-chronological resume" over other formats.
- Ninety-nine percent (99%) consider a "detailed job history" important to resume effectiveness.
- Ninety-one percent (91%) find a two-page resume acceptable, with some preferring it over a single-page resume.
- Sixty-two percent (62%) prefer that a resume not exceed two pages.
- Eighty-nine percent (89%) prefer that a job seeker provide a stated objective in some form.

So, this data suggests that job seekers should adhere to the following universal criteria when developing their employment resumes:

- Use a "reverse-chronological" format (which I explain later in this chapter).
- Include some form of job objective statement (the type of position you seek).
- Utilize a two-page format.
- Provide a detailed job history.

> **Note:** You can purchase a summary of the full SHRM resume and cover letter survey report directly through the Society's Web site at www.SHRM.org.

Advice from Top Corporate Staffing Executives

Although the SHRM survey is quite useful in addressing questions concerning resume style and format, it provides limited insight into resume content. In order to address the matter of content, I therefore discussed this topic with a select group of top corporate staffing executives, to see what their recommendations were on this subject.

Discussions with this group were very beneficial. Especially helpful was Virginia (Ginger) Moore, Director of Staffing—Global Outsourcing for Unisys Corporation in Blue Bell, Pennsylvania, who gave generously of her time to discuss this topic in some depth. Here are some key findings from these informal discussions.

Make It "Results" Focused Rather than "Activity" Focused

Modern resumes need to be focused on "results," not "activities." Simply providing a description of your position (functions you managed/performed, principal accountabilities, size of staff, and so on) will not suffice. Instead, today's employers want to know about your accomplishments. What problems did you tackle, and what results did you achieve? Results provide "tangible evidence" of performance. Activity statements or simple job responsibility descriptions provide no such evidence, and leave employers guessing about your ability to use your talents to make meaningful contributions.

Show Your Personal Impact

Resumes need to spell out your "personal impact." Don't simply describe yourself as a member of a team that produced a significant accomplishment. State what you personally contributed to this effort. What specific contribution did you make? What value did you personally add to this end result? Your resume needs to make this distinction. The employer is not hiring the team. They are hiring *you!*

Recommended Resume Styles

There are essentially two recommended resume styles, both of which are acceptable to the professional employment community. These are the reverse-chronological resume and the skills-based functional resume. Although it is clear that the reverse-chronological resume is preferred, there are times when the skills-based functional resume is the recommended format.

So that you can understand the difference between the reverse-chronological format and the functional format, I will begin with a brief comparison of the key components of these two formats. Additionally, I will discuss the advantages and disadvantages of both resume formats, so that you can decide which style best suits your needs. I will follow this discussion with a detailed description of the key components of each of the two resume types so that you will know how to construct one and what to include in each section.

To make the job easier, I've included a sample of both reverse-chronological and functional resumes for your reference (see figures 3.1 and 3.2). Spend a few moments looking over these two resume samples. This will help you better visualize exactly what I'm recommending. As they say, "A picture's worth a thousand words."

Comparing the Two Resume Types

A brief comparison of the two sample resumes (reverse-chronological and functional) illustrates that the key components are as follow:

Reverse-Chronological Resume	Functional Resume
Heading (name, address, etc.)	Heading (name, address, etc.)
Qualifications Summary	Qualifications Summary
Skills Profile	Skills Profile
Professional Experience (detailed job history)	Major Accomplishments
Education	Work History
	Education

As this comparison reveals, the first three sections of both resume styles are identical. They both start with a Heading, followed by Qualifications Summary, and then a Skills Profile. From this point on, however, they differ.

In the case of the reverse-chronological resume, the next component is the Professional Experience section. This is the heart of the reverse-chronological resume. As you can see from the sample resume, this section provides a detailed history of each position you've held, arranged in reverse-chronological order. This includes a brief description of principal job accountabilities, followed by a bulleted list of key results or achievements. The focus of this resume style is on jobs.

In the case of the functional resume, however, the next resume component is titled "Major Accomplishments." Unlike the reverse-chronological resume, the focus of this resume style is on functional skills rather than on specific jobs. So, as you can see from the sample resume, the resume lists four to five major skill areas each followed by a list of specific accomplishments related to the highlighted skill area. The focus of this resume is on skills, not jobs. In fact, as you will notice, the Work History section does not appear until the final page of the resume.

Linda A. Johnson

435 Boston Road
Appleton, WI 21811

LAJohn@AOL.com

Phone: (614) 877-9437
Cell: (614) 866-9087

QUALIFICATIONS SUMMARY

Seasoned Procter & Gamble lead project engineer with 8 years of experience in the successful engineering design, installation, and startup of towel and tissue paper machines. B.S. Mechanical Engineering, University of Michigan. Expert in wet-end forming equipment design. Hold 2 U.S. patents.

SKILLS PROFILE

Paper Machines	Engineering Design	Wet-End Design
Towel Machines	Tissue Machines	Transpiration Drying
Sheet Formation	Pulp & Paper	Yankee Dryers
Paper Converting	Paper Finishing	Charmin Tissue
Paper Machine Installation	Paper Machine Startup	Machine Design
Project Management	Control Systems	G.E. Motor Controls

PROFESSIONAL EXPERIENCE

PROCTER & GAMBLE   **2003 to Present**

Lead Project Engineer (2005 to Present)
Report to Engineering Project Manager. Lead team of 12 project engineers and 55 contract personnel in the engineering design, installation, and startup of a $150 million tissue paper machine and allied converting equipment at the Appleton, Wisconsin plant.

- Completed paper machine design phase in record time (delivered 2 months early).
- Modified existing forming section design, resulting in the award of 2 U.S. patents.
- Controlled project costs resulting in $2 million savings in Phase 1 of project.
- Assisted in resolving major labor dispute with contract workforce, avoiding costly project delay.
- Redesigned automated control systems application, resulting in savings of $1/4 million.
- Led engineering design and successful installation of novel transpiration dryer section on time.
- Headed cross-functional team responsible for evaluation of new paper converting equipment.
- Initiated use of new project planning software, improving planning and project cost control.
- Built and led high-performance work team, achieving high employee morale and efficiency.

Senior Project Engineer (2003 to 2005)
Reported to Lead Project Engineer. Supervised project team of 6 professionals (1 designer, 2 engineers, and 3 technicians) in the successful redesign, rebuild, and startup of the wet end of the #5 paper machine at the Winslow, Maine, plant.

- Redesigned and successfully installed wet-end section of #5 paper machine (a $25 million capital project) on time and 5% under budget ($1/4 million savings).
- Led cross-functional team (engineering professionals and operating technicians) in highly successful machine startup, achieving all production and quality benchmarks in under 6 weeks.
- Facilitated team project planning meetings using group problem-solving techniques to shorten project delivery time and contain costs.

Figure 3.1: A sample reverse-chronological resume.

Linda A. Johnson

WILSON PAPER COMPANY   **1999 to 2003**

Senior Project Engineer—Converting (2001 to 2003)
Reported to Plant Engineering Manager with responsibility for the engineering design, installation, startup, and troubleshooting of towel and tissue paper converting and finishing equipment at the Appleton, Wisconsin plant.

- Engineered and successfully installed the Prince Towel paper converting and finishing line ($18 million capital project) on time and within budget.
- Rebuilt Shop Towel bagging line with resultant savings of $1 million annually.
- Engineered and successfully installed TSI 2000 control system on #4 tissue converting line, reducing machine downtime and saving over $1/2 million in labor costs annually.
- Automated warehousing distribution system (a $32 million project), reducing warehouse labor costs by 20% ($3 million annual savings).

Project Engineer—Paper Mill (2000 to 2001)
Reported to Paper Mill Superintendent. Responsible for all engineering troubleshooting and maintenance in support of an 800 ton per day, 4-machine papermaking operation.

- Installed preventive maintenance program, with scheduled online servicing, reducing machine shutdown time by 20% ($2 million annual savings).
- Initiated predictive maintenance plan, allowing just-in-time parts replacement and reducing machine failure and non-scheduled downtime by an estimated 10%.
- Assisted Senior Project Engineer in the successful startup of the #3 paper machine.

Engineer (1999 to 2000)
Entry-level engineering position. Provided assistance to senior engineering staff in a wide range of engineering projects in papermaking and converting operations.

EDUCATION

B.S., Mechanical Engineering
University of Michigan, 1999
Dean's List Student (4 years)
Wilson Scholarship Award (3 years)

PROFESSIONAL ACHIEVEMENTS

2 United States Patents (Paper Forming Devices)

Linda A. Johnson

435 Boston Road	LAJohn@AOL.com	Phone: (614) 877-9437
Appleton, WI 21811		Cell: (614) 866-9087

QUALIFICATIONS SUMMARY

Seasoned Procter & Gamble lead project engineer with 8 years of experience in the successful engineering design, installation, and startup of towel and tissue paper machines. B.S. Mechanical Engineering, University of Michigan. Expert in wet-end forming equipment design. Hold 2 U.S. patents.

SKILLS PROFILE

Procter & Gamble	Project Management	Wet-End Design
Towel Machines	Tissue Machines	Team Building
Sheet Formation	Pulp & Paper	Yankee Dryers
Paper Converting	Paper Finishing	Charmin Tissue
Paper Machine Installation	Paper Machine Startup	Machine Design
Engineering Design	TSI Control Systems	G.E. Motor Controls

MAJOR ACCOMPLISHMENTS

Project Management—Paper Machines

- Led project team (12 engineers, 55 contractors) in the successful engineering design, installation, and startup of $150 million Beloit twin-wire forming paper machine, on time and under budget ($4 million savings).
- Managed $35 million redesign and rebuild of #4 paper machine wet end, increasing machine speed by 25% and improving quality of sheet formation ($5 million annual savings).
- Spearheaded project team that successfully replaced #3 tissue machine instrumentation and control systems, reducing annual labor costs by 22% ($2 million annual savings).
- Led cross-functional team (engineering professionals and operating technicians) in the successful startup of the new, 250 TPD #6 paper machine, beating all operating and quality objectives within 6 weeks of machine startup date.
- Built and motivated several high-performance, cross-functional work teams, providing key leadership in both engineering and operations startup environments.

Project Management—Paper Converting

- Led team of 3 engineers in the successful design, installation, and startup of a complete tissue converting and finishing line (project completed 1 month ahead of schedule and $120,000 under budget).
- Managed project team in the reengineering and rebuild of Gordon Towel converting line, increasing machine speed by 30% and reducing labor costs 15% ($1 million annual savings).
- Directed design team in the complete redesign of the Tailor Tissue converting and finishing line, completing project ahead of schedule and demonstrating potential cost-saving of about $1.3 million over initial design proposal.

Figure 3.2: A sample functional resume.

Linda A. Johnson   Page 2

Engineering Design

- Designed entire wet end of the #5 paper machine (a $30 million project), resulting in a 20% increase in machine speed and improved sheet formation. (Awarded 2 U.S. patents.)
- Redesigned the dryer and after-dryer section of the #4 paper machine, reducing steam requirements by 30% and increasing paper machine speed by greater than 10%.
- Designed the complete Wilson Towel paper converting and finishing line to include cutters, slitters, winders, and gluing and packaging operations (a $25 million project), meeting all deadlines.
- Designed full instrumentation and control system for an $18 million rebuild of the Stay-Dry Diaper line, scheduled to go online in 6 months.

Team Building

- Trained, facilitated, and led cross-functional team (engineering and operations personnel) in the successful startup of the #5 paper machine.
- Trained, developed, and led more than 6 different engineering project teams, meeting or beating all project deadlines, and with an estimated $16 million in cost savings to my employers.

WORK HISTORY

PROCTER & GAMBLE   **2003 to Present**

    Lead Project Engineer   (2005 to Present)
    Senior Project Engineer   (2003 to 2005)

WILSON PAPER COMPANY   **1999 to 2003**

    Senior Project Engineer—Converting (2001 to 2003)
    Project Engineer—Paper Mill   (2000 to 2001)
    Engineer   (1999 to 2000)

EDUCATION

B.S., Mechanical Engineering
University of Michigan, 1999
Dean's List Student (4 years)
Wilson Scholarship Award (3 years)

PROFESSIONAL ACHIEVEMENTS

2 United States Patents (Paper Forming Devices)

So the key difference, as you can see from this comparison, is that the reverse-chronological resume shows a clear connection between jobs and accomplishments, whereas the functional resume does not. Instead, the functional resume focuses on functional skill areas and related accomplishments, but deemphasizes specific jobs, which are not shown until the second page of the document.

As illustrated by the same resumes, the final section of both resume formats is Education.

Which Style Should You Pick?

Both resume formats are quite acceptable; however, as you saw from the SHRM survey, the preferred style is reverse-chronological. As you will recall, this survey showed that 74 percent of respondents prefer the reverse-chronological resume over other resume styles. So, with a few exceptions, the reverse-chronological format should clearly be your style of choice.

To be sure that you select the right format for your specific situation, however, let's take a more in-depth look at the strengths and drawbacks of each of the two styles. Let's first examine the reverse-chronological resume format.

The Reverse-Chronological Resume Format: Strengths and Drawbacks

Key characteristics of the reverse-chronological resume style, including strengths and drawbacks, are as follow:

- **Highlights companies.** Because company names are highlighted and stand out in this resume style, using this format is advantageous if you have worked for well-respected companies that are known leaders in their field.

> **Note:** Conversely, this could work to your slight disadvantage if your past employers are lesser known, have a poor reputation in the industry, or are known to lag significantly behind in the adoption of modern practices and technology.

- **Highlights job/career advancement.** Because job titles and dates are prominently displayed, it is to your advantage to use the reverse-chronological resume format if you have had good career progression. A reasonable history of promotions and advancement provides prospective employers with tangible evidence of your past productivity and value.

> **Note:** Lack of career progression and advancement is not of concern if you have worked in a technical field and have a history of solid contribution. However, you will probably not want to use this format if your job history shows a "downhill trend." This might suggest that your career has peaked and you are no longer as productive as you once were.

- **Highlights job stability.** Because employment dates and job chronology stand out, you might not want to use this style of resume if you have a spotty employment record. It will enable the employer to easily see a history of many jobs in a short time interval, or gaps in employment dates. This might raise concerns about your past performance and job stability.

> **Note:** Job stability is of much less concern if you have been working in an industry or occupation where high job turnover is commonplace. For example, high turnover or employment gaps in engineering project management, aerospace, and information technology is considered normal and would not raise undue concern.

- **Connects jobs with specific accomplishments.** The reverse-chronological resume makes a direct connection between jobs and specific accomplishments. Employers, for the most part, want to know what you accomplished in specific positions—especially in positions that are similar to their own and in the same industry. The functional resume does not make this connection.

> **Note:** You will probably not want to use the reverse-chronological resume format if you haven't worked in your target industry or occupation for quite some time. This is also true if you are making a complete career change into an entirely new occupation or industry. In both cases, you will want to use the functional format.

- **Highlights recent results.** What have you done lately? Employers like to see what significant contributions you have made recently. They are less interested in achievements from 10 and 15 years ago. The reverse-chronological resume allows the employer to make that determination.

The reverse-chronological resume is a great format to use if you can demonstrate some good achievements in recent years. However, if this is not the case, and most of your significant achievements occurred much earlier in your career, you might want to consider using the functional resume format instead.

From the discussion thus far, you probably already have a pretty good idea which format to use. However, let's now take a look at the functional resume format.

The Functional Format: Strengths and Drawbacks

Key characteristics of the functional resume format, including strengths and drawbacks, are as follows:

- **Highlights key functional skills.** The primary focus of the functional resume format is on key functional skills and their related accomplishments. This style of resume therefore allows you to highlight your strongest skill areas, drawing immediate attention to them. This can be an advantage if the skills you choose to highlight are those that are considered most critical to job success.

> **Note:** You will not want to use this resume style if your strongest skills are not relevant to your target position, or if you lack any critical skills, because it will draw attention to their obvious absence. You will also want to remember that most employers prefer the reverse-chronological resume format because they want to connect skills and accomplishments with specific jobs and industries (especially similar jobs in the same industry as their own).

- **Connects key skills with results.** This resume format does a good job of connecting key skills with specific accomplishments. In doing so, it not only draws attention to these key skills, but also provides the employer with "evidence" of your skill level and proficiency by making the direct connection between the highlighted skill and specific achievements or results. This is perhaps the strongest argument for using the functional format.

> **Note:** Again, however, the majority of employers (74%) prefer to see a detailed job history showing the direct connection between specific jobs and their related accomplishments. They especially want to know what you did in those jobs that are most like the one they have to offer. The functional format does not provide this linkage.

- **De-emphasizes spotty work history.** This style of resume is recommended if you have a spotty work history. If you have had several periods of unemployment, extended unemployment, or a recent, prolonged period of underemployment (employment in jobs that are sufficiently below your skill level), these issues are immediately evident to employers if you use the reverse-chronological resume format. In such cases, you will want to use the functional resume and first draw the employer's attention to your key skills and accomplishments before revealing your employment history.

> **Note:** Seasoned employers are sometimes suspicious when this format is used and may immediately go to the second page of the resume to check your work history.

- **De-emphasizes job stability issues.** This resume format is recommended when you have had a history of frequent job turnover. If you have had a number of positions, of short duration, in a relatively short time span, the functional format is clearly the recommended resume style. Using a reverse-chronological resume in this instance would highlight this issue and cause many employers to move on to the next resume. When using the functional format, the intent is to draw the employer's initial attention to your key skills and accomplishments, thereby generating interest, before revealing employment history.

> **Note:** As with spotty work history, seasoned employers are sometimes suspicious when the functional format is used, and therefore may immediately jump to the second page of the resume to review work history.

- **Recent results and accomplishments.** If you haven't accomplished much of substance in recent years, or your most significant accomplishments occurred much earlier in your career, you will want to go with a functional resume. Unlike the reverse-chronological resume format, the functional format allows you to position your most relevant accomplishments "front and center," on page 1 of the resume.

By now, you should have enough information about these two resume styles to make a clear choice. If for any reason you remain undecided, however, I recommend that you use the reverse-chronological resume because the majority of employers prefer this format.

The balance of this chapter provides a detailed description of each of the two resume formats, so that you will understand exactly what they require in terms of both layout and content. We will first begin with the chronological resume. So if you will be preparing a functional resume, skip this next section and move directly to the section entitled "Preparing a Functional Resume."

Preparing a Reverse-Chronological Resume

Before beginning discussion of the chronological resume, spend a minute or two to carefully review the sample resume in figure 3.1. Reviewing this resume shows that it is organized into the following major sections and sequence:

- Heading
- Qualifications Summary
- Skills Profile
- Professional Experience
- Education

The following sections explore each key resume component in detail, and in the order shown on the resume sample, so that you will understand what is required in its development.

Heading

The content of the Heading section is evident. It includes your name, address, phone numbers, and e-mail address. In addition to home telephone, the heading should also include a cell phone number, provided that you are able to take telephone calls during the day without tipping your hand to your boss or fellow employees who may be within earshot of your workstation or office. Do not include your current work phone number.

Qualifications Summary

The Qualifications Summary immediately follows the resume Heading. It provides a concise, one- or two-sentence overview of your principal job function and industry experience. It can also include one or two other major qualification highlights such as name of a prestigious school from which you graduated, unique language skills you possess, or brief statement of a major accomplishment.

A typical Qualifications Summary might read as follows:

Qualifications Summary

Accomplished senior-level financial executive with 10 years of Fortune 100 and major international consultancy experience in the chemical and petrochemical industries. Harvard MBA. Trilingual: English, French, and Spanish.

or

Qualifications Summary

Seasoned senior project engineer skilled in the design, installation, and successful start-up of paper machines in the consumer products industry. Led three major machine installations ($100+ million range) with consistent delivery on time and under budget. M.S. Mechanical Engineering, Georgia Tech.

Skills Profile

The Skills Profile, which immediately follows the Qualifications Summary, is sometimes called by other titles, such as Skills Summary, Core Skills, Core Strengths, or Core Competencies. Regardless of title, the Skills Profile is a list of key job-relevant skills or skill areas that are crucial for performing the target position. The Skills Profile is either written in narrative form or presented as a simple listing. I recommend using a list because it is much easier for the employer to quickly scan and spot keywords that are relevant to the qualifications sought. The narrative presentation is also quite acceptable and is used frequently.

When developing your Skills Profile, include important skills or skill categories that are widely recognized as core skills and competencies required for successful performance of your targeted position. Avoid listing any extraneous skills that are unrelated to the work you are seeking.

When choosing key skills for inclusion in this resume section, stick to nouns or noun phrases. For example, if you are seeking a position as a control systems engineer, you might include such nouns or noun phrases as control systems design, G.E. control systems, motor controls, computer controls, instrumentation, and so on. Or, if you're seeking a position as a business development executive, you might include such skill areas as joint ventures, channel partnerships, mergers and acquisitions, due diligence analysis, and so on. When employers perform a keyword search to screen resumes, they invariably use nouns or noun phrases as the focus of their searches. Therefore, by using these in your resume, you greatly increase the probability of a match.

> **Note:** I have provided a more comprehensive discussion of keywords, and how best to select them, later in this chapter. Read this section carefully before completing the Skills Profile section of your resume.

As you develop your Skills Profile, avoid overusing subjective self-descriptions such as "outstanding" team leader, "highly-strategic" manager, "dynamic" executive, "results-oriented" professional, "exceptional" interpersonal skills, "strong" project-management skills, and the like. These, and others like them, are subjective qualities that serve no real purpose in the modern resume. They are meaningless! In fact, corporate recruiters often read these descriptions with skepticism, wondering whether the person who walks through the door for an interview will look anything like the resume description. Experience has shown that this is usually not the case.

If you are going to include personal traits or qualities at all (and you should), make sure that they are truly relevant to the job. Ask yourself, "Are these traits and personal characteristics truly essential to performance of the job? Are these the personal qualities most employers would universally agree are essential to a high level of performance?" If not, discard them! They are of no value and simply take up precious resume space.

Moreover, avoid using such overused, hackneyed expressions as "team player," "strong leadership skills," "excellent interpersonal skills," "excellent communicator," "hardworking," and the like. Everyone uses these same old, shopworn expressions and they are now perceived as hollow and worthless.

Use your Skills Profile to showcase job-specific functional areas in which you have expertise, techniques you have mastered, tools you have used, equipment you can operate, special knowledge or skill areas in which you excel, and so on. For example, a senior project engineer working in the paper industry for a consumer products company that manufactures facial tissue, toilet tissue, and paper towels might use the Skills Profile section to list the following as hard-skill areas in which he or she is competent or excels:

Project Management	Machine Design	Paper Machines
Wet End Design	Transpiration Drying	Machine Start-Up
Control Systems	Yankee Dryers	Towels
Facial Tissue	Toilet Tissue	Capital Projects
Machine Installation	GE Controls	Paper Company
Pulp and Paper Industry	T.A.P.P.I.	Cost Control

Or an Internet marketing executive, for example, might include the following job-relevant skill and competency areas in his or her Skills Profile:

Internet Marketing	Lead Generation	Channel Partners
Online Acquisition Programs	Affiliate Management	Vendor Management
ROI Metrics	Strategic Partnerships	Business Development
Advertising	Online Media Buys	Financial Reporting
Budgeting	Cost/Benefit Analysis	Sales Channels
Market Strategy	Competitive Analysis	Account Penetration

On the other hand, a manufacturing operations or production manager might show the following hard-skill categories in his or her Skills Profile:

Process Improvement	Production Control	Inventory Control
Re-engineering	Process Re-engineering	System Improvement
Change Management	Cross Functional Teams	High-Performance Teams
Self-Directed Work Teams	Lean Manufacturing	Juran Quality Improvement
Process Optimization	Malcolm Baldridge	QS/ISO
Cycle Time Reduction	Six Sigma Quality	Production Planning
Cost Reduction	Continuous Flow Manufacturing	

> **Tip:** This example uses the term "re-engineering" as well as "process re-engineering." Because digital resume screening often tallies the number of times a particular skill area is mentioned in the resume and prioritizes resumes on this basis, such redundancy is actually beneficial. Additionally, the employer might elect to use "process re-engineering," which might eliminate the candidate who used only "re-engineering." I recommend that you use several different name variations for the same skill area so you are not automatically bypassed because you used only a single word to describe an important skill area.

By viewing these examples, you can clearly see the focus on using noun and noun phrases. These are the same kinds of keywords employers will use when searching for qualified persons to fill the positions highlighted in these examples. Note how easy it is to spot job-relevant key qualifications in the list format.

Professional Experience

The Professional Experience section of your resume is the guts of the chronological format, and is critical to the resume's impact and success as a marketing document. It is here that you either make the sale or lose out to the competition.

In this resume section you have the opportunity to showcase your major accomplishments and provide the employer with "evidence" of your skill proficiency and ability to make relevant contributions. If your resume is to be compelling and have meaningful impact, as the centerpiece of your overall job search, you will need to spend some quality time making sure that this section is exceptionally well written.

Modern interview theory is based on the concept that "the best predictor of future performance is past performance." If a job seeker has been highly productive and a strong contributor in past jobs (particularly those of a similar nature to the employer's opportunity), the likelihood is high that this behavior will continue in the future. So, employers focus heavily on this section of the resume, looking for evidence of a consistent pattern of productivity and contribution when performing this type of work.

As you can see from the sample resume, the chronological resume presents job history in reverse-chronological order. It begins with the current or most recent position and then sequentially lists each position held, going back in time, so that the last position shown on the resume is the first job you held.

While studying the sample resume, take particular note of its layout and formatting. Additionally, you will note how capital letters, bold print, bullets, and white space have been used consistently throughout the resume to create good visual separation of the various resume components, making it visually pleasing and very easy to read.

When viewing the sample resume, you will notice that the company name is in capital letters and is highlighted using bold type. Company employment dates, as illustrated, are positioned at the extreme right margin of the page and are also highlighted in bold type. Job dates, on the other hand, are positioned immediately adjacent to the job title and are enclosed in parentheses. Separation of dates, in this fashion, thereby avoids any confusion as to which dates are company employment and which dates pertain to specific jobs you've held at the same company.

Immediately following each job title is a brief job description that spells out your reporting relationship and principal job accountabilities. As shown, you can easily accomplish this in a single sentence.

Following the job description, highlighted with bullet points, is a list of approximately four to eight major accomplishments or results you've achieved. Although to some it might seem laborious, it is extremely important that you spend quality time recalling those specific accomplishments that the prospective employer will see as both meaningful and significant. This is where some extra effort on your part will have a huge payoff.

When citing key accomplishments, start each such accomplishment statement with a verb (for example, managed, directed, built, and so on) followed by a specific end result. Note how this has been done on the sample resume.

An extensive list of key verbs is provided in table 3.1 for your reference and use. When selecting a verb, pick the one that best describes exactly what you actually did. For example, did you "manage," "lead," "direct," "coordinate," or what?

Not every result can be measured quantitatively, but where it can, it is a good idea to include a quantitative measurement to convey the magnitude of the change or improvement, especially if the result represented a significant improvement. For example, note the difference in impact between the following two result statements:

- Implemented process-improvement program.

- Implemented process-improvement program that resulted in a 30% cost reduction ($2 million annual savings).

As you can see, a quantitative results statement has far greater impact on the reader than a simple results statement that excludes a quantitative dimension.

When you plan this section of your resume, make sure that you first list those accomplishments that are most significant and will have the greatest impact on the reader. Then, organize the rest of your accomplishment statements in order of descending priority based on their significance or impact. Adhere to the old adage, "Lead with your strength."

Table 3.1: Example Verbs for Your Accomplishments Statements

Accelerated	Appointed	Avoided	Chaired
Achieved	Appraised	Balanced	Championed
Acquired	Approved	Beat	Changed
Acted	Arbitrated	Began	Chose
Adapted	Arranged	Bid	Clarified
Addressed	Assembled	Blended	Classified
Administered	Assessed	Brought	Closed
Adopted	Assigned	Budgeted	Coached
Advised	Assisted	Built	Co-founded
Allocated	Attained	Calculated	Collaborated
Analyzed	Audited	Capitalized	Collected
Answered	Authored	Catalogued	Co-managed

(continued)

(continued)

Combined	Digitized	Held	Merged
Commenced	Directed	Helped	Met
Communicated	Discovered	Hired	Monitored
Compiled	Dispatched	Identified	Motivated
Completed	Doubled	Implemented	Moved
Computed	Drafted	Improved	Negotiated
Conceived	Drove	Increased	Networked
Conceptualized	Earned	Initiated	Opened
Conducted	Educated	Installed	Optimized
Confirmed	Enhanced	Instilled	Organized
Consolidated	Enlisted	Instituted	Outlined
Contracted	Entered	Instructed	Overcame
Controlled	Envisioned	Integrated	Overhauled
Converted	Established	Interpreted	Overrode
Coordinated	Evaluated	Introduced	Overruled
Counseled	Exceeded	Invented	Oversaw
Created	Executed	Investigated	Participated
Critiqued	Expanded	Invigorated	Partnered
Crystallized	Facilitated	Issued	Penetrated
Customized	Focused	Joined	Performed
Defined	Formed	Jump-started	Piloted
Delegated	Formulated	Laid	Planned
Delineated	Founded	Launched	Positioned
Delivered	Functioned	Led	Predicted
Demonstrated	Gained	Leveraged	Prepared
Deployed	Generated	Litigated	Presented
Designed	Grew	Lowered	Prioritized
Determined	Guided	Maintained	Processed
Developed	Halted	Managed	Produced
Devised	Handled	Marketed	Programmed
Diagnosed	Headed	Mentored	Projected

Promoted	Rehabilitated	Scheduled	Supervised
Proved	Renegotiated	Screened	Supported
Provided	Replaced	Secured	Surpassed
Published	Repositioned	Selected	Systematized
Raised	Represented	Served	Tamed
Realized	Researched	Shaped	Teamed
Reallocated	Resolved	Shortened	Took
Received	Restored	Simplified	Trained
Recommended	Restructured	Sold	Transformed
Recovered	Retained	Spearheaded	Transitioned
Recruited	Reversed	Sponsored	Tripled
Redesigned	Reviewed	Stabilized	Updated
Reduced	Revised	Staffed	Utilized
Reengineered	Revisited	Started	Validated
Reevaluated	Revitalized	Streamlined	Won
Reformulated	Salvaged	Strengthened	Wrote
Refueled	Saved	Structured	

Education

The final section of the standard or core resume is typically Education, although, as you will see, there are some additional optional sections that may or may not be added to the resume.

There is occasionally some question as to where this section of the resume belongs. Does it belong on the first page, or on the last page of the resume? The answer is, "It depends."

If your education is relatively recent and from a highly regarded school, and your job experience is relatively light, I recommend that you position Education on the first page of the resume, immediately following the Qualifications Summary. On the other hand, if your recent work experience is particularly strong and directly related to the position for which you are applying, Education is best positioned after Professional Experience. This becomes a judgment call, however, and it will depend on which credential (education or work experience) is more marketable in the context of the position for which you are applying.

As shown on the sample resume, the Education section is relatively straightforward. It includes degree earned, school, date of graduation, and any scholarships or honors earned. If you are a new or recent graduate, it might also show activities in which you were involved, as well as any leadership positions you held while on campus.

Miscellaneous Sections

Although I have covered the typical sections of the standard or core resume document, you need to understand that your resume is essentially a marketing document and needs to include any other information that is relevant and helps to "make the sale." This is again a judgment call, and you should make it based on the relevance or importance of this information to the industries and companies that you have targeted.

If you are a research scientist, for example, you would probably want to list any patents you hold, scientific books or papers you have published, technical presentations you've made, and the like. Additionally, if you have held leadership positions in your professional society or trade association, you might want to include a section titled Professional Affiliations, in which you list positions you've held and the dates. Moreover, if you have received specific licenses or certifications in your field, you would want to include these under a resume section titled Professional Licenses and Certifications. Or, if you have taken a number of courses that distinguish you in your occupational specialty, you could list these in a special section titled Relevant Courses and Training.

The Need for a Plain-Text Version

Although you should use the paper version of your resume for resume mailings, job interviews, and networking, you will also need an electronic (plain-text) version of it for use in various Internet job search activities. As you will see in the next chapter, however, you can very easily convert your paper resume to an electronic format.

The Keyword Conundrum

I'm sure you've heard by now about the importance of using keywords in your resume. Because of the huge number of resumes pouring onto employer Web sites through myriad sources (such as direct application, major job boards, search firms, print ads, and the like), employers have been forced to use computers to do the initial screening. Without it, they would be buried alive! The process used for this electronic screening is known as "keyword search." It is believed that more than 80 percent of all resumes processed by employers are now electronically searched for job-specific keywords before a human ever sees them.

What Are Keywords?

In reality, keywords are any words for which an employer digitally searches resumes, as the means of identifying qualified candidates for a given job opening. More specifically, keywords are typically nouns or noun phrases representing specific areas of skill or competency that the employer feels are important to job performance. You have just seen several examples in the Skills Profile section.

Although these examples are right on target, keywords can fall into any of several categories including the following:

- Industry names (for example, chemical process, pulp & paper, automotive, electronics, and so on)
- Company names (usually the names of competitors or prized customers)
- Business functions (for example, finance, accounting, engineering, law, packaging, and so on)
- Job titles (for example, engineer, physicist, project manager, plant manager)
- Job levels (for example, supervisor, manager, vice president, and so on)
- Job functions (for example, production planning, scheduling, salary administration, and so on)
- Product names/types (for example, digital cameras, corn flakes, satellites, whiskey)
- Services (for example, consulting, financial planning, contracting, nursing, and so on)
- Certifications/licenses (for example, CPA, RN, MD, PE, and so on)
- Educational level: (for example, Bachelor's, Master's, Ph.D.)
- College major: (for example, English, Chemistry, Biology, Mathematics, Physics, and so on)
- School name (for example, Harvard, Princeton, Penn State, University of Alabama, and so on)
- Professional skills (for example, machine design, architectural drawing, heart surgery, and so on)
- Equipment experience (for example, forklifts, cranes, computer control systems, furnaces, and so on)
- Techniques (for example, behavioral interviewing, statistical process control, and so on)
- Buzzwords (for example, customer focused, high-performance teams, channeling, and so on)
- Traits/characteristics (for example, aggressive, self-motivated, creative, diligent, detailed, and so on)

As you can see, the possibilities are numerous. The challenge, however, is to choose the right keywords, so that your resume will float to the top of the stack.

Winning at "Keyword Roulette"

So, as you can see, you are being forced to play "keyword roulette." It's a life-or-death struggle. Choose the "wrong" words, and your candidacy is dead in the water. Pick the right words, and you're the grand prize winner! So, your career is now in the balance. It rests on your ability to carefully select just the right combination of keywords for use in the Skills Profile section of your resume. (Sounds ridiculous, doesn't it?) So how do you play these odds and still come out a winner? Is it possible to stack this deck in your favor? Absolutely! Here is what you do and how to do it.

Study Employment Ads

Go onto a large Internet job board (such as Monster, CareerBuilder, or Yahoo! HotJobs) or use an Internet job aggregator (such as Indeed.com, Simply Hired, or Jobster) and conduct a job search for the type of position you are seeking. Print several of these ads and lay them on the table in front of you. Then, using a highlighter, highlight the nouns and noun phrases (the key skill and competency areas) displayed in each of these ads.

> **Note:** Although it will take longer, you can do the same thing using newspaper ads.

Now, list these nouns and noun phrases on a sheet of paper. Then, as these same skill areas are repeated from ad to ad, simply put a check mark beside the keyword each time it appears in an ad. Repeat this process for a couple of dozen ads. (Hint: Take special note of any skill areas that seem to be emphasized repeatedly. Words like "must have," "preferred," "highly desirable," and so forth should give you a clue.)

Now, step back and have a look. Obviously, those skill and competency areas that have the greatest number of checkmarks are the ones that most employers are seeking. You can consider these skills to be the universally valued skill set that most employers consider important to successful job performance. These, then, are the same words you will want to list in the Skills Profile section of your resume. You can bet these are the same ones employers will be using as keywords for resume screening purposes.

Job Descriptions

Try doing a similar analysis using job descriptions. Take a look at your own job description as well as those of professional colleagues who hold the same job as you. Again, go through and highlight nouns and noun phrases and perform the same analysis as in the preceding section.

If you are unable to access a physical job description, try pulling up some job descriptions using Internet search engines. Simply type your job title (and variations of it), along with such terms as "job description," "job responsibilities," "skills," "competencies," "key skills," "core skills," "core competencies," and "core skills and competencies." Be sure to put quotation marks around any two-word terms to ensure that the search engine finds just the pages that include the two words used together. In most cases, you will find what you need.

Professional Associations

Some professional organizations have done studies to identify the core skills and competencies required for successful performance of various types and levels of positions within their profession. This information may be readily available on the association's Web site. If not, call the association and inquire whether this information exists and how to access it.

Company Web Sites

Check out company Web sites, particularly those companies in which you are especially interested. In addition to your target job, study other company job listings for particular themes or trends. Are you seeing some of the same candidate qualities and traits continuously repeated across a variety of the ads? This might suggest a certain kind of profile that the company feels is most compatible with its culture or business strategy. Also read the company's annual report and select press releases looking for similar themes. If you are seeing a consistent trend, you might want to incorporate these as keywords in the resume you send this firm.

So, as you can see, this is not quite the game of keyword roulette I mentioned earlier. There are some intelligent ways to play and win this word game. It just requires a little extra work on your part. But it can have a huge payoff.

Repetition Counts!

This is one of the few times that repetition really counts. When employers use digitized computer scanning to select resumes, the software not only looks for certain keywords, but will often count the number of times these keywords appear in the resume document. The greater the count, the higher the probability that the resume will be selected.

Therefore, when writing your resume, you will want to repeat these keywords numerous times throughout the body of the resume document so that you increase the odds of having your resume selected as one of the finalists and positioned closest to the top of the stack.

> **Tip:** Don't overuse keywords, however, to the point that it is nonsensical or hilariously obvious that you are trying to load up your resume just so that it will be selected. Although such a tactic might impress a computer, it will not be very impressive to the human being that will be reading your resume. Overdoing this trick could well relegate your resume to the "dead bones" pile, so use this tactic wisely.

Additionally, you need to be alert to the use of synonyms (words having the same meaning). For example, the words "recruiting" and "staffing" mean the same thing as "employment." Employers use these terms interchangeably. The same is probably true of certain keywords you will be using in your resume. Be aware of these synonyms and alternate using them throughout the resume.

Likewise, if you are using acronyms such as JIT (just-in-time), SPC (statistical process control), or SHRM (Society for Human Resource Management), you will also want to use the full name, in addition to these abbreviations, to be sure you have all of your bases covered.

Preparing a Functional Resume

As previously discussed, there are times when you should choose a functional style resume over the reverse-chronological format. By now, you have probably made that decision.

Before I provide a detailed description of the functional resume format, take a few moments to study the functional resume sample in figure 3.2. Take particular note of the general resume layout as well as specific sections and the sequence in which these sections appear in the document.

Reviewing this sample resume shows that it is organized into the following major sections, in the order shown:

- Heading
- Qualifications Summary
- Skills Profile
- Major Accomplishments
- Work History
- Education

I will describe each of these resume sections so that you understand what is required in each and how it is best developed and written.

Heading

As with the reverse-chronological resume, the content of the heading section is obvious. It includes your name, address, phone numbers, and e-mail address. You should include your cell phone number as well, unless doing so could a cause an embarrassing or compromising situation. You would certainly not want your boss or a co-worker to overhear you discussing the possibility of a new position with a different employer.

Qualifications Summary

The Qualifications Summary follows the resume heading and provides a concise overview of your functional and industry experience. Sometimes it might also be used to highlight a unique qualification, such as a degree from a well-known school, a unique skill, or an exceptional accomplishment. The following is an example of a typical Qualifications Summary.

Qualifications Summary

Creative Procter & Gamble packaging design engineer with 10 years of experience. M.S. in Packaging Engineering, Michigan State. Awarded four (4) U.S. patents.

or

> ## Qualifications Summary
> Wharton MBA with three years of portfolio management for Western Asset Management, a leading bond investment company with more than $500 billion under management. Recipient of Top Trader Award three years running.

Skills Profile

The Skills Profile immediately follows the Qualifications Summary. Other headings you might use for this section include Core Skills & Competencies, Skills Summary, Key Skills, Core Strengths, or Core Competencies. Regardless of which title you use, the Skills Profile contains a listing of key skills or skill areas considered vital to job performance. It can be written using either a narrative or a simple list format. Employers might have a slight preference for the simple skills listing because it is easier to read and also makes it easier to spot specific skill areas for which the employer has a preference.

The Skills Profile is designed to highlight important skills or skill categories that are readily recognized and universally accepted as critical to successful job performance. When preparing this skills listing, you will want to avoid including unrelated skills that are not relevant to the position for which you are applying, as these distract rather than add value to the resume.

As emphasized earlier, when selecting key skills for inclusion, I strongly encourage you to use nouns or noun phrases that represent particular areas of strength or competency. This is because when employers use a keyword search to screen resumes, they typically use nouns or noun phrases as the basis for their searches. They are searching for concrete things, such as company names, specific job titles, specific skills, names of specific business functions, names of specific technologies, specific methods or practices, and so on. They are focused on searching for concrete things rather than descriptive phrases comprised principally of adjectives.

Avoid overuse of subjective self-descriptions such as "charismatic" team leader, "highly motivated" manager, "solid" producer, "results-focused" professional, "outstanding" communicator, "strong" contributor, and the like. These expressions, and similar ones, are subjective qualities, which, from the employer's perspective, are essentially meaningless. Recruiters pay little or no attention to such subjective self-evaluations, and, in fact, often joke that the candidate who walks through the door seldom resembles the superlative description contained in the resume. Subjective self-descriptions of this type are simply not believable. They add no value and only take up precious resume space that you could utilize more effectively.

If you feel compelled to include personal traits or qualities at all, make sure that they are truly job-relevant. Ask yourself, "Are these traits or characteristics really important to performance of the job? Are these the traits most employers would universally agree are critical to a successful job performance?" If not, eliminate them. They add nothing of value to the resume.

Be sure to especially avoid use of certain overused, hackneyed expressions. For example, everybody is a "team player," has "strong leadership skills," has "excellent interpersonal skills," is a "good communicator," is "hardworking," and the like. If you feel you must use such subjective descriptors at all, restrict their use to the cover letter rather than include them in the resume document. Conserve valuable resume space for displaying key accomplishments or other important qualifications that have real meaning and value to the employer.

In place of these meaningless self-descriptors, you are better served by including only non-subjective "hard" skills in your Skills Profile. Use nouns and noun phrases to list job-specific functional areas in which you have expertise, techniques you have mastered, tools you have used, equipment you can operate, special knowledge or skill areas in which you excel, and so on. For example, a financial executive might list the following "hard" skill areas as areas in which he or she has strong expertise:

Financial Management	International Finance	Mergers
Acquisitions	Capital Financing	Debt Reduction
International Taxation	Financial Planning	Asset Leveraging
Capital Acquisition	Financial Analysis	Risk Management
Shareholder Value	Cash Management	Strategic Financing

On the other hand, a telesales account executive working in the field of fund-raising might show the following hard skill categories in his or her Skills Profile:

Call Center Management	Subscription Fulfillment	Sales/Marketing
Financial Management	Inventory Management	Account Development
Fund-raising	Donor Base Building	Relationship Building
Donor Benefits	Market Analysis	Team Building

Or, a director of business development might list the following skills in his or her Skills Profile:

Partnership Management	Channel Partners	Competitor Analysis
Joint Ventures	Market Analysis	New Market Identification
Due Diligence	Negotiations	Marketing Strategy
Capital Funding	Acquisitions	Mergers

Major Accomplishments

The Major Accomplishments section of the resume is really the "guts" of the functional resume. The purpose of this section is to highlight your major achievements and accomplishments in the key skill areas that you highlighted in the Skills Profile. Employers will read this section carefully in search of hard evidence that you not only possesses the key skills required of the position, but that you can also use these important skills to achieve the results expected of the person in the position.

The basic premise on which modern interviewing and employment selection theory is based is that "past performance is the most reliable predictor of future performance." So, if a candidate is skilled in the right areas, and has used these skills to continuously achieve significant results in past jobs, the likelihood is that this pattern will continue into the future, after the candidate has been hired.

When preparing this section of the resume, begin by selecting four or five key skills from the Skills Profile to highlight. I strongly recommend that you choose these skills areas carefully and that you choose those considered most critical to overall job success. Moreover, when listing them on your resume, position them in order of their relative importance to performance success, going from most important to least important.

The "Winning at 'Keyword Roulette'" section earlier in this chapter provides an excellent process for deciding which primary skill areas (keywords) you might want to highlight. There are certain skill areas most employers recognize as essential to successful performance of your targeted position. You will want to include these among the skill areas you choose to highlight.

Once you have chosen those key skill areas you want to highlight, list at least three to five (or more) specific accomplishments or results you have achieved for each skill area. A quick look at the sample resume in figure 3.2 will give you the right idea.

Each key accomplishment or results statement should begin with a verb (for example, leveraged, launched, consolidated, expanded, reengineered, and so on) followed by a "quantitative" result. Some examples of good result statements are the following:

- Consolidated two divisions into a single unit, reducing headcount by 32% ($5 million annual savings).

or

- Funded new venture in record time, raising over $.5 million in 3 days.

or

- Reduced manufacturing costs from $4 per unit to $3.50 ($300,000 annual savings).

A listing of commonly used verbs is provided on page 47 for your reference. When selecting a verb to introduce your result statements, try to be as precise as possible. Select the verb that most accurately depicts the action you took. For example, did you "lead," did you "direct," did you "supervise," or did you "coordinate"? Which verb most precisely represents the action you took?

As cited earlier, not every achievement can be measured quantitatively. If possible, however, where you cannot furnish an exact measurement, try to ascribe an approximate measurement. For, example, it is okay to say you improved something by "approximately 30%" rather than simply stating that you improved it. This is especially true when the improvement was a significant one. Certainly the addition of the words "approximately 30%" has far greater impact than not including this particular qualifier.

Education

The Education section of the resume is relatively simple and straightforward. It includes degree earned, school, and date of graduation. It may also include any scholarships awarded and honors earned. If you are a recent graduate, the resume should also list any campus activities in which you were involved, as well as campus leadership positions you held.

Miscellaneous Sections

Because the resume is intended as a marketing document, you might want to include additional sections beyond the Education section, if doing so will enhance your overall qualifications in the eyes of the employer. The decision whether to add such sections should be based on the relevance of this additional information to the industries and companies you have targeted.

If you are an engineer or other technical professional, for example, you should probably list any pertinent patents you hold, relevant papers you have published, technical presentations made, and the like. In doing so, you might want to title this section "Publications and Patents," "Professional Achievements," or some other appropriate heading. Additionally, if you have held leadership positions in your professional society or trade association, you might want to include a section titled Professional Affiliations, in which you list the dates and positions held.

Moreover, if you are licensed or professionally certified in your field, include this information under a section titled Professional Licenses and Certifications. Or, if you have taken a number of special courses that serve to uniquely qualify you for the position you seek, you might want to include a listing of these courses under a special section titled Relevant Courses and Training. This is especially true if this additional training is well recognized in your profession and would cause you to stand out from other job seekers with who you must compete. However, avoid listing courses that have no relevance to your targeted position. Such extraneous information is essentially meaningless to an employer, and may cause the employer to wonder about your judgment.

The Need for a Plain-Text Version

Although the resume formats described in this chapter are ideal for use in the job interview, for a direct-mail campaign, and for networking, you will also need a plain-text version of your resume for use on the Internet. Fortunately, the formats covered in this chapter are fairly Internet-friendly and can easily be converted into a plain-text (ASCII) resume version, as you will see in the next chapter.

Chapter Summary

Key points to remember when designing an effective resume are the following:

- Choose the resume style (either reverse-chronological or functional) that best markets you to your target employers.

- Remember that most employers (74 percent) prefer the reverse-chronological resume format over other resume formats.

- Use the standard format and resume sections recommended in this chapter. They are those with which employers are most familiar and comfortable.

- Make effective use of universally accepted keywords throughout your resume to increase the probability that your resume will pop to the top of the stack when it is scanned by a computer.

- Be sure that your resume is "results focused," not "activity focused." Employers are looking for your achievements, not a job description.

- When describing results you achieved, be sure to include quantitative descriptions that illustrate the magnitude and importance of your accomplishments.

CHAPTER 4

The Internet Resume: Converting Your Resume to a Plain-Text Version

In chapter 3, you learned to use standard word processing to prepare the traditional reverse-chronological and functional resume formats. As stated earlier, you will definitely want to use this version at the time of your job interviews, as well as when you're preparing a direct-mail campaign to targeted managers. In most cases, however, this is not the version you will want to use when e-mailing your resume to an employer or search firm via the Internet. In such cases, you will want to use an electronic form of your resume, known as an ASCII or plain-text version.

Don't despair. This doesn't mean that you are now going to have to write an entirely new resume. You can simply convert your existing resume into an electronic version. The basic content of your current resume will remain unchanged; however, you will simply need to shuffle some text to properly fit and align with the new plain-text format. As you will see, this process is fairly simple.

What Is a Plain-Text (ASCII) Resume?

ASCII stands for American Standard Code for Information Interchange, which is a universally accepted, plain-text format adopted by the "gods of the Internet" that allows text to be transmitted, received, and read by all computers regardless of type or location. The term "plain-text" means just that. It is plain, and doesn't contain any out-of-the ordinary treatment such as boldfacing, underlining, bullets, italics, graphics, and so on.

When preparing a plain-text (ASCII) document, the only "tools" available to you are those on your immediate computer keyboard. Special effects such as boldfacing, underlining, bullets, and justifying margins (which are contained only in your word-processing software), are simply not present or available for your use. In fact, if you convert a word-processing document (such as a resume prepared in MS Word) into a plain-text (ASCII) file, any existing special effects will automatically disappear, leaving only "plain" text remaining.

So, to create a plain-text (ASCII) resume, you essentially have two choices:

- Use Notepad (a basic word-processing program that comes with Windows) to create your resume from scratch as a plain-text (ASCII) document.

or

- Save your MS Word (or other word-processing) resume as a plain-text (ASCII) file.

Either way, once the document exists as a plain-text (ASCII) file, you can't use any of the aforementioned special effects. The resulting document is rather dreary looking and lacks the oomph and pizzazz of the traditional word-processing resume, which has been dressed up using all the bells and whistles of these special effects.

Why Do I Need a Plain-Text (ASCII) Resume?

When you're applying for a job using the Internet, you will quickly find that many career and employer Web sites now insist that you submit a plain-text (ASCII) resume, and that this document be pasted directly into the e-mail message that you are using to transmit your resume. To accomplish this, you would first save your resume as a plain-text (ASCII) file, and then copy and paste the plain-text document into the body of the e-mail itself.

You might wonder why all employers don't allow you to send your MS Word resume document as an attachment to your e-mail. This would seem to be so much easier, and the resume would also look much better. The reason is simple. Computer viruses are often embedded in e-mail attachments. When these attachments are opened, the virus can be released and, if not caught, could potentially bring down the employer's entire computer system. So, there is good reason for concern.

Additionally, the applicant-tracking and resume-management software some employers use cannot properly process and store resumes submitted in MS Word or other word-processing software format. Moreover, some people might not want to take the extra time required to open a resume that has been sent as an e-mail attachment.

It should be noted, however, that not all employers require you to use a plain-text format. Some may permit you to paste your MS Word version into an area provided for that purpose on their Web site, or send it as an e-mail attachment. The important thing to remember, however, is to follow the employer's instructions *exactly*, sending your resume in whatever form they request that it be in. In this way, you will be assured that your resume will get into their applicant-tracking or resume-management system and will be available for computer search as appropriate job opportunities develop.

So, the bottom line is that you need two separate versions of your resume. One is either the reverse-chronological or functional format, as described in chapter 3, and the other is the plain-text (ASCII) version of the same resume.

Converting Your MS Word Resume to Plain Text

At this point, if you have read chapter 3, you have probably prepared a standard resume (either reverse-chronological or functional style) using MS Word (or other word-processing software). Here are the steps to follow in making the conversion to plain-text format:

1. Open your existing MS Word resume document.

2. Using the main toolbar "File" menu, scroll down and select "Save As." The "Save As" box will now appear.

3. Using the "Save As" box, proceed as follows:

   a. In the "Save In" window, select the location where you want to store the new file (suggestion: "Desktop").

   b. In the "File name" window, assign the new file a name (suggestion: "Plain-Text Resume").

   c. In the "Save as type" window, scroll down and select "Text Only" or "Plain Text."

   d. Click on "Save" to save the new plain-text file to your Desktop.

Note: Depending on which version of Word you are using, a screen may appear advising you that "The file you are about to save may contain features that are not compatible with a Text Only format. Do you want to save the document in this format?" If this occurs, click "Yes" (saving the file to your Desktop). You might also see a File Conversion box. If so, accept the default settings and click OK to continue.

---

4. Now close the original MS Word file remaining on your screen and return to the Desktop.

5. On your Desktop, click on the new file, which is named "Plain-Text Resume.txt." This opens the plain-text resume for the polishing process, which you'll tackle in the next section.

Polishing Your Plain-Text (ASCII) Resume

When you open your new plain-text resume file, you will find that all of the special effects (boldfacing, underlining, and bullets) are now missing, leaving only plain text. You will also notice that although all of the original resume text is present, it is somewhat scattered and needs to be aligned. It is certainly not very attractive in its current state.

In order to properly align your new plain-text resume document and make it more attractive and user-friendly, there are certain rules you need to follow. These are outlined in the following sections. So that you can better understand and visually see what I am recommending, I have converted the Linda A. Smith reverse-chronological resume (figure 3.1), from the preceding chapter, into a plain-text (ASCII) resume, which I will be using as my example (see figure 4.1). Take a moment or two to look it over before proceeding.

Aligning the Resume Text

If you have converted your standard MS Word resume into a plain-text document, the first thing that you will notice is that the text has become misaligned and is scattered across the page. So your first chore will be to realign the text using the tools now available to you (in other words, your computer keyboard and the limited toolbar located at the top-left corner of the plain-text screen).

In aligning the text, one important thing you will need to know is that you cannot use your computer Tab key to accomplish this alignment. The Tab key is the one keyboard function that does not work properly in the plain-text format. Instead, you will need to use the spacebar, rather than the Tab key, to properly align text on the page. This means that you will need to remove the previous tabs and re-create the spacing using your spacebar.

Moreover, because the text-centering feature is no longer available to you, all text (including key resume headings) must now be aligned at the left margin of your resume. Don't bother to use the spacebar to attempt to center these headings. When an employer opens the resume, this center alignment will probably be lost due to the employer using different software.

As you can see from figure 4.1, these key resume headings will still stand out as such if you use capital letters to visually separate them from the rest of the resume text.

Controlling Resume Width

When realigning text in your new plain-text resume version, you will need to pay particular attention to the width of the lines. If your resume is too wide and there are too many words on the same line, when an employer opens it, differences in software may cause the text to wrap in an ugly fashion. This will totally destroy the lovely alignment you have worked so hard to get.

To prevent this from happening, limit the number of spaces occupied by text on a single line to no more than 60 letters. An easy way to accomplish this, and avoid a lot of manual counting, is to do what I did on the sample resume. You will note how I have used a line comprised of equals signs to separate each of the key resume components. Well, if you were to count the number of equal signs, you would find

Linda A. Johnson

435 Boston Road
Appleton, WI 21811

LAJohn@AOL.com

Phone: (614) 877-9437
Cell: (614) 866-9087

==

QUALIFICATIONS SUMMARY

Seasoned Procter & Gamble lead project engineer
with 8 years of experience in the successful
engineering design, installation, and startup of
towel and tissue paper machines.

B.S. Mechanical Engineering, University of
Michigan.

Expert in wet-end forming equipment design.
Hold 2 U.S. patents.

==

SKILLS PROFILE

Paper Machines   Wet-End Design
Towel Machines   Transpiration Drying
Sheet Formation   Yankee Dryers
Paper Converting   Paper Finishing
Paper Machine Installation Paper Machine Startup
Project Management   Control Systems
Engineering Design   Charmin Tissue
Tissue Machines   Machine Design
Pulp & Paper   G.E. Controls

==

Figure 4.1: The plain-text version of Linda A. Johnson's resume.

PROFESSIONAL EXPERIENCE

PROCTER & GAMBLE   2003 to Present

Lead Project Engineer (2005 to Present)

Report to Engineering Project Manager. Lead team of
12 project engineers and 55 contract personnel in
the engineering design, installation, and startup
of a $150 million tissue paper machine and allied
converting equipment at the Appleton, Wisconsin,
plant.

* Completed paper machine design phase in record
  time (delivered 2 months early).
* Modified existing forming section design,
  resulting in the award of 2 U.S. patents.
* Controlled project costs, resulting in $2 million
  savings in Phase 1 of project.
* Assisted in resolving major labor dispute with
  contract workforce, avoiding costly project
  delay.
* Redesigned automated control systems application,
  resulting in savings of $1/4 million.
* Led engineering design and successful
  installation of novel transpiration dryer section
  on time.
* Headed cross-functional team responsible for
  evaluation of new paper converting equipment.
* Initiated use of new project planning software,
  improving planning and project cost control.
* Built and led high-performance work team,
  achieving high employee morale and efficiency.

Senior Project Engineer (2003 to 2005)

Reported to Lead Project Engineer. Supervised
project team of 6 professionals (1 designer, 2
engineers, and 3 technicians) in the successful
redesign, rebuild, and startup of the wet end of
the #5 paper machine at the Winslow, Maine, plant.

* Redesigned and successfully installed wet end
  section of #5 paper machine (a $25 million
  capital project) on time and 5% under budget
  ($1/4 million savings).
* Led cross-functional team (engineering
  professionals and operating technicians) in
  highly successful machine startup, achieving all
  production and quality benchmarks in under 6
  weeks.
* Facilitated team project planning meetings using
  group problem-solving techniques to shorten
  project delivery time and contain costs.

WILSON PAPER COMPANY   1999 to 2003

Senior Project Engineer--Converting (2001 to 2003)

Reported to Plant Engineering Manager with
responsibility for the engineering design,
installation, startup, and troubleshooting of towel
and tissue paper converting and finishing equipment
at the Appleton, Wisconsin, plant.

* Engineered and successfully installed the Prince
  Towel paper converting and finishing line ($18
  capital project) on time and within budget.
* Rebuilt Shop Towel bagging line with resultant
  savings of $1 million annually.
* Engineered and successfully installed TSI 2000
  control system on #4 tissue converting line,
  reducing machine downtime and saving over $1/2
  million in labor costs annually.
* Automated warehousing distribution system (a $32
  million project), reducing warehouse labor costs
  by 20% ($3 million annual savings).

Project Engineer--Paper Mill (2000 to 2001)

Reported to Paper Mill Superintendent. Responsible
for all engineering troubleshooting and maintenance
in support of a 800 ton per day, 4-machine
papermaking operation.

* Installed preventive maintenance program, with
  scheduled online servicing, reducing machine
  shutdown time by 20% ($2 million annual savings).
* Initiated predictive maintenance plan, allowing
  just-in-time parts replacement and reducing
  machine failure and non-scheduled downtime by an
  estimated 10%.
* Assisted Senior Project Engineer in the
  successful startup of the #3 paper machine.

Engineer (1999 to 2000)
Entry-level engineering position. Provided
assistance to senior engineering staff in a wide
range of engineering projects in papermaking and
converting operations.

===

EDUCATION

B.S., Mechanical Engineering
University of Michigan, 1999
Dean's List Student (4 years)
Wilson Scholarship Award (3 years)

===

PROFESSIONAL ACHIEVEMENTS

2 United States Patents (Paper Forming Devices)

that there are exactly 60, which happens to be the new resume width you will need to use. So, this makes it easy. When aligning your text on the page, align it with this line of equals signs, and don't allow any of the text to go beyond the line on the right side of the page. If it does, simply hit the Enter key and move that word (or words) to the next line.

You will also note from figure 4.1 that I had to realign the "Skills Profile" section, using only two columns instead of the original three columns of skills contained on the MS Word version of this resume. It was necessary to do this in order not to exceed the new, more narrow, 60-space resume width required in the plain-text resume format. When shifting from a three-column listing of skills to two columns, don't forget to use the spacebar rather than the Tab key to get the new spacing.

Replacing Bullet Points

As with other features, such as bold print and underlining, when your MS Word resume is converted to plain text, those bullet points you used to highlight each of your key accomplishments disappear. Because you will want to continue to highlight these accomplishments and provide at least some visual separation between them, you have two choices.

The first, as I have done in figure 4.1, is to use an asterisk in the place of each bullet point. The other is to precede each key accomplishment with a single hyphen to achieve the desired effect. Doing so will preserve the visual separation and cause each accomplishment to stand out on its own.

Without using either the asterisk or the hyphen to accomplish this separation, your accomplishments won't stand out, and will appear as a boring and difficult-to-read solid block of text. So, take the time to replace your bullet points with one or the other of these two features. Your resume's appearance will be greatly enhanced by doing so.

Eliminating Page Numbers and Page Breaks

If you have numbered the pages of your resume, you will want to remove these numbers because they serve no real purpose in your ASCII resume. This is because when the employer opens you resume document, depending on the software he or she is using, the page break might not occur in the same place as your numbered pages in the original document. So, if you have included your name and "page 2" at the top of the second page of your resume, for example, you will want to remove both of these items before saving your resume document for future use.

Using "Underlining" and White Space

As previously explained, traditional underlining is not available when you're working with a plain-text resume. The equals sign and the hyphen, however, are available for use because they are keys on your computer keyboard.

A quick look at figure 4.1 will show you how you can use these two features very effectively to create a resume that is far more attractive and more easily read. You will notice how I have used a line of equals signs to separate each major component of the resume. Notice also how I have used white space (extra returns) to further separate these sections and create a document that is more visually appealing.

You will also notice the use of a line of hyphens on the next line below the job title to simulate the underlining of job titles. As you can see, this makes it much easier for the employer to visually separate one job from the next. All in all, I think you would agree that the use of this type of "underlining" (using equal signs and hyphens) does a fairly good job of dressing up what would otherwise have been a rather boring and difficult-to-read resume document.

Testing Your Plain-Text Resume

At this point, it's a good idea to test your new plain-text resume. According to renowned career columnist and author Joyce Lain Kennedy, it is a good idea to e-mail a copy of this resume to yourself and, perhaps, someone else you know who is using a different e-mail program than you are. This will allow you to make whatever adjustments you need to make before "going live" with an employer. You don't want to discover, after several days of job search, that the resume version you have been sending out to several hundred employers and search firms is improperly aligned or in some other way distorted. So, be on the safe side and conduct a trial run.

Sending Your Resume Via E-mail

Once you have reformatted your new plain-text resume and made it more presentable, you will want to save these changes and store this resume version for future use as you need it.

When responding to an online ad or e-mailing your plain-text resume directly to an employer, be sure to precisely follow the instructions provided by the employer. If the employer requests an MS Word version sent as an attachment to an e-mail, then send an MS Word version as an e-mail attachment. If the employer instructs you to paste a copy of your MS Word resume into a specific space provided on the employer's Web site for this purpose, by all means follow these instructions precisely. Should the employer request that you copy and paste your plain-text resume version into the body of your e-mail, do so. Failure to follow precise instructions will likely cause your resume to be excluded entirely because you didn't follow instructions and therefore your resume is incompatible with whatever resume-management software the employer is using to capture, store, and search candidates' resumes.

When the employer has provided no specific instructions, I recommend that you copy and paste your plain-text (ASCII) resume into the body of the e-mail message that you are using to transmit the resume to the employer. In order to do this, follow these simple instructions:

1. Open the plain-text resume that you have stored on your Desktop (or elsewhere).

2. Using the "Edit" feature located in the toolbar in the top-left portion of the window, scroll down the menu and choose "Select All." This will highlight all of the resume text.

3. Now using the same "Edit" feature, scroll down the menu and select "Copy."

4. Then close your plain-text resume file and exit to your Desktop.

5. Now, open your e-mail screen and choose the "Send" feature.

6. After typing the appropriate e-mail address and subject line, type a brief introductory cover letter (if one is needed). See the section titled "Creating an E-mail Cover Letter" below for tips on writing this letter.

7. Finally, following this introductory message, paste the plain-text version of your resume into the body of your e-mail. To do this, simply choose the "Edit" command from your toolbar, scroll down the Edit menu, and select the "Paste" command. Your plain-text resume should now appear in the body of your e-mail, following your brief introductory message.

8. Now, click on the "Send" command and your e-mail message and resume are on their way to the designated location.

Creating an E-mail Cover Letter

When composing the subject line of your e-mail cover letter, try to use something a little more original than simply "resume" or "profile." You need to use a subject line that will capture the reader's attention. So, you might try something like the following:

- Procter & Gamble Design Engineer
- Financial Executive/Harvard MBA
- Award-Winning Sales Professional
- Talented Human Resources Professional
- Profit-Minded Plant Manager

Subject lines of this type tend to grab attention much faster than the mundane subject lines of "Resume," "Introduction," "Professional Profile," and the like. Be careful, however, not to use too many words in the subject line, or it might not be read. The optimum number of words, as illustrated in the preceding examples, is probably about 4 or 5.

E-mail cover letters are essentially used to transmit your resume to the employer or to answer a specific ad on a job board or the company's Web site. Busy staffing managers or other executives are simply too busy to read lengthy cover letters, so your cover letter needs to be brief, concise, and to the point. However, it does need to contain sufficient information and be written attractively enough to create interest in your candidacy and motivate the reader to continue on to your resume.

Basically, there are two types of e-mail cover letters. The first is what is typically referred to as a general broadcast letter. The second is an ad-response cover letter.

The General Broadcast Letter

This type of e-mail cover letter is used when you are simply e-mailing your resume to a number of employers for the purpose of creating interest in your candidacy and getting your resume into the employer's resume database so that you will be considered for either current or future positions as these opportunities may exist or develop. Figure 4.2 is an example of this type of cover letter.

As you can see in figure 4.2, the letter contains the traditional salutation followed by a brief introductory paragraph of one or two attention-grabbing sentences, which serve to highlight your qualifications and generate interest. This is your "opener" and, as such, it must immediately command the reader's attention. If it

---

Dear Sir/Madam:

I am a successful Wharton MBA financial executive interested in career opportunities with your company. Core strengths and competencies include

- 10 years of financial management in the petrochemical industry.

- Expert cash management, generating millions in savings.

- Record of highly profitable mergers and acquisitions.

- New business development, including five successful launches.

- Capital acquisition to support multimillion-dollar projects.

- Strong background in international finance.

My resume is included for your review and consideration.

Should you be interested in acquiring the services of a seasoned financial executive with a propensity for helping companies make money and expand their business, I would love to speak with you.

I can be reached via e-mail or on my cell phone, which is (612) 875-9512.

Thank you.

Sincerely,

Barbara Schneider

Figure 4.2: An example of a general broadcast e-mail cover letter.

doesn't, the employer might never even bother to read the resume that you have spent so much time crafting.

The second component of the cover letter, as illustrated in figure 4.2, consists of a series of about five or six key qualifications and accomplishments, which make a strong case for the type of position you are seeking. Obviously, Barbara Schneider has done just that!

You then need only a single sentence to reference the resume, which you have included in the e-mail along with the cover letter. Note how this has been accomplished in the sample cover letter.

Next, as demonstrated on the sample letter, you will want to include a brief one- or two-sentence paragraph that attempts to motivate and stimulate action on the part of the reader, followed by a stated desire to talk with or be interviewed by the employer.

The final paragraph provides contact information—typically e-mail address and cell phone number, or another phone number where you can be readily reached. This information is then followed by a "thank you" and a traditional letter closing (such as "Sincerely").

Despite the brevity of the sample letter, I think you would admit that it is a fairly effective document that packs some punch. If you are to be noticed, your e-mail cover letter will need to do the same. So, commit some quality time to constructing a comparable letter that serves to encapsulate your core qualifications/contributions and makes the reader want to meet you.

The Ad-Response E-mail Cover Letter

An example of a typical ad-response e-mail cover letter is shown in figure 4.3. Take a moment or two to read it and look it over.

After the traditional salutation, the first paragraph of the letter is used to accomplish three things, as follows:

- Reference the employer's job listing to include job title and location of the advertisement.
- Make a strong affirmative statement signaling your confidence in your ability to perform in the job.
- Introduce and draw the reader's attention to your qualifications.

As illustrated, the next section of the cover letter provides an excellent opportunity to highlight your key skills and major accomplishments, which demonstrate not only your competencies but also your ability to deliver results.

William Criswell has certainly highlighted some key accomplishments that should attract the attention of any HR executive who is seeking a staffing expert. Reducing hiring cycle time, saving agency fees, skilled use of the computer to identify passive candidates, and behavioral interviewing expertise are bound to be on

Dear Ms. Hudson:

I am responding to your current CareerBuilder job listing for the position of Corporate Staffing Specialist, and believe I am an excellent candidate who can bring some strong skills to your staffing operation. Please consider the following:

- Five years of corporate staffing experience with demonstrated success in landing hard-to-find technical specialists.

- Reduced hiring cycle time by 25 percent in two years.

- Cost-conscious recruiter who saved more than $300,000 in agency fees in 2005.

- Skilled in Internet recruiting and use of Web spiders to identify passive candidates.

- Expert trainer who has trained hundreds in the use of behavior-based interviewing and selection techniques.

- Master's degree in Industrial Psychology, Michigan State University.

My full resume follows.

I believe you will find me an exciting prospect for your current staff opening and look forward to meeting with you personally.

Please contact me at this e-mail address, or on my cell phone at (912) 775-0927.

Thank you.

Sincerely,

William Criswell

Figure 4.3: An example of an ad-response e-mail cover letter.

the "qualifications shopping list" of any senior executive in search of a top-drawer staffing professional.

So, as Criswell did, you will want to list about five to six key skills and accomplishments that make a strong, compelling case for your employment candidacy and encourage the employer to quickly move on to scan your resume.

As with the broadcast letter, you should follow your list of core skills and achievements with a brief statement drawing the employer's attention to the fact that your resume follows, as part of the e-mail.

The paragraph following the resume reference is used to demonstrate confidence in your ability to perform the position and to encourage a personal meeting.

Finally, the last paragraph of the letter provides the employer with basic information to facilitate personal contact with you. This is then followed by a "thank you" and a traditional letter closing.

When responding to a job advertisement using this approach, you will want to closely tailor your list of qualifications and accomplishments to those areas that the employer appears to emphasize in the ad. Read the ad carefully and, at the same time, look for clues that suggest the employer has a preference for certain qualifications over others. Then, when itemizing your list of competencies and accomplishments in the letter, be sure to put these "high-preference areas" at the top of your list.

Using the Internet to Mass-Mail Your Resume

When using the Internet as your main distribution tool to mass-distribute your resume to hundreds or perhaps thousands of employers or agencies, be aware of steps you will need to take to ensure that your e-mail resume is received and appropriately processed at its destination.

As I'm sure you are aware, companies, particularly large ones, get thousands upon thousands of unsolicited resumes sent via e-mail. Most of these can be totally unrelated to the types of profiles typically hired by the employer. So, in order to cut down on this huge volume, some companies have set their spam filters to block out resumes that have been mass-mailed. These resumes might be deleted or stored in a temporary file for some specified time frame and then discarded. Additionally, your Internet Service Provider's spam filter might prevent you from sending out a single e-mail to a large number of recipients at the same time.

So, when mass-mailing your resume via e-mail, it is best to limit the number of addressees on a single e-mail to 25 or less, so that your message will pass under the radar of both your ISP and the employer and be delivered, as you had intended. Of course, when time and circumstances permit, you will want to customize your e-mail and send it to a single employer. Although this method is time-consuming, it has proven to be superior to the mass-mailing approach. Also, where practical, it is probably a good idea to follow your e-mailed resume with a snail-mailed version sent directly to the employer as well. In this way, you can be sure it has been delivered.

Chapter Summary

You will need a well-formatted plain-text version of your resume for use when apply-ing to many jobs advertised on the Internet. The conversion from a standard MS Word version of your resume to a plain-text (ASCII) version is a fairly simple and painless process. Key points to keep in mind when preparing and using a plain-text resume are as follows:

- Always use the exact resume format specified by the employer (plain-text, MS Word, and so on) when applying for a position over the Internet.

- When in doubt, use a plain-text (ASCII) resume and paste it into the body of the e-mail cover letter you are using to transmit your resume to the employer.

- To convert your standard MS Word resume document, open it and then save it as a plain-text (ASCII) document. Then open your new ASCII resume document and realign the text. Use the hyphen and equals sign to create an "underlin-ing" effect and separate the key components of your resume.

- Special effects such as bullet points, underlining, and boldface type are lost when converting to an ASCII resume. Replace bullet points with either an asterisk or a hyphen.

- When bulk e-mailing your resume to multiple sources, limit the number of recipients for each e-mail message to 25 or less to prevent your e-mail from being classified as spam.

- Proper cover letter design is also essential to effective Internet job search. A well-designed e-mail cover letter grabs the reader's attention and compels him or her to read your resume.

CHAPTER 5

Internet Job Search: Boom or Bust?

How effective is the Internet as a job-hunting source? Is it really worth your time as a job seeker? Is it a tremendous resource that can save you considerable time in finding that ideal job, or a distraction that can gobble up precious hours without much to show for your effort?

The answer is, it can be both! It all depends on which Web sites and Internet tools you use, and how you use them. Based on these factors, using the Internet to find a job can prove to be a frustrating, time-wasting experience or an enormously successful vehicle for finding that ideal job in record time!

I have scoured the Internet and talked with some of the top authorities and experts in the world of Internet recruiting to get answers. The focus of this research was get to the bottom line—a specific strategy for job seekers that will enable them to get the most out of this tremendous resource—to find a satisfying job within the shortest time frame possible and with the least amount of effort wasted.

The objective of this chapter is to help you quickly wade through the Internet mire, cast aside all the electronic static, and get down to a specific strategy that will help you become extremely proficient in using the Internet as a job search tool. The idea is to let the technology do all the work for you, or as much as possible, so that you don't have to.

The Foundation for the Ultimate Internet Job Search Strategy

The Internet job search strategy recommended in this chapter is based on the findings of studies conducted by some of the leading experts and organizations in the employment field. They help us determine which aspects of the Internet (both Web sites and tools) have produced the best hiring results, and reflect the learning gleaned from direct surveys of both companies and actual job seekers alike. These studies help us to answer two important questions:

- How productive is the Internet as a job hunting source?
- Which specific Internet sectors and Web sites are the most productive for landing jobs?

The following sections address these questions.

How Productive Is the Internet as a Job Hunting Source?

Although the data vary somewhat depending on whose study you read, it is clear that the Internet plays a significant and increasingly important role as a source of employment. It appears that the Internet now accounts for about 30 percent of all jobs landed. Therefore, you should use it as a major resource and important focus of your overall job search strategy.

Two recent studies are of particular note. The first study, conducted by Gerry Crispin and Mark Mehler of CareerXroads and published on the CareerXroads Web site (www.CareerXroads.com), shows that the Internet accounts for 29.6 percent of hires. This survey, entitled *CareerXroads 4th Annual—Sources of Hire 2004*, was based on data reported by 40 large, high-profile companies whose combined hiring is more than a quarter-million jobs annually. You can read the full study and results for free on the CareerXroads Web site. Crispin and Mehler are top experts in the field of Internet recruiting who provide Internet training and consulting services to many of the world's leading corporations.

The second study, the results of an online survey of more than 1,500 job seekers conducted by weddles.com, shows that 34 percent found their last job on an Internet job board. Peter Weddle is a world-recognized authority in the fields of recruiting and Internet job search. His WEDDLE'S 2005/6 *Guide to Employment Websites* is considered an authoritative guide to the world of Internet job search. Moreover, among numerous accomplishments in the career field, Weddle was the founder and former Chairman and CEO of Job Bank USA, one of the largest electronic employment service companies in the United States.

These and other studies on Internet effectiveness suggest that the Internet has now risen to either the number-one or number-two position as the most productive source for finding employment.

Which Are the Most Productive Internet Sectors and Web Sites?

The CareerXroads study cited above appears to provide the best breakdown of Internet sectors, showing the percentage of jobs filled by each of three main sectors as follows:

- 8.6%: Monster.com
- 8.1%: CareerBuilder
- 6.1%: Yahoo! HotJobs

All this data is well and good, but what does it tell us about the Internet job search strategy you need to use in order to save time and still get the most out of the Internet as a source of jobs? Considering that there are an estimated 40,000 job boards and career Web sites out there, this still leaves considerable guesswork and a lot more research for the average job seeker to do in order to end up with an effective strategy that saves time and identifies the best job opportunities. Certainly, the last thing you would want to do is try to manually explore some 40,000 job sites in order to find the best ones without some tools and techniques to do the legwork for you. Fortunately, such tools are now readily available on the Internet. If used properly, they can cut an estimated 50 to 75 percent off your job search time, and in many cases produce several viable career opportunities simultaneously. Having multiple job offers from which to choose is any job seeker's dream, and should be the objective of your ultimate job search strategy.

So, what are these tools and what is the ultimate strategy for efficiently tapping the full power of the Internet as a top-producing employment source? Find out in the next section.

The Ultimate Internet Job Search Strategy

Figure 5.1 outlines my recommended strategy for tapping the full power of the Internet to quickly find interesting job opportunities without wasting time doing so.

Without proper guidance, you can unwittingly waste hours and weeks of precious job search time exploring the overwhelming array of Internet options available and end up with little or no concrete results for your effort. This is especially true when you consider that there are more than 40,000 Internet job and career sites from which to choose. Just how long would it take to explore all 40,000 and pare it down to the few sites and tools that will produce the best results? One can only guess!

The Internet job search strategy illustrated in figure 5.1 should take the guesswork out of the process, and enable you to effectively use this tremendous resource to your advantage. It will definitely save you considerable time, and allow you to get significant results with only a small amount of effort and time on your part.

I have broken down the Internet into three major segments: the "Big 3" job boards, niche boards, and company Web sites. These three sectors together account for an estimated 93 percent of company Internet hires. You will want to target these same three sources for the purposes of your own job search.

This Internet strategy diagram in figure 5.1 lists specific techniques and tools that you can use to efficiently penetrate and tap all three of these major Internet sectors. By using these tools and techniques, you will find that technology will do

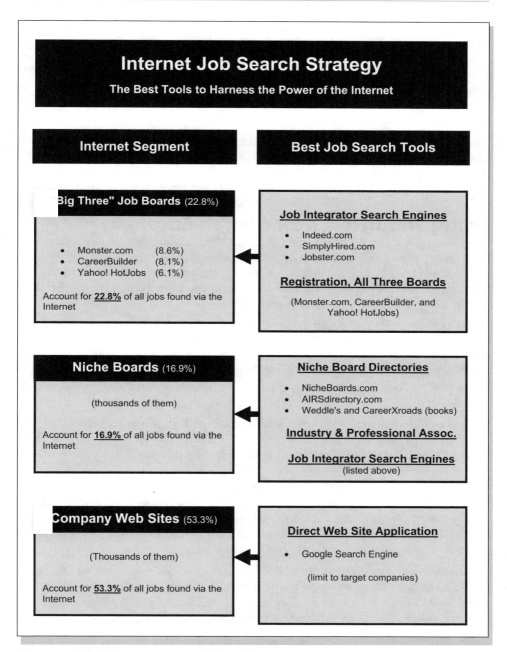

Figure 5.1. The Ultimate Internet Job Search Strategy.

much of the work for you, saving considerable time and limiting your frustration in the process. The tremendous time savings will enable you to simultaneously use other employment sources (for example, networking, looking at classified advertising, working with employment agencies, and so on), thereby cutting valuable time off the process and increasing your chances of identifying multiple job opportunities within a much shorter time frame. This is, of course, the goal of the Ultimate Job Search.

The balance of this chapter is devoted to explaining how to use each of these tools and techniques to effectively penetrate the three major Internet segments (the "Big 3" job boards, the niche boards, and company Web sites), which combined represent an estimated 93 percent of Internet job market employment results.

Using Job Integrator Search Engines

How would like to save hours upon hours of time reading tons of newspaper ads, days on end weeding through thousands upon thousands of jobs posted on Internet job boards, and evening after evening posting your resume on career site after career site? What if you could accomplish the same thing and get the same results using only a few minutes of your time?

What if your computer could do all of this for you? What if it could scour the entire Internet—going through thousands of Internet job boards, newspaper want ads, search firm job listings, and employer Web sites—and automatically bring back to you only those jobs in which you would be interested, and only those job opportunities located in the geographical area you have targeted? Would you be interested?

Well it can, and the solution rests with the use of RSS job aggregators that will scour the Internet for you. What is an RSS aggregator and how can you use these tools to automate and manage most of your Internet job search for you? Read on.

What Is an RSS Aggregator?

Although this is a relatively unimportant fact to most job seekers, RSS stands for *Really Simple Syndication, Rich Site Summary, RDF Site Summary,* or a variation on one of these. It is a method for allowing Internet users to automatically obtain up-to-date information from their favorite Web sites.

Although it was conceived in 1999, RSS was basically unknown to most of us until 2004, when Web bloggers began to use it to hound the presidential candidates and humble Dan Rather by keeping a current log of events, which automatically fed updated developments to the blogger community using RSS feeds almost as soon as any new event occurred.

Aggregators, using RSS feeds, can now automatically collect information from hundreds if not thousands of Web sites and offer this information, often free of charge, to anyone electing to subscribe or register to receive the news feed from the aggregator's Web site. RSS is now being used to shake up the Internet job search business in a major way. Internet job aggregators have sprung up using RSS news feeds to automatically update registered job seekers on new jobs almost as soon as they are posted on the Web. These aggregators scrape job content from thousands of Internet Web sites (including major job boards, niche job boards, employers' Web sites, newspaper want ads, search firm online job listings, and so on), based on keywords you supply, and automatically bring these job listings back to you based on your personal job search criteria.

This being the case, you can only begin to imagine the huge time savings and efficiency these new Internet-based tools have brought to the job seeker. What could have taken days if not months to accomplish (manually registering and scrolling through these Web sites) now takes a matter of seconds. These news feeds are commonly updated about every hour, so you will receive these job listings almost as soon as they are posted on the Internet.

What Are the Major Aggregators?

Although I am sure there are more, my research has led me to three such major Internet job aggregators (although probably by the time this book is published, there will be more). These three are the following:

- **Indeed** (www.indeed.com)
- **Simply Hired** (www.simplyhired.com)
- **Jobster** (www.jobster.com—formerly WorkZoo)

Because each of these job aggregator Web site news feeds is free and only takes seconds to use, you may want to experiment to see which is best for use in locating the type of position you seek. You will be amazed at the results! Having done so, you might then want to permanently register on the one or two sites that produce the best results, so that you will be notified automatically of any new positions that meet your keyword search criteria as these positions are posted on the Internet.

A brief description of each of these three Internet job aggregators follows.

Indeed (www.indeed.com)

According to its Web site, Indeed is a search engine for jobs. It provides job seekers free access to millions of jobs from thousands of Web sites. It includes all job listings from the major job boards as well as from newspaper, association, search firm, and company Web sites. According to Indeed's CEO and co-founder, Paul Forster, at the time of this writing, the site is adding more than 130,000 new job listings each day, or close to 4 million listings in the last 30 days alone. This number continues to grow as new job sites are added.

As with most search engines, the site is extremely easy to use. In one box (the "what" box), you simply type a job title, keywords, or a company name. In the second box (the "where" box), you input a city and state or ZIP code. The results are instantaneous and impressive, to say the least!

I gave the search engine a trial run, to see what it could do. By typing the term "Human Resources" in the first box and inputting "Maryland" as the location,

Indeed instantly brought back 186 job listings, all very much on target. Narrowing my search further, by adding "Manager," the search engine immediately pared the list down to 50 positions. It would have taken me days of registering and combing through hundreds of job boards and Web sites to produce the same result. All of this was delivered to me in a matter of seconds!

Each job listing displayed during the search included job title, company name, source of the posting (for example, Monster, CareerBuilder, SHRM, company, search firm, newspaper, and so on), a brief job and qualifications description, as well as a link that took me directly to the site where the original job listing was posted. An additional nifty feature includes the length of time since the job was posted, expressed in days, hours, and minutes. This enabled me to quickly weed out older postings to which I might not want to apply.

If you want to narrow your search somewhat by choosing a specific ZIP code, the search engine will deliver any appropriate job listings located within a 25-mile radius of your ZIP code location. This is particularly helpful for people who don't want to relocate, and who would like to keep commute time to a minimum.

Additionally, job listings are ranked solely by relevance or date. Indeed does not accept payment to include jobs in the search engine or to improve a given job listing's ranking.

The search engine also allows you to save your search criteria and set up automatic e-mail alerts by simply clicking on "Job Alert." This feature automatically sends daily e-mails containing links to any new jobs that match your job search criteria.

Another very interesting feature of this site is a map of the United States, with red dots showing where the most jobs are concentrated. Large dots indicate a large concentration of current job openings, with smaller red dots showing areas of the country where job listings are more sparse. This neat feature enables you to efficiently target areas of the country that appear to be booming, and where chances of finding your ideal job are likely much greater.

Simply Hired (www.simplyhired.com)

As of this writing, Simply Hired's Web site provides the ability to currently search some 4,388,672 jobs from more than 5,000 job boards and thousands of classified ads and company Web sites. The search engine utilizes "deep filtering" and metadata integration to provide extensive drill-down capabilities based on the job seeker's search criteria. Filtering capabilities include the following:

- Job type (part-time, full-time, volunteer, contract, or internship)
- Education or experience level
- Company size (by number of employees or revenue)
- Ranked lists (Fortune 500, Working Mother 100, Forbes 100, Minority, and so on)

This search engine is very similar to that of Indeed. Simply type a job title or key-words and a location, and up pop job listings instantly. Each listing provides a job title, employer's name, short description of the position, and a link that takes you straight to the original Web site listing where you can directly apply for the job. Additionally, the job listing shows the source of the original job posting (for example, Monster, CareerBuilder, USAJobs, the newspaper, company career sites, and so on) as well as how long ago it was posted (shown in days and hours).

I took a test-drive of this search engine by typing "Human Resources" into the keywords box and "Maryland" into the location box. The search instantly produced 81 job listings for positions in the Human Resources field. I then attempted to narrow my search somewhat, by adding the word "Manager." To my surprise, I got 82 such job listings, one more than the broader search using "Human Resources" alone.

> **Note:** Because a large percentage of job listings often refer to the Human Resources Manager or ask you to e-mail your resume to Human Resources, in my search results count I made sure to select only those positions that advertised for Human Resource professionals.

Here again, as with Indeed, the search results were immediate. Within seconds I had a complete list of appropriate positions matching my search criteria. I can only imagine how long it would have taken me to find the same openings by manually searching more than 5,000 job boards and thousands of want ads and company Web sites. Although I didn't attempt to use the available filtering technology to fur-ther refine my online search, it would appear, based on the above filtering criteria, this would further narrow search results and save even more time by reducing the number of job listings I would need to sort through.

The Simply Hired Web site also allows you to save your job search criteria as well as specific positions you might want to review or recall at a later time. You can also activate an e-mail alert feature, which will automatically e-mail any new posi-tions that have been posted since your last search and that fit your original job search criteria.

Once you have developed a short list of jobs using the site's filtering capabilities, you can use the Web site to further evaluate the job opportunities you have iden-tified. Additional features allowing you to do this include the following:

- **Who Do I Know?:** Simply Hired has hooked up with LinkedIn, a huge online networking database of more than 4.2 million professionals, allow-ing you to connect with employees at your target company, or people who have relationships to those at your target firm, for networking purposes (see chapter 8 for more on how to use networking to your advantage).

- **Research Salary:** Once you have finished your Simply Hired search and have a short list of opportunities that interest you, one click on this feature and you get geographically linked salary ranges for this type of job. This salary data comes from a link with PayScale.com.

- **Company Research:** Adjacent to each company, a comprehensive company profile is available, containing company details, financials, and descriptions.

- **Apply Now:** Clicking on this feature takes you directly to the application process for any job in which you have interest.

Obviously, this is a powerful and feature-rich search engine that can get you to jobs of interest quickly, and can instantly provide you with valuable contacts and information at the click of your mouse.

Although the affiliation with LinkedIn is fairly recent, this partnership could prove to be a tremendous advantage for job seekers by allowing them to quickly link with an employee of (or a person who has contacts with an employee of) the companies identified through their Simply Hired online search.

With networking and employee referral believed to account for between 30 and 90 percent (depending on job level) of all jobs filled, having a networking contact at your target company has the potential to provide you with a big competitive advantage over other candidates who are simply e-mailing resumes to the employer in response to their online job listing.

Jobster (www.jobster.com)

A relative newcomer to the Internet job aggregator arena, Jobster seems to be off to a good start with the recent acquisition of WorkZoo, one of the pioneers in the job aggregator field. As with both Indeed and Simply Hired, Jobster allows you to use its search engine, free of charge, to automatically scour numerous job sites from across the Web to identify jobs that meet your criteria. Currently, the Web site has access to approximately one million "fresh" jobs, all posted on the Internet within the last seven days.

Jobster's search engine is easy to use, requiring you to type a job title or other relevant words into the Keywords box, and then the desired location (city and state or ZIP code) in the Location box. Results are instantaneous and provide a complete listing, including job title, company name, brief position description, job location, original job listing source, and when the job was first posted on the Internet (in days and hours).

In addition, an "advanced search" feature enables you to further refine your search using a number of options. An "e-mail alert" feature also gives you the opportunity to have new job listings automatically e-mailed to you as they are posted on the Web.

Furthermore, job listings are linked to the original listing site; so with a click on the link, you are instantly transported to the original job posting. At the bottom of this posting, with the click of the mouse, you can apply now, print a copy of the posting, save the job for future reference, view all saved jobs, or conduct a new search. It is therefore possible to quickly scroll through all jobs listed and save any that are of interest for more careful screening at a later time.

I put the Jobster search engine to the test, typing the terms "Human Resources" in the Keywords box and "Maryland" as my targeted location. Response was immediate, providing me with some 70 Human Resources job listings in the state of Maryland. Narrowing the search by adding the term "Manager" produced an immediate list of about 10 positions; however, results on the second page of the search had some oddball positions, such as Store Manager, mixed in.

A truly unique feature of this Web site is its job referral system, which Jobster calls its "talent network system." Jobster has created a professional networking system whereby active job seekers and passive browsers alike can register and volunteer to serve as a referral source for people seeking employment with their companies through the Jobster Web site. When a job seeker conducts a search using the Jobster search engine, certain job listings will have a small yellow icon positioned next to the listing, signaling that a member of the Jobster network is employed by that company and has volunteered to assist the job seeker by personally referring them to the company's hiring team.

What makes this idea particularly intriguing, from the job seeker's standpoint, is that due to the number of companies that have employee referral programs (especially those that pay a reward to their employees for successful employment referrals), many company employees have an incentive to join the network, whether or not they are actively looking for a new job. The more such people who join the network, the merrier, and the more viable the overall network becomes as a referral source for those seeking employment.

This feature also allows employers to tap into this pool of networking contacts to reach passive job seekers who might not be actively looking but might be interested if the right job opportunity should come along. So far, about 150 companies, including several major employers, have signed on to this program and are participating in this networking community.

The "Big 3" Job Boards

As you can see from my description of the three job integrator search engines in the preceding section (Indeed, Simply Hired, and Jobster), these are enormous timesavers that enable job seekers to use a single search engine to search multitudes of job listings from thousands of job listing sources across the Web. Despite the fact that these search engines can currently search the job listings contained on CareerBuilder, Monster.com, and Yahoo! HotJobs, in my mind there are some important questions still to be answered before you can completely rely on these job aggregators to do the entire job for you:

- How long will it be before CareerBuilder, Monster.com, and Yahoo! HotJobs find a way to prevent the job aggregators from scraping job listings from their Web sites?

- How significant is the time gap between the point a job is posted on one of the "Big 3"'s Web sites directly and its availability to you through the job aggregator search engine?

When it comes to Internet job search, time is of the essence! With a global audience of millions of job seekers, a time gap of minutes, let alone an hour or so, could make the difference between getting an interview or not. In a matter of seconds, thousands of job seekers can respond to a single job listing, with the employer's own in-house software instantly scanning and processing these resumes and applications. By the time you respond to the job listing through a job aggregator's search engine, the employer may already have identified qualified candidates for the position and be in the process of inviting them in for job interviews.

This is not to say you shouldn't use the aggregators—to the contrary, you should! What I am pointing out here, however, is that you don't want to be disadvantaged by doing so. And, because the "Big 3" job boards account for an estimated 22.8 percent of all jobs filled through the Internet, you would be well advised to also register directly on each of these individual Web sites as well.

I want to emphasize that the reach of job aggregators goes well beyond the "Big 3" Web sites to encompass thousands of other Web sites and job boards as well, so you will want to definitely use them. To only register on the "Big 3" would cause you to miss out on potentially millions of other job listings that would never surface by using the "Big 3" alone. Additionally, the networking opportunities afforded by these job-aggregator Web sites, if utilized, could provide you with a huge competitive advantage over other "Big 3" applicants, allowing you to network directly to key hiring managers or the hiring team.

So, I encourage you to do both—use the major job aggregator search engines (as previously described) as well as register on each of the "Big 3" Web sites. There is likely to be some duplication of job listings; however, you can always eliminate these and quickly pare down the list to the handful that are of particular interest to you.

Let's now examine each of the "Big 3" job boards so that you have an understanding of each of their capabilities as well as how to use them to your advantage.

Monster.com (www.monster.com)

Monster, the undisputed long-time champion of all job boards, as of this writing, is still the largest. However, it should be mentioned that CareerBuilder has closed the gap significantly in recent months. Estimates are that Monster now holds about 8.6 percent of the Internet job market, with CareerBuilder holding about 8.1 percent. So, it appears to be a virtual toss-up between the two Web sites, with the potential of CareerBuilder taking the lead shortly.

I spoke with a Monster.com service representative, who revealed that current job listings total approximately 1.23 million, although this can vary from day to day. The representative to whom I spoke indicated that some 44,000 new jobs were listed on the Web site yesterday alone. So, obviously, this is a huge database against which to launch your job search.

The volume of Monster's listings illustrates why it is important to use Monster and some of the Internet job aggregators simultaneously. For example, Simply Hired, with some 4.38 million job listings, has more than three-and-a-half times the job listings as does Monster. So by using Monster alone, you would miss out on searching an additional 3.1 million job opportunities. Moreover, Indeed.com indicates that its search engine has added 697,870 new jobs over the last seven days. At an average of 99,695 new job listings a day, Indeed appears to be adding more than twice as many new jobs per day as does Monster.

This is certainly not an argument suggesting you not use Monster. You definitely should. It simply goes to show that your job search needs to go beyond Monster in order to access the much larger total job search community. Internet job aggregators allow you to do this with little or no effort on your part.

In order to compare search results with those achieved using the job aggregators, I decided to also test-drive Monster's search engine as well. By using the "advanced search" feature, selecting "Human Resources" from the targeted job search menu, and then using the locations menu to select all seven Maryland options, I instantly generated 231 job listings, the oldest dating back approximately two-and-a-half months. Of these, 58 jobs had been posted within the last seven days, By further refining my search to include the keyword "Manager," search results were further pared down to 39 job listings within this same time frame.

When you click on a job listing, you are instantly transported to a full description of the position. From here, you can either e-mail the employer directly or click on the convenient "apply now" button, to choose a pre-stored resume and cover letter for use in completing the application.

As you might expect from this granddaddy of all job boards, Monster's Web site is feature-rich and offers a number of attractive options to help you automate and manage your overall job search. Here is a summary of these key features.

Resumes

Once registered with a free account, you can create and store up to five versions of your resume for future use. You have the option of copying and pasting an existing resume, downloading a resume from your personal computer, or creating a resume using online templates provided by Monster. It is recommended that these resumes be converted to plain-text documents prior to storing them on the Web site because most employers are now leery about opening other resume formats, attached to job seeker e-mails, because doing so might expose them to computer viruses.

You can also elect to include your resume in the public database for use by employers when searching for qualified candidates to fill their openings. A Monster service representative advised me that more than 810,000 employers are actively registered with their Web site.

Importantly, if you are currently employed, Monster's "Privacy Plus" feature allows you to block up to five companies, preventing these blocked companies from accessing your resume document.

Cover Letters

As with resumes, registered Monster users can store up to five different versions of their cover letter for instant recall and immediate use when needed. This can be an added convenience and timesaver.

Quick Apply

A "Quick Apply" feature enables you to click a button and instantly e-mail a preselected version of your resume and cover letter to an employer without having to return to your stored resumes and select one. This can be an added timesaver when the majority of job listings to which you will be applying are substantially similar, and there is no need for a more customized resume version.

Job Search Agent

Registered job seekers can create up to five job search agents, allowing continuous search of new job postings as employers list them on the Web site. When these new listings match your search criteria, a job alert e-mail is automatically sent to you, alerting you to the new listing. This eliminates the need to manually search the site's new listings, thus saving you considerable time and effort.

Other Job Search Management Tools

Monster also provides registered job seekers with a host of other features designed to facilitate management of their job search. An "Apply History" feature stores a complete history of positions for which the job seeker has applied as well as the resume that was used when applying for each position. An online calendar is also provided for use in scheduling interviews or various follow-up reminders on specific dates.

Online Networking Community

A unique feature of the Web site is Monster's online member network, which provides registered users with the opportunity to connect and network with other members throughout the entire Monster community. Use of this feature starts with creation of a personal profile, which serves to provide other members with a brief synopsis showing work experience, education, skills, and areas of interest. Members can search these online profiles for other members with similar backgrounds and interests for networking purposes.

Members can also select from a total of 36 different networking message boards, each with a different focus, where they can trade messages on topics of common interest or get advice from other professionals with whom they may be networking. A message center is also provided, allowing you to track and manage these messages.

CareerBuilder (www.careerbuilder.com)

CareerBuilder, founded in 1996, is one of the "Big 3" job boards you will want to include in your job search. It is owned by three major newspaper dynasties (Gannett Company, Knight Ridder, and Tribune Company) and was their answer to competing with Monster and other job boards as these online job advertising sites began to offer serious competition to the traditional standby of newspaper classified want ads.

Today, with more than 1.3 million job listings, CareerBuilder has become the mother of all online newspaper classified ads. When an employer places a recruitment ad in one of the more than 130 national and local newspapers that are part of the CareerBuilder network, for a small extra fee their ad will also be listed online on the CareerBuilder site.

CareerBuilder claims its Web site has around 26 million unique visitors monthly. Comparing this number to the 1.3 million job listings posted on the Web site, you get some perspective as to just how competitive the online job market is for the average job seeker. This is certainly a good reason for you to carefully fine-tune your resume to make sure that it stands out (see chapter 3 for more on resumes).

As with Monster.com and the job aggregator search engines previously discussed, I decided to test-drive the CareerBuilder search engine as well. The results were impressive!

By using the "Quick Job Search" feature on the homepage, and selecting "Human Resources" as the search category and Maryland as the location, the search engine immediately produced 190 openings that had been posted on the Web site within the last 30 days. Refining my search by adding the category of "Management" further narrowed the search results to 62 positions, all of which had been posted on the Web site within the last 30-day period.

The site's "advanced search" feature is fairly sophisticated and easy to use. In addition to standard search options such as searching by keywords, city, and category, this feature provides the ability to search by company and pay level. Additionally, there is an "exclude" box that allows you to exclude job listings with specific keywords, job titles, or companies. You can also elect to exclude national and regional jobs. These advanced search features are an added bonus of the Web site that will save valuable time when you're attempting to quickly narrow down search results to only those positions that interest you.

Applying for a single job is simple. By clicking on the listing, you are immediately transported to the employer's Web site and presented with two options. You can elect to apply instantly via e-mail by clicking on the e-mail option. You would select this option if you want to send your cover letter and resume using your own e-mail account. Alternatively, you can select the "apply with a posted resume" option, which allows you to apply using a pre-stored resume that you previously saved in your "My CareerBuilder" account.

While you're on the company's Web page, other options are also available to you. You can save the job in your "My CareerBuilder" account, print a copy of the listing, see all job listings at the company, or e-mail a copy of the listing to a friend.

A brief summary of other key Web site features follows.

Resumes
CareerBuilder enables you to store up to five different versions of your resume for future use in responding to postings. If you already have a resume, you can simply upload your document or copy and paste your resume into the CareerBuilder form. Optionally, if you don't have a resume, you can use CareerBuilder's step-by-step process to create one. There is also a privacy option that allows you to exclude your resume from being posted on the CareerBuilder online database. Electing this option allows you to store your resume for use in responding to job listings, but does not allow employers access to your resume document.

Cover Letters
As with resumes, this Web site also allows you to save cover letters for future use; however, there was no indication of the number of such letters that could be stored.

Job Alerts
Registered Web site users can also elect to use the "job alerts" feature. Using this feature allows you to have CareerBuilder automatically e-mail job alerts for any new jobs posted since your last search. You can choose to receive these alerts immediately (as soon as the new job is posted), daily (everyday by 9 A.M.), or weekly (every Monday by 9 A.M.).

Recommended Jobs
The "recommended jobs" feature automatically brings to your attention any jobs the Web site feels are appropriate and may be of interest to you.

Salary Wizard
CareerBuilder's "Salary Wizard," powered by Salary.com, allows you to get salary information for the type of position you are seeking as well as for the location of a given job listing in which you have interest. A helpful cost-of-living calculator also helps you determine what the cost of living is in a specific location, which, of course, could affect the salary you ask for when receiving a job offer from a particular employer.

Other Job Search Management Tools
Other job search management tools offered by CareerBuilder include the ability to save and recall previous searches, including criteria used, as well as the ability to save job listings and jobs to which you have applied.

Reference Check

For a fee of $40 (currently on sale for $29.95), job seekers can order a basic reference check, thereby seeing what employers might see in checking their references. A cursory review of this feature, however, suggests that it is more of a verification check than a full-blown reference check. This leaves some question marks in my mind as to whether this feature is truly worth the $40 fee.

Resume Blasting

A unique feature of CareerBuilder is the ability to use "Resume Direct" to blast your resume out to a number of search firms and employment agencies for a basic fee of $49.99. Under this arrangement, CareerBuilder will send your resume instantly to these firms in any three industries and three locations you select. There are additional fees if you want to select more than three industries or locations.

I attempted to find out how many such firms could receive my resume through use of this feature. In my judgment, there is a much better way to blast your resume to these firms through use of Kennedy Information's Executive Agent program, which is quite reasonably priced and appears to offer considerably more options than CareerBuilder does. For more information on this subject, and a complete description of Kennedy's Executive Agent service, see chapter 6 on search firms and employment agencies.

Yahoo! HotJobs (http://hotjobs.yahoo.com)

Yahoo! HotJobs, the third major job board recommended for use by job seekers, is the smallest of the "Big 3" boards. Although I was unable to get the number of job listings contained on the site, at the time of this writing, it is estimated that Yahoo! HotJobs accounts for approximately 6.1 percent of Internet hires. It should therefore be included in every job seeker's search strategy.

An interesting development is worth noting. In July 2005, Yahoo!, Inc., announced a new search engine that enables job seekers to use the Yahoo! HotJobs Web site to find job listings from across the Internet. According to the news release, this new search engine allows job seekers to not only search for client-paid positions already listed on the Yahoo! HotJobs Web site, but also to use Yahoo!'s Web-crawler technology to crawl the Internet and identify job listings from other employer and job board sites as well. So, Yahoo! HotJobs is now one of the newer entries into the world of Internet job aggregators.

When Yahoo! HotJobs presents search results, however, top billing is given to clients who have paid for their job postings. These paid position listings therefore appear first on the job seeker's search results, with the free job listings, scraped from other sites across the Internet, appearing at the end of the list.

I decided to give this new search engine a whirl to see what would happen, and to see how these results compared with their competition. By typing "Human Resources" into the Keywords box and "Maryland" as the location, the search engine immediately delivered 93 job listings, with 70 of these posted in the last 30 days and 36 posted in the last 7 days. Search results were instant and very much on target.

I then narrowed my search criteria by adding the word "Manager." This instantly produced a listing of 43 positions posted during the last 30 days, with 18 of these positions posted within the last week. As advertised, the search engine went beyond the paid listings already posted on the Web site to grab additional position listings from other sites across the Internet. This included both company Web sites and other niche job boards. A quick review of these results, however, showed no positions scraped from either of Yahoo! HotJobs' two main competitors (Monster and CareerBuilder). Consequently, this suggests that job listings from these two other major job boards will need to come either through direct registration on these boards, or from the use of one or more of the Internet job aggregators.

Yahoo! HotJobs's "advanced job search" features allow you to narrow your search by selecting a number of modifiers. Keywords used for search purposes can be modified to include certain specific words and exact phrases, as well as to eliminate job listings that contain certain words. You can also select up to three different job categories and specify up to two search locations, designated by city, state, or ZIP code.

Moreover, by specifying a minimum acceptable salary amount as well as years of experience required by the position, you can further narrow the results. You can also restrict job search results to only employers or only staffing firms.

It is clear that, by using Yahoo! HotJobs's advanced search feature and its many options, you can save considerable time that would otherwise have been consumed by manually screening each job listing for the desired criteria. This kind of efficiency gain can cut considerable time from your overall job search and enable you to find your ideal career opportunity much faster.

As with the other job boards, applying for a single position contained in the search results is quite simple. By clicking on a listing, you are instantly transported to the original job posting, where you can apply for it. From this listing, you can e-mail a copy of your resume, along with an optional cover letter, directly to the listing source; or you can follow specific employer-provided instructions as shown in the job posting.

A brief summary of other key Web site features follows.

Resumes
You can store up to 10 different versions of your resume, any of which can be chosen and edited to customize it for any opening for which you apply. If you have a preexisting resume in MS Word format, you can copy and paste it into the Yahoo! HotJobs resume box, where a text editor feature will automatically convert it into a plain-text document, which is preferred by most employers. Optionally, if you need a resume, you can create it from scratch using Yahoo! HotJobs's online resume tools.

After you have created a resume, you can opt to include it in the Yahoo! HotJobs online resume database where it can be searched by both companies and third-party staffing firms. You also have the option to restrict access to your resume to either employers or staffing firms, by simply checking the appropriate boxes provided for this purpose.

Additionally, you can choose the "Hotblock" feature to designate companies that you don't want to view your resume. And, of course, you can choose not to have your resume included in the public resume database. In doing so, it is simply stored for your own use when applying to jobs in which you are interested.

Cover Letters
As you create individual cover letters for response to specific job listings, you are given the option of storing the cover letters for future use. You can then modify or edit these stored cover letters to tailor them to other positions to which you apply in the future.

Job Search Agents
After you have input your search criteria for a given search, you can click the "Save Search" button to save this search for future reference or edit. Once you have saved a search, Yahoo! HotJobs will automatically e-mail you any new listings fitting your search criteria as soon as these positions are posted. Using this feature will ensure that you are the first to know when an appropriate position is posted.

Salary Calculator
If you click on the salary calculator feature, Yahoo! HotJobs will help you get a feel for salary levels paid to people in your field in the geographical area in which the job is located. Simply select the appropriate job category and then enter either the ZIP code of the employer's location or the state and metro area closest to the job's location. In doing so, you will get salary range information that should prove helpful in your negotiations if you receive a job offer.

Summary: The "Big 3" Job Boards
With the "Big 3" job boards representing an estimated 22.8 percent of Internet hiring, it is obvious that if you are serious about finding your ultimate job, you should register on these major Internet job boards. When you combine direct registration on these Web sites with use of the three major job aggregator search engines, you will unleash a tremendous force to assist you in finding that one ideal job opportunity.

Although there is bound to be considerable job listing overlap and duplication between these sites, the critical mass of jobs being searched using the online capability of this powerful combination of Web sites and search engines is in the range of more than 14 million total job listings. Searching this huge critical mass of jobs, if done intelligently, will surely produce a number of interesting career opportunities within a relatively short time frame. If you manage this process effectively, the bottom-line result should be a number of interviews and the opportunity to select that one ideal job from among multiple employment offers. This, of course, is the goal of the ultimate job search.

It is important to realize, however, that managing this huge combination of online job sources will be a challenge. You are therefore strongly advised to make full use of the advanced search features as well as the job search agents offered by most of these sites. You will want to use all available technology to the fullest to effectively manage the search process. And, of course, you will want to do as little manual search as humanly possible, allowing the site-provided screening technology to do most, if not all, of the work for you.

Also to facilitate rapid response to those job listings in which you have interest, you will want to pre-store several versions of both your resume and cover letter. This will enable you to instantly respond to most employment opportunities without wasting time. Not only will this make you far more efficient, but it will also provide you with a competitive advantage over those candidates who must take the time to prepare these documents before responding to the job listing. With the Internet, time can be either your ally or your enemy. Sometimes employers make initial candidate selection decisions within minutes of posting the job listing. In those cases, you don't want to be applying an hour or so later! (See chapters 3 and 4 for more on creating your resume.)

Moreover, full use of such automation as advanced search features, job alert agents, and rapid job application options will permit you to significantly save time as opposed to carrying out these processes manually. You can then use the time you save to simultaneously utilize other productive employment sources such as employment agencies, search firms, networking, and print advertising. Not all jobs are posted on the Internet. So you do not want to waste unnecessary time on the Internet when you could put this time to better use through networking. (See chapter 8 for more on networking.)

Niche Boards

As you will recall from figure 5.1, niche boards account for an estimated 16.9 percent of Internet hiring and have an important role to play in any well-conceived job search plan. Because there are more than 40,000 such boards, however, to save time and fully exploit this important job hunting resource, you will need a highly focused and well-planned strategy. Without such a strategy, you will be lost in the morass and waste an enormous amount of time and effort in attempting to find the handful of specialty sites that produce good results.

What Is a Niche Board, and What Role Should It Play in Your Overall Job Search Plan?

As the name suggests, a niche board is a specialty job board that is focused exclusively on providing job listings for a specific segment of the job seeking population. Such boards provide employers with the opportunity to narrow the audience they reach with their job listings to a designated group whose members are a closer match for the employer's requirements. By using niche boards, for example, employers can target such specific segments of the workforce as executives, minorities, females, temporary workers, contractors, specific occupational special-ties, specific industry experience, and so on. As previously stated, there are an esti-mated 40,000 niche boards, so the array of categories is almost dizzying to contemplate.

Much has been written recently about the growing use of niche boards as employ-ers begin to move away from the large general boards such as Monster and CareerBuilder in search of specialty boards that are far more focused. There are far fewer candidates registered on the niche boards, and their overall qualifications are more specific to the employer's needs. Whereas Monster and CareerBuilder can produce hundreds if not thousands of responses to a given job posting, the same posting on a niche board might produce only a handful of candidates; however, their profiles are likely to be a closer match to the employer's needs. This elimi-nates the need for employers to process huge volumes of candidate resumes, many of which are not even close to the employer's requirements. Because of this, employers are beginning to show an increasing preference for these specialty boards over the mega-boards.

Interestingly, the same rationale that applies to employer use of niche boards also applies to the job seeker as well. With their growing use by employers, you need to be sure to incorporate these boards into your overall job hunting plan. Posting your resume on such specialty boards, or using it to search for jobs, allows you to more quickly locate jobs of interest that are a closer match to your employment profile. Additionally, and most importantly, because there tend to be far fewer resumes posted on these sites, the competition is far less intense than when com-peting for the same position posted on one of the mega-boards.

Niche Board Strategy

With more than 40,000 niche boards and specialty career sites out there, how do you begin to get your hands around this critical mass and begin to make some sense of it? What is the best process for identifying that handful of boards that will produce the best results for your investment of time and energy?

When planning your job search strategy, there are essentially two main types of niche boards on which you should focus attention. These are the following:

- Trade/industry boards (those that cater specifically to your target industry)
- Career boards (those that cater to specific career fields/occupational specialties)

The following strategy, although it requires a little front-end research, will help you bring these two principal niche board categories into greater focus and save you considerable time in identifying and zeroing in on those two or three specialty boards that will produce the best results.

95

Identifying Trade/Industry Niche Boards

By now you have likely identified a specific industry, which you intend to target for purposes of your job search. In order to identify the best niche job boards, which contain job postings for this target industry, you will want to start by identifying the principal industry or trade association to which most companies in that industry belong. In many cases, there may be two or three such predominant associations.

If you are not already familiar with these key associations, I would suggest you network with other professionals now employed in this industry and ask them. Optionally, you might consider calling the public affairs departments of a couple of major target industry companies and asking them which are the two or three key industry associations to which their companies belong. A quick phone call or two will save much time and get you the information you need in short order.

Reference Books

If you are uncomfortable making such calls, you will need to do a little legwork to get this information. This process begins with identifying all target industry associations (and there may be several of them), and then narrowing down the list to those two or three that have the largest number of member firms. Here are some resources that you can use for this purpose:

- *Encyclopedia of Associations:* This encyclopedia lists more than 22,200 industry and professional associations in the United States. Using the index to look up your target industry will yield a comprehensive list of trade and industry associations associated with this industry target. Reviewing the descriptions of each, including purpose and membership size, will enable you to quickly zero in on those two or three that are dominant in their field.

  Once you have identified these key associations, use an Internet search engine (such as Yahoo! or Google) to see whether they have a Web site (most will), and whether this site contains a "jobs" or "career" section that lists member-company job postings. If you are unable to find an association Web site, or you can't find a job board on the site, simply call the association's national office and ask whether such a Web site or job board exists. In addition, you will want to ask them to help you identify other job boards that cater to that specific industry and are most frequently used by member companies for online job opportunity posting. Although the *Encyclopedia of Associations* is accessible online, the cost of access is prohibitive for most job seekers. This reference book, however, is commonly carried by many libraries and should be readily available in print form, free of charge.

- *The National Trade and Professional Association Directory:* You can use this directory as a backup to the *Encyclopedia of Associations*. Although not quite as comprehensive, it provides descriptions of more than 7,500 trade associations, professional societies, technical organizations, and labor unions in the United States. Despite having fewer listings, it provides much of the same kind of information as the larger encyclopedia. You may also find that your local library has this directory among its selection of reference books.

The important thing to know about these two reference books is that, in addition to providing complete descriptions of each association, they also show the size of the association (the number of member companies). This information is important because it serves as the basis for determining which two or three associations are the largest—the dominant players in their industry.

Whether you are identifying key industry associations or top professional societies, which cater to given professions or career fields, there are three books I highly recommend you consider buying or finding in your local library. These three publications are affordably priced, and are excellent resources for identifying those top niche boards associated with your target industry and profession. These are the following:

- *CareerXroads:* For those who are knowledgeable about the use of the Internet as a job search tool, the book *CareerXroads,* last published in 2003, is considered to be perhaps the most authoritative work on the subject, and it is well worth acquiring. Although as of this writing, the 2003 edition is completely out of stock, I would suggest checking Amazon.com to see whether there are any used copies available. As of this writing, there appears to be an ample supply.

  Despite the 2003 publication date, this is a book well worth having as part of your job search library. The book's authors, Gerry Crispin and Mark Mehler, are world-class experts and consultants in the field of Internet recruiting, who have a number of top American and international companies as clients. Among other services, they conduct research and run seminars for employers and search firms on everything from effective career Web page design to how to best use technology and the Internet to efficiently fill job openings. Their directory, *CareerXroads,* lists thousands of job, resume, and career-management Web sites, including many of the more popular niche boards. The authors have personally reviewed and evaluated more than 500 sites and selected 50 of these as "the best of the best." There are multiple indexes at the end of the directory, by which you can identify thousands of Web sites arranged by industry and occupational specialty, as well as other categories.

- *Weddle's Guide to Association Websites:* This guide, published in conjunction with the Association of Internet Recruiting, lists more than 1,800 professional, technical, and trade associations and shows what kind of employment services (for example, job board, resume database, network listserv, or discussion forum) they provide. Weddle's guide can be ordered online at www.weddles.com. Peter Weddle is a leading expert and consultant in the employment and career fields. He is a recruiter, HR consultant, and business CEO turned author and commentator. He is widely published and is frequently quoted on career and employment matters by major media. He is also the former Chairman and CEO of Job Bank USA, Inc., one of the largest electronic employment services in the United States, which he founded in 1991 and sold in 1996. He is considered to be a foremost authority in the field of electronic recruiting.

- *Weddle's Directory of Employment-Related Internet Sites:* This directory, which is published annually, provides the URLs for more than 8,000 Web sites that specialize in employment. It lists sites that post a wide range of jobs, as well as those that list openings for a specific career field, industry, geographic location, or affinity group. The book includes Web sites that post full-time, part-time, contract, and consulting opportunities. It is perhaps the most complete and up-to-date Internet address book of job boards and career portals anywhere. The directory is organized by career field, industry, and geographical focus. You can order it online by visiting www.weddles.com.

Online References

In addition to the print resources previously discussed, there are also some Internet-based resources that you can use to identify industry associations. Although they are convenient resources that should not be overlooked, each has certain shortcomings when used as the basis for formulating a focused, efficient niche board strategy. On the plus side, they enable quick identification of industry-focused niche boards with links that can take you directly to these Web sites. Shortcomings, however, may include the following:

- Limited listing (only a partial listing of industry job boards)
- No ranking (no way to tell which are the most popular and heavily used boards)

Despite these drawbacks, it is an easy way to dip your toe in the water while you do the previously described fundamental research needed to formulate a more comprehensive and efficient niche-board strategy. Nonetheless, here are a few online resources you might try:

- **Yahoo! Business and Economic Section:** This section of Yahoo! provides a free listing of many trade and industry associations, along with links that will take you directly to each association's Web site. It may take quite a while to scan though these Web sites to determine association size, and the information does not appear to be nearly as well organized or easy to use as either of the preceding two reference books.
- **AIRS Directory:** The AIRS directory, found at www.AIRSdirectory.com, provides a comprehensive listing of popular niche boards frequently used by employers and executive search firms to post job openings online. This directory of online sites lists some 4,961 popular niche job boards, broken down into 13 major categories as follows:

- Top Traffic (10 boards—the Internet job boards with the most Web site visitors)
- International (618 boards—10 categories by geographic location)
- Career Hubs (958 boards—6 regional categories)
- Function (294 boards—7 business functions)
- Industry (968 boards—38 industry categories)
- Technical (499 boards—12 categories)
- Healthcare (319 boards—22 categories)
- Financial Services (91 boards—4 categories)
- Government (827 boards—2 categories)
- College/Alumni (81 boards—6 categories)
- Diversity (115 boards—10 categories)
- Newsgroups (132 boards—10 categories)
- Contractors (49 boards—10 categories)

Although the list links directly to these job boards, you may find it difficult to wade through all these and determine which two to three boards are the ones predominantly used by those firms that are members of your target industry.

- **BigTimeJobs.com:** This Web site contains a comprehensive listing of Web sites broken down into 112 categories. If you click on any of the 112 categories, an extensive list of niche job boards appears, each linked directly to the niche board itself. The 112 categories are arranged in alphabetical order and are a mixture of both specific industries and occupations listings. This seems to be one of the better online resources for quickly identifying niche sites pertaining to your industry and occupational targets. The fundamental problem with using the site, however, is that there is no way to determine how these sites were selected for inclusion, and whether they really represent the predominant niche boards used by those employers wishing to target that specific industry or occupational category.

- **Nicheboards.com:** As the name of the Web site implies, this site provides easy access to a small number of niche boards organized by industry and occupational category. The number of categories and boards is extremely limited, but the site suggests that these are some of the boards experiencing higher usage by job seekers. According to the Web site banner, these leading niche boards attract more than 3 million unique visitors per month. A simple click on each job or industry category instantly takes you to the board and its job listings.

Identifying Career Boards

As the name suggests, niche boards that focus solely on listing job opportunities for a given profession or occupational specialty are known as career boards. Although this is certainly not always the case, the top career boards are often hosted by professional societies or professional associations, and are provided as a convenience to members seeking employment. The use of career boards by employers is growing because these niche boards enable employers to reach a more targeted audience of qualified professionals in a given occupational field than do the mega-boards such as Monster and CareerBuilder.

Because of their growing popularity and increased employer usage, you should incorporate career boards as a part of your overall job search strategy. As with industry job boards, however, the key is to find those two or three major niche boards that account for the bulk of the job listings and are most frequently used by employers to target your profession. There are thousands of career boards out there, so in the interest of efficiency and achieving maximum results, you must do some front-end research to pinpoint those Web sites that will be most productive.

The process for identifying the best niche boards for your career field is not much different from that recommended for use in pinpointing top industry niche boards. If you don't already know which career boards are "tops" in your field, you may want to call or e-mail some fellow professionals who are "in the know" and conduct a short survey. If your professional network is limited, you may then want to contact regional or national officers of your professional society and conduct a similar survey. You will probably find that there is fairly uniform agreement among these professional colleagues on which are the best two or three career boards to use.

If you do not belong to a professional association, or have a limited network of professional colleagues, you will need to do a little more work to arrive at a good decision on which niche career boards to use. In this event, I recommend use of the *Encyclopedia of Associations* or *The National Trade and Professional Association Directory* to identify the larger professional associations or societies that dominate your occupational field, and then place a call to their national office. Most national officers are quite knowledgeable and should be able to quickly point you in the right direction. And, while you are at it, you may want to also get the names of some of the local chapter officers for networking purposes. It may not hurt to seek their advice on this subject as well.

You will probably find that some of the recommended career boards are hosted by the professional society itself, whereas others are commercial boards run by independent companies. Although commercial boards are typically open for use by any member of the profession, this might not be the case with job boards sponsored by professional associations. Professional association job boards are often restricted to use by association members. In such a case, you may want to consider joining the association. Association fees are typically nominal in comparison to the many benefits you will receive. Not only will you gain access to the association's job board, but association membership will likely provide you with an invaluable resource for job search networking purposes as well.

Job Aggregators Can Replace the Use of Many Niche Boards

It is important to note that the major Internet job aggregators (Indeed, Simply Hired, and Jobster) already target thousands of job boards, including numerous niche boards. So, from a strategy standpoint, I recommend that you limit use of industry and career niche boards to a combined total of no more than four to six larger boards. Because all niche boards combined account for only an estimated 16.9 percent of Internet hires, it would be foolish to go much beyond this total. Moreover, smaller niche boards may already be covered though your use of Internet job aggregators.

After a few searches using both the job aggregators and your selected niche boards, you will want to compare search results. In doing so, you may discover that the job aggregators are already scraping job listings from the niche sites you have chosen and automatically returning these listings to you through their job search agent or e-mail alert feature. In such a case, you will want to avoid this unnecessary duplication by discontinuing use of the appropriate niche board(s).

Company Web Sites

As you already know from the Internet job search strategy illustrated in figure 5.1, if you are to have a complete job search plan, you will also need to use the Internet to apply directly to companies through their own Web sites. It is believed that approximately 53.3 percent of all Web-based hiring occurs through such direct application.

This is by far the most productive source of Internet hiring for companies. However, from the job seeker's perspective, it is by far the most time-consuming to use. There are thousands upon thousands of companies out here, so where do you start?

Clearly, you need to narrow your focus considerably by focusing solely on those companies that are target industry members and are located within your preferred geographical area. Once you have created a complete list of such companies, prioritize this master list so that you are focusing primarily on those firms in which you have greatest interest. This will get you down to a more manageable list of target companies and establish some reasonable priorities from an efficiency standpoint. Without such focus and prioritization, you will waste considerable time exploring Web sites and applying to companies in which you have little or no interest. This is valuable time that you could well put to far more productive use.

So, what is the process for identifying these target companies? In order to save time and avoid being redundant, I would suggest you refer to chapter 8, "The Incredible Power of Networking," where you will find a logical, step-by-step process for use in identifying target firms. After you have identified and prioritized these target companies, your online application process will run more smoothly and efficiently, and you will be making far better use of your time.

If you already have a list of preferred target companies, the fastest way to their Web sites and job listings is through use of Google's search engine (www.google.com). Simply type the company's name and the word "career" or "jobs" into the search box and click on the search button. In most cases, you will be provided with a company listing and link that will take you directly to the company's website or online job listings. From there you can scan current job opportunities, click on those in which you have interest, and then follow the online instructions for completing the company's application process.

Chapter Summary

The Internet now accounts for an estimated 30 percent of all jobs landed. To realize the full benefit of the Ultimate Job Search process, having a carefully planned strategy for exploiting this powerful employment source is a must. The three major segments of the Internet on which your strategy must focus are

- The "Big 3" job boards
- Niche job boards for your industry and profession
- Company Web sites

Effective use of these essential tools will enable you to cut job search time considerably and identify many more exciting job opportunities faster than ever before. If properly utilized, the Internet is a truly powerful resource that will prove to be the very heart of the Ultimate Job Search process.

CHAPTER 6

Using Search Firms and Employment Agencies to Generate Job Opportunities

Executive search firms and employment agencies continue to be a major source of jobs, and should therefore be part of any well-formulated job search strategy. Most studies show that these firms account for filling about 10 percent of all jobs, with some research showing this number to be higher. An online survey of more than 2,000 job seekers, recently conducted by Staffing.org, showed that 13.5 percent of respondents had found their last position with the help of a search firm or employment agency.

When you properly use search firms and employment agencies, in combination with the Internet sources recommended in this book, you have the opportunity to generate many job opportunities rather quickly, and thereby greatly increase the probability of landing your ultimate job. Using search firms and employment agencies is an important component of this combined strategy; therefore, make it a part of your overall job search plan.

The Difference Between Executive Search Firms and Employment Agencies

Before discussing search firms and employment agencies (how they operate and the best way to exploit them as a job source), it is important that you understand the difference between these two types of firms. Awareness of this difference will help you better understand the distinct roles of each and how to best utilize these two types of firms as an important source of job opportunities.

Executive Search Firms

The basic difference between the executive search firm and the employment agency centers around how they work with client companies, how they are paid, and the extent of the services they provide. The following summarizes the common characteristics of the executive search firm:

- Retained by the employer, under a legally binding written contract, to function as its exclusive agent and consultant in filling a given position.

- Will never represent the job seeker (they represent only employers).

- Is paid a predetermined consulting fee by the client company, regardless of the outcome of the search project. This fee is intended to pay the search consultant for his or her professional consulting services and time.

- In addition to consulting fees, is typically reimbursed for certain agreed-upon out-of-pocket expenses incurred while carrying out the search assignment, as part of the consulting contract.

- Legally, acts as the agent of the employer and is fully responsible to the client company for the results of the search project.

- Works only on an "exclusive" basis. The employer will use no other firm or employment source to fill the position on which the search firm is working.

- Always conducts a thorough interview of the candidate (often face to face), and writes a complete report summarizing interview results, observations, and specific employment recommendations.

- Always conducts a thorough reference check and prepares a complete written reference report on finalist candidates before recommending candidates to the client company.

- At the conclusion of the search, typically meets with the employer to present, and thoroughly discuss, no more than two to three finalist candidates who have been thoroughly interviewed and reference-checked. The employer is provided with an overview of the search process as well as written summaries and recommendations on all finalist candidates.

Executive search firms are sometimes referred to as *retained* executive search firms, referring to the fact that they are paid a consulting retainer fee for their services. This is quite different from the employment agency, as you will see in the next section.

Generally speaking, retained search firms tend to fill senior-level management positions paying well over $100,000 per year. Often these positions are at the director, vice president, or senior officer level. Occasionally a retained search firm may also work on assignments below the executive level, but this is normally not the case.

Employment Agencies

It is rare that an employment agency is ever paid any kind of retainer fee. Almost all work is performed on a straight "contingency" basis. This simply means that the employer does not pay an employment agency a fee of any kind unless and until they are successful in actually filling the job. Thus, their fee is strictly "contingent" upon successful placement of a qualified candidate. They are therefore sometimes referred to as *contingency firms*.

The following are general characteristics of an employment agency or contingency firm:

- Is not under contract with the employer to perform the search assignment, and does not legally represent the employer, as its agent, in conducting the search.

- Seldom has an "exclusive" on the search assignment. Must frequently compete with other employment agencies and other employment sources (for example, advertising, employee referral, direct sourcing by the employer, and so on) when working on an assignment.

- Is not paid by the employer unless they actually "place" a successful candidate in the position.

- Is not reimbursed by the employer for any out-of-pocket expenses incurred while conducing the search assignment.

- May represent either the job seeker or the employer, depending on its relationship with either party. Will represent and actively market the job seeker, if the firm believes that they can successfully "place" this person and earn a fee. (Employment agencies typically will not represent a job seeker unless they feel the individual is "marketable.")

- May or may not interview a job seeker before presenting his or her credentials to an employer. Will sometimes simply mail the job seeker's resume to several employers hoping to generate interest and make a "placement."

- Deals strictly with resumes. Would rarely provide an employer with a written interview summary or written reference report.

Whereas executive search firms focus primarily on filling executive-level management positions, employment agencies more typically focus on middle management, front-line supervisory positions, and individual professional positions. This is not to say that employment agencies *never* handle executive-level positions; sometimes they do. Proportionately speaking, however, the lion's share of such senior-level positions is handled by retained executive search firms as opposed to employment agencies.

So, if you are seeking a senior-level management position (for example, director, vice president, corporate officer, board chairman, and so on), focus primarily on using executive search firms rather than employment agencies. You can always decide to broaden your search to include employment agencies later, should your initial search efforts with executive search firms fail to provide the kind of results for which you had been hoping.

On the other hand, if you are looking for a position at the middle-management level or below, focus primarily on employment agencies. However, because some search firms handle a reasonable volume of middle-management searches, if you are seeking a position at this level, you will likely want to target these retained firms as well.

No Phone Calls!

One of the biggest mistakes job seekers frequently make is to spend valuable time calling these search firms and employment agencies. Unless you have an established relationship with a particular firm or consultant, or know for certain that a particular firm has a current search assignment for which you are well qualified, making such phone calls is a terribly inefficient use of your time.

When you make phone calls to these firms, you are playing a numbers game with an extremely low probability of winning. Your odds would be better playing a roulette wheel in a casino. To begin with, if the firm is a retained search firm, calling them is a fruitless exercise because these firms represent employers, not individual job seekers. They are simply not going to have an interest in taking your call.

Although some employment agencies might take your call, you are still playing a losing game. The odds are extremely slim that the firm will coincidently happen to have an opening, for which you are an exact fit, at the time of your call. This would just be plain "dumb luck."

If you are going to play the numbers game with these firms, you are far better off doing so through use of either e-mail or snail mail. As you will see shortly, it is quite possible, in a matter of minutes (and at nominal expense) to get your resume in front of literally thousands of such recruiters. Think of the time and cost of performing this same feat by phone. Chances are, you would still be making phone calls a year from now!

How Search Firms and Employment Agencies Work

Because I spent several years as a consultant in the executive search industry, I can give you an insider's view of how these firms work and why it is far better to send your resume than to call these firms individually by phone.

In the search industry, whether you are a retained search firm or an employment agency, time is a very precious, valuable commodity. As a search consultant, you need to focus your efforts on the handful of search assignments on which you are currently working, rather than take random phone calls from job seekers who may or may not have the qualifications you are seeking for one of your assignments.

Typically, when a search firm or employment agency lands a new assignment, they begin the search process by conducting preliminary research to identify appropriate persons who are most likely to have the profile the employer seeks. For the most part, such research is exclusively aimed at penetrating competitor companies and then targeting employees who hold the same or similar job title as the position for which the search firm is recruiting. In retained search firms, full-time researchers perform this basic research function, whereas in employment agencies, the search consultant often performs this research personally.

Once a large list of potential candidates has been identified, the search firm or agency begins the process of *direct sourcing*. This means that they begin calling the list of targeted candidates to identify those who might be both qualified and interested in the position. To supplement this research, they might also search their online resume database (or hard-copy resume files, depending on the extent of their automation) for additional candidates who fit the search criteria.

The typical search consultant can efficiently handle only about six to eight searches simultaneously, each at different stages of the search process (for example one in the research phase, one in the sourcing phase, one in the interview phase, one in the reference-check phase, one in the final presentation phase, and one in the job-offer/negotiations phase). Moreover, the consultant is probably dealing with between four and six potential candidates per search assignment at any given point in time. This means that in addition to the six to eight client companies with whom the consultant is dealing, he or she must actively juggle relationships with between 24 and 48 candidates. Add to this mix the fact that employers are anxious to get their positions filled promptly and are continuously pressuring the consultant to do so. Are you beginning to get the picture?

Now, put yourself in the consultant's shoes for a moment. Assume that your firm receives the typical 30 to 40 unsolicited phone calls a day from job seekers, randomly calling to find out whether your firm just happens to have a search assignment for which they are qualified. Considering your workload and narrow focus, how many of these random calls would you likely take? And, if you did take any of these calls, what do you think the probability would be that the person who is calling will just happen to match one of the six to eight search assignments on which you are currently working? And, in the highly unlikely event that one of the callers did fit the search profile, what is the likelihood that this random caller would also just happen to have stronger credentials than the candidates already identified through direct sourcing of your client's competitors?

Does the word "remote" enter your mind at this point? Well you would be right! The probability is truly remote. So, why waste your time making such calls? There are far better ways to accomplish this same thing much faster, and with considerably less time and expense wasted in the process.

Direct-Mail Campaigns

Mailing your resume directly to search firms can be a quick and effective way to find a large number of job opportunities. In this section I discuss the ins and outs of conducting such a campaign.

A Successful Experiment

A few years ago, while under contract to provide outplacement-consulting services to some of America's largest corporations, my firm was working with literally thousands of displaced employees who were going through career transition. During this time, we experimented with several different job-hunting strategies to find out which produced the best results.

At the time, we began experimenting with large-scale, direct-mail campaigns, which were used to send a displaced employee's resume to a large pool of employment agencies and search firms. A typical mailing involved using snail mail and included about 300 to 400 such firms.

This technique proved to be quite effective, and a high percentage of our clients ended up finding jobs using this approach. Moreover, this approach tended to produce multiple job opportunities within a relatively short time span (usually two to three weeks). We then proceeded to make literally thousands of these resume mailings, with consistently impressive results.

Assuming each candidate had a well-prepared cover letter and resume, what we discovered was that a typical mailing could consistently produce about a 2 to 3 percent positive response rate. This meant that with a 400-piece mailing, a typical job seeker might expect to initially receive between 8 to 12 phone calls from agencies expressing preliminary interest in the job seeker for current search assignments on which they were working. In roughly half of these cases, after some preliminary conversation, either the search firm or the job seeker would decide they were not interested in pursuing the matter further. This, then, netted down to about four to six bona fide opportunities and, after employer interviews, about two to three job offers.

Can you begin to imagine just how long it would take to make 400 phone calls and achieve the equivalent result?

So, when using these mailings, we were playing the numbers game, but stacking the deck in favor of the job seeker. By using snail mail (rather than the telephone), we substantially increased the number of agency contacts to several hundred (rather than just a handful), thereby surfacing a number of viable job opportunities within a relatively short time span (typically two to three weeks maximum).

Try a Second Mailing

It is important to know that in rare instances, you might get zero response to this type of mailing. Although this is extremely unusual, it can happen. In my years of career consulting I have seen this occur in only a couple of instances. In these few isolated cases, however, by making the identical mailing about two to three months later, the job seeker did receive a positive response. Much of this can be explained by the search cycle and assignment turnover.

A single search assignment normally takes an employment agency or search firm from two to three months to complete. This means that in two to three months, the firm is now working on a completely new slate of jobs, compared to the assignments they were working on before. This search assignment turnover is what accounts for the fact that the second mailing can sometimes be more productive than the first mailing, despite the fact that both the resume and cover letter are identical, and despite the fact that the second mailing was sent to exactly the same firms as the first mailing.

> **Tip:** Although both snail mail and e-mail should work equally well, e-mail is considerably cheaper, is much less labor intensive, and is much faster.

Regardless of whether you are using e-mail or snail mail, I recommend that you complete this mailing as one of the very first tasks of your job search plan. Experience has shown that things will happen quickly, with most results occurring within two to two-and-a-half weeks of your mailing. So, it is quite possible that, within two to three weeks, you will already be into the interview phase of your job search.

So, in the meantime, use the "Big 3" career Web sites as well as the three major job aggregators (see chapter 5) to search through several million online job opportunities, quickly bringing back the positions in which you have interest. The critical mass of job opportunities generated by this powerful combination of job search sources should enable you to bring your job search to a head quickly, hopefully allowing you the luxury of selecting the best possible career opportunity from among multiple job offers.

Finding and Targeting Executive Search Firms and Employment Agencies

In order to set up your own direct-mail campaign, you need to uncover a list of the search firms and employment agencies that are most likely to be looking for someone with your skills. The following sections discuss the top places to look for these firms.

The Directory of Executive Recruiters

Those who work in the career-consulting field know that the best listing of executive search firms and employment agencies is *The Directory of Executive Recruiters* (commonly known as the "Red Book"), which is published by Kennedy Information, Inc., of Peterborough, NH. The "Red Book" is widely used as the "bible" by most professional career consultants and virtually all leading national/international outplacement consulting firms. My firm has consistently relied on this directory when making large-scale resume mailings for our clients.

Published since 1971, the famous "Red Book" details more than 13,000 executive recruiters at 5,600 search firms. This book contains only select firms, both executive search firms and employment agencies, that have been carefully screened by Kennedy Information, Inc., prior to inclusion in the directory. As a result of Kennedy's thorough screening, the firms listed in this directory are believed to be among the best search firms and employment agencies in the industry. Both the online version and hard-copy edition of this book are currently priced at $49.95, and can be ordered through Kennedy's Web site at www.kennedyinfo.com or by phone at (800) 531-0007.

The "Red Book" has a separate category breakout for retained executive search firms and employment agencies, so it is possible to easily distinguish between these two types of firms.

The online version is searchable by more than 120 industries and more than 80 job functions. So it is possible to find firms that specialize in your target industries and targeted job functions.

The book provides considerable information for each firm listed in the directory. Each listing, for example, includes the firm's mailing address, phone number, fax number, Web site address, and e-mail address. The listing also includes a brief descriptive summary of the firm's business, its specialties (for example job functions and industries), and the names and titles of principal contacts. Additionally, the directory includes a complete listing of all branch offices for each firm, and provides similar detail for each branch as well.

Because of the known accuracy and completeness of *The Directory for Executive Recruiters*, combined with the proven effectiveness of a large mail campaign targeting executive search firms and employment agencies, I strongly recommend that you use this directory to prepare such a mailing. In carrying out this mailing, you should minimally target 500 to 600 of these firms (preferably more), so that you have sufficient critical mass to ensure a reasonable return for your effort. This is a great way to quickly generate multiple career opportunities and provide yourself with several options rather than be forced to make an important career decision based on only one employment offer in hand.

ExecutiveAgent.com

Although using snail mail to make a search firm/employment agency mailing can be both labor intensive and expensive, there is a much faster, simpler, and far less expensive way to accomplish the same thing. This is to use Kennedy Information's new ExecutiveAgent to do all of the work for you.

ExecutiveAgent.com is an automated resume-distribution service built on Kennedy's Executive Recruiter Database. This is the same database used to generate *The Directory of Executive Recruiters*, which contains more than 13,000 consultants and more than 5,600 executive search firms and employment agencies. For the current bargain price of $87, you can use ExecutiveAgent's online service to instantly e-mail your resume and cover letter to thousands of the firms in the ExecutiveAgent database—within a matter of minutes. To do the same thing manually, using snail mail, would likely cost in excess of $700 and take three to four days to accomplish.

> **Tip:** There are dozens of other "resume blasters" out there, but ExecutiveAgent.com is undeniably the best, due to Kennedy's thorough screening of firms before including them in their database. They are truly fastidious in compiling their data, and their database is updated annually and has a high degree of accuracy. This is the only resume blaster I recommend you use for contacting search firms and employment agencies.

After registering on the Web site and paying the $87 fee, you will have the opportunity to use the Web site's search engine to search the database by industry and job function, and to identify the search firms and employment agencies that fit your criteria. You also have the option to e-mail your resume to retained search firms only, to employment agencies only, or to both types of firms. In making your selection of firms, it is important to keep your selection criteria sufficiently broad so that your resume is e-mailed to at least 500 to 600 firms (hopefully more).

Firm-Selection Pointers

Here are some basic pointers to follow when selecting firms:

- **Geography:** Don't select firms based on the geographic location of their office. These firms typically operate on a national (and sometimes international) scale. Firms located in Los Angeles, for example, may well have clients all over the country. In fact, there could be times when they have numerous active search assignments, but currently have no California clients.

- **Multiple branch locations:** Don't assume that if you e-mail your resume to the firm's corporate office, it will automatically be made available to the firm's branch offices. Although some may have common resume databases, many do not. Don't take the chance. E-mail your resume to both the corporate office as well as all branch locations.

- **Job function and industry specialty:** When registering with Kennedy Information for inclusion in its directory, search firms and employment agencies are essentially forced to declare areas of specialty. Don't automatically assume that because a firm does not list your target industry or job as one of its specialties, that the search firm or agency doesn't do search assignments of this type. Experience shows that this would be a mistake. Although they specialize in a given area, most firms will undertake a variety of search assignments covering an array of job types and industries. So, don't be limited by what the firm declares as its specialties in the ExecutiveAgent database. Remember, it will cost the same $87 whether you send your resume to 100 firms or 1,000 firms. Go for the 1,000 firms!

- **Second mailing:** It will normally take up to two to two-and-a-half weeks for a mailing to completely cycle its way through the system. Although some response can be practically instantaneous, by two-and-a-half weeks,

111

almost all response will have occurred. If for whatever reason response to this initial e-mail campaign is minimal, consider making a second e-mail mailing of your resume to an additional selection of firms. There are more than 5,600 firms to choose from, and for the price of $87, you can hardly go wrong! Additionally, as mentioned earlier, if response is minimal or nonexistent, consider repeating the identical mailing to the same list of firms, as initially targeted, about two to three months later, By then they will be working on an entirely different slate of search assignments.

ExecutiveAgent Testimonials

To give you some idea as to how effective this technique can be, here are a couple of current testimonials from the ExecutiveAgent Web site.

"First let me say that I have been overwhelmed by the responses I have received within just one day of using www.executiveagent.com to send out my resume. I have had hundreds of e-mail responses, about 10 phone calls and discussions, two probable interviews, and some pretty good advice/encouragement. Well worth the fee."

"I think your service is great! I have received nearly 30 e-mails already. Most are automatic replies, but with some good information. I also have had two direct phone calls in the first 24 hours."

"I've received about 90 e-mails to date and two phone calls. This is excellent, particularly in this economy. Simply getting onto the radar screen of so many recruiters so quickly is a major accomplishment, and at a great cost."

The Association of Executive Search Consultants and BlueSteps.com

The Association of Executive Search Consultants (AESC) has long been recognized as the premier professional association to which the major retained executive search firms belong. Some of the well-known international firms that are currently members include Spencer Stuart, Russell Reynolds, Heidrick & Struggles, and Korn/Ferry International, just to mention a few.

If you are searching for a senior-level management position such as director, vice president, chief financial officer, chief operating officer, president, chief executive officer, or board chairman, this is the group of firms you will want to target with a resume mailing. Although many of these firms are included in the Kennedy/ExecutiveAgent.com database, you may also want to post your resume on BlueSteps.com, a career Web site sponsored by the AESC.

Through the AESC, more than 200 of the top retained search firms in the world have joined together to create a common database of resumes, searchable by all member firms. According to the Web site, "BlueSteps.com is the only executive career management service that gives senior executives continual exposure to over

4,000 search firm professionals in more than 70 countries. There are now over 200 of the most prestigious retained executive search firms now using this database."

As these firms land new search assignments, it is fairly routine for a member's research associate to run a search of the BlueSteps resume database for potential candidates and valuable industry contacts. If you are a senior-level executive, therefore, it is an excellent idea to register with this site online, post your resume, and complete the required individual career profile.

BlueSteps.com currently offers two levels of membership, as follows:

- **Executive Profile Only:** For $189, you are entitled to a lifetime membership in Executive Profile. This allows you to register your individual career profile and resume (or C.V.), making it quickly and easily accessible to all member search firms.

- **Executive Profile and SearchConnect:** For $269, you are entitled to the same lifetime career profile and resume registration as "Executive Profile Only," plus a one-year subscription to *SearchConnect,* the AESC's online directory of more than 200 member search firms, which you can search for firms and consultants who specialize in your industry or occupational grouping.

Only member firms can search the BlueSteps resume database. Employers do not have access. Because these member firms are exclusively retained search firms, they never represent the job seeker. Therefore, there is little likelihood that a member firm would ever circulate your resume to a client company without first seeking your permission and interviewing you for the position. This, of course, is not always the case with employment agencies that, as previously explained, work only on a contingency fee basis.

Chapter Summary

Employment agencies and search firms account for an estimated 10 percent of all employment hires. You therefore need to fully exploit this important job source as part of your Ultimate Job Search strategy. A well-designed search firm/employment agency strategy can rapidly generate a number of great job opportunities quickly—if you use the right sources and execute the strategy properly. Key components of this search firm/employment agency strategy should include the following steps:

- Conduct a large-scale mailing of your resume to a group of 500+ carefully selected search firms and/or employment agencies using the Directory of Executive Recruiters database as the basis of your mailing.

- Use the ExecutiveAgent.com resume e-mail services to instantly "blast" your resume to up to 5,600 top-quality search firms and employment agencies.

- Repeat the identical mailing in two to three months.

- If you are searching for a senior executive position, register with BlueSteps.com, making your background available for search by more than 200 of the most prestigious national and international executive search firms.

CHAPTER 7

Getting the Most from Newspaper/Journal Advertising

Although some people would suggest otherwise, newspaper and trade/professional journal advertising is not yet dead as a source of employment. Although the use of such advertising by larger companies has certainly declined in favor of Internet job boards in recent years, remember that smaller companies employ an estimated 85 percent of the United States' working population. Many of these smaller employers hire infrequently and are less sophisticated in their use of the Internet as an employment source.

Therefore, many still run want ads in the Sunday classifieds of their local newspaper—or in industry, trade or professional journals—without ever giving much thought to using a major Internet job board to advertise their jobs. So if you limit your job-hunting approach to searching Internet job boards, you might never see many of these job openings.

Evidence that Print Advertising Still Works

Two recent studies provide testimony to the continued use of print advertising as a hiring source. The *CareerXroads* study, referenced in chapter 5, shows that among the 40 large companies responding to the survey, print advertising still accounts for 5.5 percent of their total hires. The Weddle study (also in chapter 5) shows that 8 percent of people who responded to its online survey had found their last positions through newspaper advertising.

To further complicate the matter, as time goes by, more and more employers are buying combination-advertising packages (print plus online) from newspapers or other traditional print media. It is getting more and more difficult, therefore, to determine exactly what hiring is attributable to the print ad and which positions have been filled as a result of the ad appearing online. Although many local or smaller regional newspapers typically do not charge extra to run an employer's ad on their Web site as well as in the newspaper, others have formed partnerships with commercial online job boards and now charge a premium for placing the ad in both.

The three largest newspaper chains—Gannett Company, Knight Ridder, and the Tribune Company—jointly own the giant job board, CareerBuilder.com. More than 130 local newspapers are now affiliated with CareerBuilder. These newspapers, for an extra fee, will not only run an employer's ad in the local newspaper, but will also post the ad on the CareerBuilder job board as well. This gives the employer's ad far greater geographical exposure than just the local job market. This one-two punch combination has proven quite popular with employers. CareerBuilder now claims to have more than 1.3 million job listings posted on its Web site.

All of this is well and good, except that not all employers are willing to pay the added premium for a combined newspaper and major commercial job board ad. Furthermore, some just don't feel the need for the added exposure because history has shown that an ad in the local newspaper (and now also the newspaper's own Web site) has always produced a sufficient number of qualified candidates to fill their employment needs.

So, the bottom line is that not all jobs are listed on the large commercial job boards, and you might miss out on some excellent career opportunities if you limit your search to these major boards. As a result, a well-planned, well-balanced job-hunting plan must include an overall strategy that will enable you to capture these newspaper and other print ads as well.

A Strategy for Using Print Advertising to Find Jobs

Some job seekers may unwisely use daytime or early evening hours to read and respond to newspaper and advertisements. This is valuable time that can be used far more effectively for networking than for reading want ads. Networking, as you know, accounts for an estimated 25 percent of hires, whereas print advertising, as you have seen, accounts for only about 5.5 to 8 percent of jobs landed.

These statistics alone suggest that you should reserve daylight and early evening hours principally for networking and making personal contacts with those who can help you with key referrals and introductions. In the interest of running an efficient and productive campaign, therefore, consider reading and responding to newspaper and trade journal ads later in the evening.

Typical job seekers often take a rather haphazard approach to the use of recruitment advertising as a job-hunting source. It is not uncommon for a job seeker to limit his or her efforts to picking up the Sunday edition of a local newspaper or two. Perhaps, as an afterthought, he or she might thumb through an occasional trade association publication or professional journal in search of job opportunities. This rather limited approach is clearly not the way to fully exploit the potential of print advertising as a source of employment. A more strategic and comprehensive approach is certainly called for.

Formulating a winning strategy for getting the most from job advertising requires you to target four distinct segments of the job advertising market. These segments are the following:

- The national market
- Your target geography
- Your target industry
- Your profession/career field

Visualize this combined strategy as comparable to saturation bombing used by the military. There may be only a handful of really desirable but low-visibility positions in the mix, so the more complete or blanketed your overall strategy is, the higher the probability that you will get a "direct hit" (the job you really want).

The following sections discuss the four components of your strategic attack.

The National Market

There are several "national" newspapers you might want to consider using in you job search. Most of these now have online job search capability, allowing you to scan their classified ads directly from your computer. In most cases, this service is provided free.

These are the nation's largest newspapers that enjoy mass circulation well beyond the major cities in which they are published. Due to this mass circulation and large geographical coverage, these newspapers are particularly popular with employers as preferred advertising media. Their large circulation, combined with searchable job listings on their Web sites, often translates into large resume response and, therefore, a higher likelihood of finding better overall candidates than smaller community papers. Furthermore, their extensive circulation throughout a given region makes them the preferred choice when employers are attempting to attract candidates from a broader regional area than just the city in which these papers are published.

The following is a list of these large national newspapers, along with the Web addresses for their job listings:

- *Boston Globe:* BostonWorks.boston.com
- *Wall Street Journal:* www.CareerJournal.com
- *New York Times:* jobmarket.NYTimes.com
- *Philadelphia Inquirer:* www.philly.com/mld/philly/classifieds/employment/
- *Baltimore Sun:* www.baltimoresun.com/classified/jobs/
- *Washington Post:* www.washingtonpost.com
- *Atlanta Journal-Constitution:* www.ajcjobs.com/JOBSWeb/
- *Cleveland Plain Dealer:* www.cleveland.com/jobs/

- *Chicago Tribune:* www.chicagotribune.com/classified/jobs/
- *Houston Chronicle:* www.chron.com/class/jobs/
- *Dallas Morning News:* www.dallasnews.com/classifieds/jobcenter/
- *Los Angeles Times:* www.latimes.com/classified/jobs/
- *San Francisco Chronicle:* www.sfgate.com/jobs/
- *Seattle Times:* http://marketplace.nwsource.com/jobs/
- *Denver Post:* www.postnewsjobs.com/

In planning your advertising strategy, be aware that most of these large newspapers have their own searchable Web sites, where you can find job listings that replicate the print ads now running in the newspapers. Some of the more sophisticated Web sites also include job search tools and features designed to save job listings, store resumes, save cover letters, and generally help you manage your job search as well.

A handful of these major newspapers' online job classifieds are powered by CareerBuilder. So if you are already using CareerBuilder as one of your job search engines, there is no need to go to these newspaper Web sites individually to review their classifieds. You are already doing this automatically through your use of the CareerBuilder search engine. In fact, if you click on a main "jobs" icon on these newspaper Web sites, it will automatically take you directly to the CareerBuilder search engine. As of this writing, those newspapers whose job listings are powered by CareerBuilder include the *Philadelphia Inquirer,* the *Baltimore Sun,* the *Chicago Tribune, and* the *Los Angeles Times.*

As you plan your advertising search strategy, you will want to look through this list of major national newspapers and select those that provide the best coverage based on your geographical preferences. I would also suggest you scan their job listings once a week, probably on Sundays, because that is the day you will find the greatest saturation of employment ads.

Moreover, if you are not computer literate, or don't have access to an online connection, you might want to contact the newspaper directly and have the Sunday edition mailed directly to your house. Optionally, depending on your location and geographical target, you might want to check with your local newsstand or drugstore to see whether they already carry the Sunday edition of these papers, and have them put one aside for you. Additionally, major bookstore chains tend to sell the Sunday editions of these major newspapers as well.

Your Target Geography

Beyond the large national newspapers, you will also want to access the classified want ads of the local newspapers published in some of the smaller cities within your preferred geographical target area. Choice of these cities and newspapers will, of course, be driven strictly by your own geographical preferences.

A simple step-by-step process for accomplishing this selection follows:

1. Using a state or regional map, select the cities that are most central to your preferred geographical target area.

2. Make a list of these cities.

3. Using the Google search engine, type the city name, the state, and the word "newspaper" into the search box. Then click the "go" button.

4. Review the search results to identify the appropriate newspapers. Then click on the link to the newspaper's Web site.

5. Check the Web site thoroughly to see whether the newspaper provides online access to its job listings.

6. If no online job listing is available, consider subscribing to the newspaper's Sunday edition on a month-to-month basis. (Subscription information is normally provided on the newspaper's Web site.)

If you are unable to determine the name of the principal newspaper for a chosen city, contact the target city's or county's chamber of commerce for this information. You should be able to find the chamber of commerce phone number or e-mail address on its Web site. A quick inquiry by e-mail will usually do the trick. If you're not using a computer, simply use your telephone to contact Information in your target city to get the chamber's phone number. Then call them for the information you need.

When ordering a smaller city's newspaper or checking its online job listing for jobs of interest to you, focus your time on the Sunday edition. When it comes to smaller city or regional newspapers, you will find that most employers place the bulk of their ads in the Sunday edition because it is most widely read. Additionally, when the employer is running an ad for a full week, these ads typically appear for the first time during the early part of the weekend. If the employer is using a one-time display ad, however, it is almost always placed in the newspaper's Sunday edition.

While you're on the newspaper's Web site, also check to see whether they are part of the CareerBuilder network, and therefore include their employment ads as part of the CareerBuilder job-listing database. If so, and you are already using the CareerBuilder search engine as part of your overall job search strategy, you can eliminate this newspaper from your list. CareerBuilder will already have this newspaper's job listings included in its database and, thus, you already have online searchable access to them.

Your Target Industry

Not all job advertising is run in newspapers. Some employers instead choose to run some of their employment ads in industry or trade journals. This is particularly true if they want to target people with job experience in their own industry. Certain of these trade publications are published directly by the major trade or industry associations and distributed to their members. Others are commercially published by independent publishing companies and distributed to industry members on a subscription basis.

When planning your advertising strategy, be sure to include on your "must read" list any key publications of this type that routinely include recruiting advertisements aimed at people who have experience in your target industry. Most people are already aware of which journals these are; however, this might not always be the case. If you are not, I suggest that you network with professionals already working in your target industry and ask their advice on this subject. Optionally, you might want to call national or regional officers of some of the key industry associations to get their recommendations on which of these publications you should be reading.

Not Just for Job Listings

Beyond the job advertisements, there is a secondary reason for reading these publications. Doing so will enable you to not only remain current on current industry events, but might also provide you with a "heads up" on specific events that may well be the advance herald of job opportunities. For example, be alert for such news as expansion announcements, key retirements, major industry problems (especially those for which you may have a solution), and so on. These could well be the foreshadowing of some excellent job opportunities if you are thinking strategically about your general value and industry marketability.

Stay alert and use your networking skills to get the right introductions where events suggest there could well be job opportunity. This will get you ahead of the wave, and may help you land a significant opportunity long before the job reaches a newspaper or trade journal advertisement. You'll learn more about this kind of networking in chapter 8.

Industry Saturation Strategy

One thing to keep in mind is that many industries tend to concentrate in certain geographical areas. For example, the pharmaceutical industry has a significant concentration of companies in the Philadelphia, Pennsylvania area. The pulp and paper industry has a major concentration of companies in Wisconsin and Maine. Additionally, the oil industry has a large concentration in Texas and Oklahoma. These are but a few examples of such industry geographical saturation.

When planning your advertising strategy, take this factor into consideration. Consider whether your target industry has geographical concentration in certain areas of the country. If so, consider targeting the key newspapers from that geographical region as part of your overall job search strategy. This makes good sense because you will find that many industry employers target much of their job advertising in these very publications due to the high concentration of qualified candidates, with industry experience, who live and work in these geographical areas.

When thinking about using this approach, don't automatically eliminate key newspapers from these areas on the basis that you are not interested in living there. This could prove to be rather shortsighted. The job advertised in these newspapers, in many cases, may well not be located in that region. In fact, the actual job location could easily be in another state—or across the country, for that matter. Consider the following: If you were the corporate staffing manager for a pharmaceutical company located in Charlotte, North Carolina, and you were looking for some research scientists for your Charlotte research facility, you might want to run some ads in the *Philadelphia Inquirer*. This would be an excellent choice due to the large concentration of pharmaceutical companies in the Philadelphia area. So you would run the ads in Philadelphia, despite the fact that the jobs are actually in Charlotte.

So, if you were a research scientist with appropriate credentials living in Charlotte, you might be totally unaware of this opportunity because you did not think to look at job advertisements in the *Philadelphia Inquirer*. If you were using CareerBuilder's search engine, however, this might not happen because the *Philadelphia Inquirer* is part of the CareerBuilder network, and its job listings also appear online in the CareerBuilder database.

The example of the *Philadelphia Inquirer*, however, does point out another possible fallacy when it comes to how job seekers conduct their searches. Most of the major online databases, such as CareerBuilder, provide the ability to narrow your search to specific geographical areas such as states, cities, and ZIP codes. Although this can be a timesaving feature, it can also exclude opportunities in which you might well be interested. In the preceding example, if you limited your online CareerBuilder search to the Charlotte area, you might have missed seeing the Charlotte opportunity because you did not include Philadelphia as one of your CareerBuilder search parameters.

In final analysis, then, the key point to remember is "think strategically." When formulating your advertising strategy, for job search purposes, remember not to limit your geographical focus to those areas in which you prefer to live, but also focus on those areas of the country that have a large concentration of your target industry companies. Either subscribe to the Sunday editions of the key newspapers covering these regions or check their online job listings on their Web sites.

> **Tip:** Remember also to check the Web sites of major industry associations. Many now include job listings posted by employers who are looking for candidates with prior industry experience. This could mean you!

Your Profession/Career Field

Much the same rationale that applies to industry publications also applies to publications targeted to your particular career field. There are professional journals and newsletters, published by both professional societies and commercial printers, which contain job advertisements targeted at those with experience in a given profession. For example, if you are a marketing professional, there are certain marketing professional journals and newsletters containing job advertisements for people with marketing backgrounds. This is true for almost every profession or career field. So, as part of your advertising strategy, include these publications on your "must read" list.

As with industry journals, if you are unsure which profession or career field publications to acquire, consider informally surveying colleagues now working in your field. Alternatively, you might consider calling or e-mailing national or regional officers of the major professional societies or associations whose membership is comprised of persons working in your profession. You can readily acquire this information through these knowledgeable professionals.

If you are not already getting these publications, and you are somewhat strapped for cash, most local chapter officers or association members would gladly loan you their copy of these journals and newsletters. You might also find copies of them at your local public or college library.

And, don't forget to regularly check association Web sites for any job listings in which you might be interested. Many of the larger professional associations maintain online job listings for this very purpose. If you're not a member of the association, you will want to consider joining so that you have access to this online resource. Moreover, many of the professional journals and newsletters published by these organizations are included in the price of your membership. This is not to mention the additional job search benefit of being able to network through fellow association members as an integral part of your plan. Clearly, these benefits can be well worth the membership fee.

Using Newspapers to Find More Leads

Although your primary reason for reading newspapers is to scan the classified ads, effective use of these publications dictates that you also pay close attention to other factors that could provide excellent employment leads. These include

- Company expansion announcements
- Employee promotion announcements to key positions
- New-hire announcements
- Companies in trouble
- Obituary notices

Each of these events suggests the possibility of newly created jobs.

Healthy, expanding companies typically need to hire from the outside to support their growth and expansion plans. Companies that are experiencing difficulty, in turn, may need to hire people with specific knowledge or skills to help them cure their ills. On the other hand, employee promotion announcements may suggest the need to hire replacements from outside the company, while new-hire announcements might suggest the need to hire replacements at the new hire's former place of employment.

Although seemingly a bit morbid, more than one major executive search firm has made a good living from carefully reading the obituary column of the newspaper, only to land a nice search contract a few days following the announcement of a key executive's untimely demise. Not a very pleasant thought, but a practical one!

So, the message is: Read the newspapers carefully. Be alert to the possibility that any one of these events can give rise to an excellent career or job opportunity. Moreover, this can give you a shot at these opportunities long before they materialize as want ads in the local newspaper.

Adicio and CareerBuilder: A Powerful Combination for Searching Newspaper Ads Online

Move over, CareerBuilder! There's another major player on the online newspaper advertising scene. This player is Adicio. Although CareerBuilder has dominated the newspaper advertising industry from an online perspective, there is another major applications service provider, Adicio, now powering the job search engines of a number of major newspaper Web sites. Formerly known as CareerCast, Adicio now boasts more than 100 newspapers as part of its network. This includes the likes of the *Wall Street Journal*, the *Boston Globe*, the *New York Times*, the *San Diego Union-Tribune*, and the *Orange County Register*, among several others.

Adicio, through its private-label branding of its search engine, provides job seekers with the opportunity to use any of the participating newspaper Web sites to aggregate and scrape the appropriate job listings from all of the other newspaper Web sites that participate in Adicio's network. Access to this job aggregator is through each member newspaper's own Web site. To access it, simply select the "jobs" link on the participating newspaper's Web site, which then allows access to the entire network. As of this writing, Adicio has access to more than 2.4 million newspaper job listings on member newspapers' Web sites.

A very important point to be aware of is that, in order to thoroughly search online newspaper job listings, you must use both CareerBuilder and Adicio. At this time, unless an employer is simultaneously running an ad on CareerBuilder and one of the Adicio newspaper sites, there is no duplication of ads. To simplify your decision and ensure that all your bases are covered, I suggest registering on CareerBuilder as well as on one of the following Adicio newspaper Web sites:

- *Wall Street Journal:* www.CareerJournal.com
- *New York Times:* jobmarket.NYTimes.com
- *Boston Globe*: BostonWorks.boston.com
- *San Diego Union-Tribune:* careers.signonsandiego.com/index.cfm
- *Orange County Register*: www.ocjobfinder.com/

- *Seattle Times:* marketplace.nwsource.com/jobs/
- *St. Louis Post Dispatch:* www.stltoday.com/jobs

You can use the job search engine of any one of these newspapers to search the job listings of all 100 newspapers that are part of the Adicio network (a total of 2.4 million jobs).

With CareerBuilder claiming more than 130 newspapers (1.3 million jobs) and Adicio claiming more than 100 newspapers (2.4 million jobs), by using the combined power of both search engines, you can completely automate the search of more than 230 newspapers and a combined total of 3.7 million job listings! This automation will cover a good portion of the overall newspaper job-advertising market, and enables you to search an enormous cache of jobs efficiently.

When using the CareerBuilder and Adicio job search engines, make sure to automate the search as much as possible. Make full use of the advanced search features of both search engines to pinpoint your requirements as specifically as possible. Let the technology do all of the legwork for you, so that you spend your time reviewing only those positions that are a close match to your ultimate job objective.

Chapter Summary

Accounting for between 5.5 percent and 8 percent of all hiring results, newspaper advertising deserves a role in your Ultimate Job Search strategy. Rather than a haphazard approach, you will need to formulate a comprehensive strategy that leaves little to chance. Key components of your advertising job search strategy include the following:

- A "national market" strategy
- A "target geography" strategy
- A "target industry" strategy
- A "profession/occupational specialty" strategy

You can eliminate most manual screening of job advertising through the use of screening technology now available on the Internet. Key search engines, such as those available from CareerBuilder and Adicio, allow you to scan millions of jobs in a matter of seconds and return only those ads that meet your criteria. This can be a powerful addition to your Ultimate Job Search strategy, helping you to find more interesting job opportunities faster than ever before.

CHAPTER 8

The Incredible Power of Networking

Numerous studies of employment sources clearly show networking to be one of the most productive sources for landing a job. Estimates of jobs found through networking range from an average of 25 percent to a high of over 90 percent. Moreover, it has been clearly demonstrated that the higher in the organization you are, the more likely networking is to play a key role in finding employment. At the executive level, for example, some believe networking accounts for well over 90 percent of all jobs landed.

One recent study makes the point. A joint study conducted by the Society for Human Resource Management (SHRM) and the *Wall Street Journal*'s CareerJournal.com showed that some 95 percent of job seekers and 95 percent of human resource professionals use networking and personal contact to find and fill positions. Both groups rated this method as the most effective.

Regardless of whose study you read, which statistics you believe, or at what organizational level you reside, these studies unanimously agree on one point: Networking is by far one of the most productive tools for landing a position—bar none! Study after study supports this fact. Networking therefore needs to be a key component of your job search program. It is the purpose of this chapter to explain exactly how networking works and what you can do to become proficient in using it.

Why Is Networking So Powerful?

The power of networking, as a job-hunting tool, rests in the fact that networking gives you the means to access the "hidden job market." This term refers to employment opportunities that have not yet become known to the general public. These are jobs that exist, but the company has not yet advertised them in newspapers, posted them on Internet job boards, listed them with employment agencies and search firms, added them to the job opportunities section of the company's Web site, or otherwise brought these opportunities to the attention of the public.

Networking Reveals the Hidden Job Market

These jobs are "hidden" from the public's view and are known by only a small handful of internal employees (typically the hiring manager, the functional executive, and the human resources manager). In many cases, word about these openings has not yet reached the company recruiter. So, at this stage, if a corporate recruiter received your resume, you would likely be receiving a "no interest" letter or e-mail, despite the fact that a job opportunity actually existed for which you were ideally qualified.

Using networking contacts to get to these jobs, before the public knows of them, can obviously provide you with an enormous competitive advantage over other candidates with whom you might otherwise have had to compete. Think about it. If you can network to the hiring manager and generate interest in your candidacy before anyone else is even aware of the job opportunity, you have effectively reduced your competition to zero. This is what happens when you skillfully use networking.

Networking, thus, becomes key to an effective job search. Failing to take advantage of this important tool substantially reduces your chances of landing the job, as you now are one in a "cast of thousands," all competing for the same position. These are not odds on which an experienced gambler would choose to bet. So, why should you?

Networking Makes You a "Known Quantity"

There is another important reason why job search networking is so successful in landing jobs. It is a well-established fact that hiring managers prefer to hire a "known quantity." When a candidate's introduction is orchestrated through a company employee, hiring managers have a tendency to feel more comfortable with the candidate than with someone who has just "walked in off the street." Additionally, when another employee takes the time to make a candidate referral, the hiring manager typically feels a sense of obligation to give special consideration to that person's candidacy. Such personal introductions are to the candidate's advantage, and greatly enhance the probability of success.

Consider, if you were the hiring manager, how you would respond to a personal referral made by a fellow employee or someone else with whom you have a personal or professional relationship? Wouldn't you feel a sense of obligation to give this candidate careful consideration for your job opening?

Networking Actually Creates Jobs

Furthermore, studies have shown that networking can sometimes actually create jobs that did not previously exist. In fact, research conducted by Mark S.

Granoveter, a Harvard sociologist, and published by the *Harvard University* Press under the title "Getting a Job: a Study of Contacts and Careers," showed that a surprising 43.8 percent of all jobs found through the networking process were newly created and did not exist prior to the networking contact. Additionally, Granoveter's study showed that those who found their jobs through personal contacts typically found their jobs more satisfying and rewarding versus those who used other sources to find employment.

I can attest to the fact that a networking call can sometimes create jobs, even executive positions. While I was employed as manager of technical employment at Scott Paper Company's corporate offices a while back, Dr. Vincent Russo, then vice president of technology, contacted me. Dr. Russo told me that he had just received a phone call from a Dr. Jerry Bresinsky, a professor at the Institute of Paper Chemistry, inquiring about employment opportunities at Scott Paper. Dr. Russo told me that, although he didn't have a current opening in the technology group, he would like to bring Dr. Bresinsky in for an exploratory interview. Shortly thereafter, Dr. Bresinsky was hired as vice president of product development, an executive-level position that did not exist prior to Bresinsky's phone call.

So, as you can see, networking is a powerful employment tool that deserves to be a major component of any job seeker's employment plan.

Networking Perceptions

You may occasionally see newspaper or magazine articles proclaiming, "Networking is dead!" Often, such articles go on to cite, in painstaking detail, the ordeals of a particular job seeker who is frustrated with the networking process and feels it just doesn't work.

Many times, such articles cite the alleged aversion of managers toward accepting networking calls as the principal culprit responsible for the job seeker's feeling of futility. The story line typically goes on to say that managers have been "networked to death," and have fortified themselves with impenetrable defenses designed to filter out these kinds of calls.

Granted, employment networking can be challenging and requires a degree of resilience and intestinal fortitude. If you're poorly trained in networking techniques, the task can be particularly daunting, especially if you are screened out time and again by an abrupt but effective administrative guard dog, who has been charged with the responsibility of keeping such calls off the boss's back. Surely, unless you are skilled at overcoming such obstacles, networking can prove humiliating and quickly zap your confidence and self-esteem.

But, then, there's the other side of the story. There are those who have reaped the rewards of proper networking and would gladly tell their story to any reporter willing to listen. These are the ones who have used networking to cut months off their job-hunting campaign and ended up with positions they find stimulating and rewarding. These are the persons who have learned the secrets of effective networking, and have used these skills to penetrate the hidden job market and discover exciting opportunities of which others have never been aware.

Obviously, with an estimated 25 percent of all jobs filled through networking (up to 90 percent at the executive level), it is clear that many job seekers have already discovered the value of networking and reaped the rewards of using this practice. Certainly the market has shown that networking can have a huge payoff if you are willing to take the time to use it, and to use it well.

What Is Networking? How and Why Does It Work?

The general term "network" is commonly defined as a series of connected persons or objects. For example, a computer network is a series of computers hooked together so that information can be transmitted and shared between members of the network. Through the network, the computer user can access data from, or transmit data to, any or all of the other computer users connected to the same network. Likewise, a "social" network is a group of people who are connected or affiliated through a common interest or need. The objective of social networks can be either personal or business-related.

Regardless of the reason for being, an important by-product of all such networks is the relationships that frequently develop among the group's members. There is a certain level of personal allegiance and responsiveness that evolves quite naturally as the result of the group's common interests and the relationships spawned through personal affiliation with the group.

Social networks, both personal and business, are at the very heart of the employment networking process. It is through these contacts that you must work to identify employment opportunities. The objective of job search networking is to approach these contacts (either directly or through others) and to solicit their assistance finding employment.

The members of your immediate network, either directly or indirectly (through their contacts in other networks), are often in a position to provide valuable job leads. When you stop to consider that each member of your immediate network, in all likelihood, is a member of several other social or business networks (to which you do not belong), the opportunity to reach well beyond your own personal sphere, through proper networking, is huge.

The Networking "Multiplier Effect"

A reason why networking is so successful has to do with a phenomenon known as the "multiplier effect." An explanation of this effect follows.

If you had the opportunity to contact only those people you know personally, in all likelihood, networking would probably not be all that effective. It is the ability to tap into other people's networks, through a combination of personal contact and introduction, that accounts for the success of employment networking.

If executed properly, employment networking can enable you to quickly explode a small handful of personal contacts into a huge network of hundreds of "indirect" contacts, all of who become in some way involved in helping you with your job search. Multiplying these few initial direct contacts into a vast army of helpers can be an enormous force that can rapidly accelerate your job search and lead to a successful result, often much sooner than when using other, less productive employment sources.

A way of visualizing the power of this phenomenon is to think in terms of biological cell division. Organisms grow by multiplying their cells. Each organism starts as a single cell, which then divides in two. The resultant two cells then again divide into two more cells (now a total of four cells). Each of these four cells then again divides into two more (now a total of eight cells). And so the process of growth continues to explode as cells continue to divide and multiply themselves.

The networking process (as illustrated in figure 8.1) is very much like cell division. The process starts with a handful of personal contacts. Then, by networking to each of their contacts, the process (much like cell division) begins to multiply itself. As illustrated, the process can quickly become exponential. By level 6, for example, a single contact has suddenly become 32 people. Thus, by the sixth networking level, you have already recruited an army of some 32 persons, willing and able to represent your cause by providing you with job leads and further introductions to their contacts (the seventh networking level).

Figure 8.1 visually shows the multiplier effect of good networking. By starting with only one direct contact (whom you know personally), and averaging only two referrals per each subsequent networking contact, in just six levels of networking, you can rapidly multiply this single contact into a network of 32 people.

Because a good networker can average 30 to 40 networking calls daily, the total network can quickly expand to several hundred contacts in a matter of days. At this rate, it shouldn't take long to unearth several interesting job leads.

According to the theory known as "six degrees of separation," you can use your contacts to network to anyone in the world within a matter of six phone calls, just by tapping into the networks of others. So, if you have planned your networking carefully, you should be able to get to some key people with knowledge of (or having) the appropriate job opportunities by level six in the networking chain.

What Holds the Networking Chain Together?

People I have trained in employment networking are sometimes skeptical that the networking chain can continue much below the second or third level of contacts. After all, they theorize, at this level in the networking chain, you no longer even know the person who has referred you to the new contact, and the "relationships connection" now seems superficial, at best. Such thoughts often cause the networker to feel uncomfortable and lose confidence in the process. They frequently ask, "Why would someone at this level be willing to help me with my job search?" Good question, and it deserves a response!

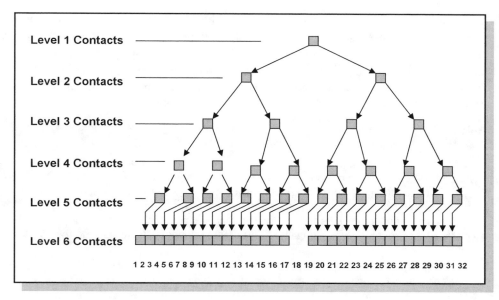

Figure 8.1: The "multiplier effect."

Thus far, I have explained only "how" employment networking works; I have yet to explain "why" it works. The "why" is best explained by what I like to call the "social obligation phenomenon."

To begin with, networking is essentially a "referral" process. At the heart of the process is the personal referral that forms the link between the person you are speaking with and the contact to whom you are subsequently referred. It is this personal referral that is the glue that holds the networking process together and makes it work, regardless of how far down the networking chain you have gone.

When you tell an individual that someone they know has referred you to them, the natural assumption is that you also know the person who has made the referral. Consequently, the new contact feels an obligation to respond, and to be of whatever assistance they can. The unwritten rules of social etiquette dictate this behavior and all but demand that any person referred by someone you know be treated in a friendly and helpful manner.

Consider, for a moment, a recent occasion when someone called you for help and told you a friend or other personal acquaintance had referred them to you. What did you do? Did you refuse to help? Were you rude? I doubt it! Chances are you listened carefully to their request and then did your best to be of assistance. Am I right? Obviously! Well this is exactly what happens with networking, if you are polite and handle yourself appropriately.

So, no matter how far down the networking chain you go, simply telling the other party you were referred by someone they know will, in almost all cases, elicit a friendly and helpful response. Your own response to the questions I asked in the preceding paragraph should reassure you that this will be the case. So, don't worry about actually knowing the person making the referral. It really doesn't matter.

The key to effective networking, then, is to make full use of the referral process, at all levels of networking, and to not be unreasonable in your request for the other person's assistance. If you follow these two simple rules, there is a high likelihood that you will become very effective at employment networking.

The Stats Favor Networking

By now the statistical advantage of using networking as a principal means of generating job opportunities should be evident. First, it is a fact that networking lands more jobs than practically any other employment source. It is better than newspaper advertising, better than employment agencies and search firms, better than career fairs, better than college recruiting—more productive than any other job source. If you focus a good part of your job search time and effort on networking, you are stacking the odds greatly in your favor.

Furthermore, if properly performed, good networking is an "exponential" process. Each new networking contact is fresh and, if fully exploited, will multiply itself several-fold. The cumulative effect of intelligent networking is that, in a short time, you can generate a critical mass of interested people willing and able to lend a helping hand to your job search effort. This can amount to thousands of eyes and ears alert to job opportunities that may be of interest to you, and willing to at least make the initial introductions needed to pursue them.

So, the choice is yours. You can elect to ignore these statistics and suffer the consequences, or you can conduct an informed job search that places the odds decidedly in your favor. The mathematical advantages of using networking as a principal job search tool simply can't be ignored.

Emotional Barriers to Networking

Experienced career counselors, who support job seekers during career transition, are particularly sensitive to the need to help individuals overcome the awkwardness so frequently encountered when contemplating networking for the first time. Most job seekers are torn. They recognize the importance of networking to job search success, but they feel awkward about doing it. For most, asking someone for help, especially a complete stranger, is not an easy thing to do. This is a very common issue for job seekers and is a natural reaction.

Embarrassment, Awkwardness, and Fear of Rejection

Emotions typically run high when you have recently been laid off or fired from your last position. In such cases, you might not only feel awkward about making a networking call, but are also embarrassed by the circumstances surrounding your employment termination. Many people feel especially uncomfortable with the prospect of having to explain the reasons for their departure. So, they might elect to deal with the situation by avoiding the issues, and decide to forego networking entirely. This is, of course, a mistake.

Beyond the initial feelings of awkwardness and embarrassment, a certain percentage of job seekers (probably better than half) will also experience some level of fear and anxiety when contemplating the thought of networking. Among job seekers, this is a frequent occurrence. What if people are annoyed by my networking call? Will they consider me a nuisance? What if they won't want to help? Maybe they'll be outright nasty? What if they're rude and just hang up? These and similar questions often rattle through the minds of job seekers as they consider the prospect of making networking calls. The fear of rejection, for most, can cause networking paralysis. They just can't bring themselves to pick up the phone.

For many would-be networkers, the combination of emotions is sufficiently strong to cause them to ignore networking entirely. Why force yourself to feel awkward, embarrassed, or fearful by doing something that seems unnatural? After all, there are other ways of finding jobs. Certainly reading newspaper ads, combing Internet job boards, contacting employment agencies, or sending letters to employers is far less threatening.

Failure to rationally deal with these feelings early, and jump into the networking waters, places job seekers at a distinct disadvantage. They are ignoring one of the most productive methods of finding employment. Furthermore, they are relegated to focusing on the public job market, where competition is far more intense. They have forgone the opportunity to effectively penetrate the hidden job market and thereby substantially reduce or even eliminate competition. Furthermore, they might forfeit the opportunity to generate sufficient interest in their qualifications for an employer to actually create a job. (Remember the Granoveter study, which showed that 43.8 percent of jobs were newly created, and did not exist prior to the networking contact.)

Overcoming Your Emotions

This is all well and good, but how do you quell these emotions and get on with the process of networking? Here are some tips and pointers:

- **Avoid asking for a job.** Most job seekers feel embarrassed about the need to ask others for a job. They are unaccustomed to asking others for help, particularly a job, and find this embarrassing, if not degrading. The solution to this dilemma is simple: Don't ask for a job! Simply tell people that you are in the process of making a career transition, and are calling them at the suggestion of "John Doe" (the name of the person who referred you) to ask for some general advice and ideas. There you go! You are no longer asking for a job or job lead; you are simply asking for advice and ideas. Most people are quite willing to provide advice, and it gets the whole networking conversation off to an easy start.

- **Don't fear imaginary ghosts.** Fear is often an irrational and unfounded emotion. It is normally associated with the unknown. When people are faced with an unknown, they frequently imagine the worst. They fill the void with all kinds of ghosts and goblins lurking in the shadows, waiting to pounce. In the case of networking, the ghost is rejection. Job seekers fear networking because they feel others will be annoyed, unkind, or nasty, or have other negative reactions to their networking call. They fear rejection. Nothing could be further from reality. I have watched hundreds of people making numerous networking calls and can tell you, without reservation, that such negative reactions are extremely rare. To the contrary, if the networker is polite and asks for assistance in the right way, the overwhelming majority of people will respond positively and provide whatever help they can.

So, put your fears and anxiety aside. They are imaginary and totally unfounded. You will find, as I move on to the discussion of specific networking techniques, that there are some very effective ways to approach a networking contact, which will create a positive atmosphere and stimulate the networking contact's desire to help you. There is absolutely no rational reason to feel embarrassed, awkward, or anxious when networking.

Explaining Job Separation to Networking Contacts

Whether recently separated from their last job as a result of company downsizing or for performance reasons, job seekers often feel uneasy about having to explain the circumstances of their separation to others during a networking call. This might cause them to be hesitant about making such calls or, worse yet, provide an excuse for not making networking calls at all.

Certainly, in some cases it will be difficult for you to avoid offering at least some limited explanation for your employment separation. When networking with close friends, for example, you will likely want to volunteer at least a minimal explanation. Additionally, in some cases, contacts through whom you are networking might ask point-blank the reason you left. In either case, you will want to be well prepared to address this matter.

If You Were Downsized

In cases where you have been affected by company downsizing, coupled with job elimination, you can handle the matter in a fairly straightforward manner. A brief explanation such as the following will suffice:

> *"Unfortunately, Baxter Corporation has downsized its corporate staff by nearly 20 percent, and my position was eliminated."*

or

"My position was eliminated as part of a 20 percent reduction in Baxter's corporate staff. Although I was offered another position, I felt it in my best interest to pursue other career opportunities outside the company."

If you were offered another position by your previous employer during the downsizing process, it's a good idea to mention this. Doing so suggests that the company at least thought enough of you to make the alternative job offer. This fact will not be lost on your networking contact.

If You Were Downsized and Replaced

If the networking contact elects to probe your company separation more deeply and learns that during the downsizing process, your employer replaced you with another employee, this is bound to raise some concerns. The obvious underlying questions are, "Why did they let you go, yet fill the same position with another worker? Were there some performance issues? Were you a marginal employee? Are your skills questionable?" These concerns, unless addressed, will linger in the contact's mind, and might cause the contact to shut down. Why would they want to refer someone who is questionable to others whose relationships they value? It probably won't happen.

First and foremost, don't automatically volunteer that you are unemployed (if you are). Simply tell the contact that you are "in the process of a career change," and that "John Doe" (the referring source) suggested you call, feeling the contact could provide some ideas and suggestions. In most cases, the contact will never ask the reason for your career change, and you can quickly move on with your networking conversation.

Although it is rare, the contact might ask whether you are still with your previous employer. If you say you are not, they might then inquire as to why you left. If the reason was company downsizing, it would be even more unusual for the contact to ask whether you were replaced in your previous position. If this occurs (although it's extremely unlikely), here are some examples of how you might address this question and neutralize the matter.

"Jane had more seniority than me, and was therefore offered the position. I am sure this was not an easy decision for the Controller, since I have been a solid performer and a key contributor to the department."

or

"My boss, John Weldon, told me he very much regretted having to let me go since (as my last four performance evaluations will show) I have been a good performer. Although I was replaced by Jim Smith, I feel confident that John would speak favorably about my skills and abilities, as well as my contributions to the group. I'm sure this was not an easy decision for him."

or

> *"Frankly, Mary, I was never offered an explanation. However, I'm honestly not concerned, since I have had a good performance track record over the years and have the skills and abilities needed to make a strong contribution elsewhere. At this point I am looking toward the future, which is really the reason for my call."*

In each example, note how the job seeker made reference to being a "solid performer" or "strong contributor." Such references shift focus away from "why" you were replaced and draw attention to the fact that you have historically been a valued employee. Positive statements of this type reflect the old adage "the best defense is a strong offense." They quickly shift the networking contact's focus to the positive side. The point is, if your performance was reasonable, make that fact known. It will neutralize the contact's concerns and move the conversation on.

If You Were Fired for Performance Reasons

We are now down to the toughest issue of all. If asked during a networking call, how should you respond to questions about company separation when your last employer fired you for poor performance?

Obviously, never volunteer that you were fired. However, if you are asked point-blank, be straightforward. Here are some ideas on how you might handle the matter.

> *"Sally, I'm not going to be evasive. Frankly, I was let go. The decision came as a real shock to me, especially since I have never before had a problem with an employer. In fact, I have always had a good relationship and enjoyed an excellent performance record with past employers. I guess this was just one of those situations that just didn't work out. I suppose we all encounter one of these unfortunate situations in our career lifetime. This was apparently mine. Nevertheless, I find myself in the position of needing to move on with my career—which leads me to the reason for my call."*

or

> *"Frankly, Keith, I was let go. There is no point in boring you with the details, except to say that I can provide excellent references from my co-workers, who are quite familiar with the quality of my work. Additionally, I know my previous bosses at both Wilson Corporation and Dupont will speak highly of the job I did for them. This current situation is unfortunate, but I need to move on with my career and find an appropriate job opportunity. I hope that you will be able to help me."*

There is no easy way to handle conversations of this type. If your networking contact insists on knowing, you are obliged to provide an answer. The preceding examples, however, demonstrate some basic principles to employ when structuring your response. These are the following:

- Keep your answers short and sweet. Avoid the tendency to "overexplain."

- Never volunteer more than is absolutely necessary.

- Be straightforward and positive in your response. Don't beat around the bush.

- Be matter-of-fact. Avoid being apologetic in any way.

- Always allude to other past work experiences that were positive and where you were perceived to be a valued contributor.

- Reference past performance evaluations that historically demonstrate your work ethic and solid contributions to the organization.

- Where feasible, offer to produce references (other than your recent boss) who can speak to the quality of your work.

- Be brief, and try to transition the conversation to the reason for your call: the need for help with your job search.

- In any event, if you were fired by your previous employer, avoid speaking negatively or critically about your past company or former boss. This does not sit well with others, and can create a negative perception of you as being someone who is a complainer, has a negative attitude, or is prone toward holding a bitter grudge. This serves no real purpose, and can only raise questions or doubts in the mind of the networking contact that are likely to be detrimental to your networking effort.

By employing these principles, I think you will be well equipped to minimize any negative fallout and transition the conversation, in a fairly smooth manner, to the purpose of your call.

Let me assure you that preparing to address these issues in advance will do a lot to quell your anxiety. Additionally, after a few calls you will find that things will go more smoothly than you thought, and most of your anxiety will evaporate. Networking is much easier than you might think, and issues of the type just described are a rarity.

Researching Your Targets

Having a good plan is essential to effective networking. You need to start by setting some clear objectives and then structuring a well-thought-out plan that will get you there. A good plan will also enable you to be more efficient and cut precious time off your job search.

What is your target? Where do you want to work, and where do you best fit? Here are some questions to help you frame your networking plan and give some focus to your efforts.

- **Target geography:** What are your geographical preferences or restrictions?
- **Target industries:** In which industries are you most qualified to work?
- **Target companies:** Which are the companies for whom you would most like to work?
- **Target functions:** What are the functional areas in which you are most qualified to work?
- **Target managers:** Who are the managers that manage your target functions?

Figure 8.2 will help you visualize where we are headed.

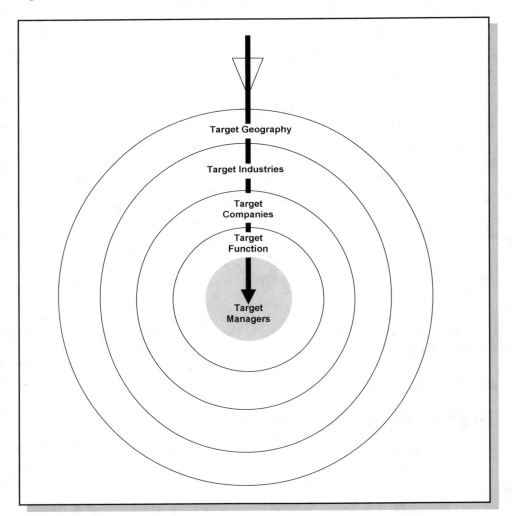

Figure 8.2: Focusing the networking process.

Six Degrees of Separation

According to the "six degrees of separation" theory, you are only six people away from anyone you might want to reach. By making six well-planned phone calls, using your own network and tapping into the networks of others (and their contacts), you should be able to reach (through introduction or personal referral) any manager on your target list.

Because you don't want to waste time, you need to start by identifying the target managers you want to reach. Then, as you begin making networking calls, think carefully about those people you personally know who might know these individuals. Or, to think more strategically: Who do you know that might know someone who is acquainted with (or related to, in some way) the manager you have targeted? Chances are, someone in your networking chain knows, and can lead you to this target person.

So if your target manager is John Jones, a hypothetical vice president employed by Johnson & Johnson, for example, you might start by asking your networking contacts if they know John Jones or someone who might know him. If this fails, you might want to then simply ask whether the networking contact knows anyone who works at Johnson & Johnson.

For example, your "six degrees of separation" might look like this:

1. Sally Mathews: A close friend of yours.
2. Martha Fallon: Sally's sister, who lives in New Brunswick, NJ (Johnson & Johnson's corporate headquarters location)
3. David Folsom: Sally's minister, whose congregation has several Johnson & Johnson employees in its congregation
4. Grace Holcomb: A vice president of Johnson & Johnson, who sits on the church board of directors
5. John Jones: vice president (your target manager)

Yes, with some good planning, in just a few phone calls, it can really happen—just like this! It requires only a little strategic thinking, along with some effective networking techniques.

If you don't know who your target managers are right from the beginning of your job search, your networking process will lack both direction and focus. It will be nothing more than a shotgun approach whereby you spend time randomly talking to large numbers of people just hoping, by some chance, that they will coincidentally know of an opening for which you are qualified and interested in. Such a disorganized, nondirected approach is bound to add several unwanted months to your job search.

It is exactly this lack of planning and focus that causes many job seekers to become disgusted and give up on networking. Because networking is a key employment source that yields one of the highest percentages of hires, I don't think you will want to be one of them!

Define Your Target Geography

The process for developing your networking plan starts with defining target geography. This is a simple process, and is easily accomplished by answering the following basic questions:

- Where do I want to live?
- What are my geographical restrictions (if any)?
- Am I willing and able to relocate?

This is one time in which bigger is better. It's a matter of simple mathematics. The larger your geographical target, the more jobs and job opportunities, and the shorter the job search. Conversely, the smaller this target area, the fewer the job opportunities and the longer the job search will take.

Next you must identify target companies that have operations within your geographical target. You are simply not going to be interested in organizations not located in the areas you have chosen.

Decide on Industry Targets

This one is a little more difficult to answer. Certainly your knowledge and skill set are going to be most marketable in the industries in which you have had experience. In most cases, you are better equipped to compete with other candidates when your skill set places you on a level playing field. This is particularly true if you work in such functions as operations, technology, or logistics. These functions typically require a fairly in-depth knowledge of the industry.

On the other hand, service or support functions such as human resources, accounting, and legal are not as anchored in a specific industry, and can more easily make the transition across industry lines. Although this is generally the case, all things being equal, employers have a natural tendency to prefer hiring people from the same industry as their own. After all, these people require less training and orientation, and can "hit the ground running" much faster than those from elsewhere.

So, unless you are really unhappy with the industry in which you work, my advice is to make that industry a priority target. You are far better equipped to compete in the arena in which you have earned your spurs and punched all the required tickets from a knowledge and experience standpoint.

If You Want to Change Industries

If, however, you feel you absolutely must change industries, you then need to give careful thought to which industries your combination of knowledge, skills, and abilities best fits. This is not an easy task, and will likely require some research and investigation prior to making a determination. Here are a couple of good questions, designed to at least get the thought process underway:

- What other industries sound interesting or appealing?
- With which of these do I have some familiarity?

- What specifically do I know about these industries?
- Do I know anyone employed in these industries? Who are they?
- What special knowledge do I have that might be of interest to these industries?
  a. Technology?
  b. Products?
  c. Markets?
  d. Customers?
  e. Key contacts?
  f. Specialized skills, education, or training?
- Which industries, other than my current industry, are likely to value my special knowledge and skills?
- In which of these industries do I have interest?
- With my qualifications, how well can I compete with others who already have experience in these industries?

Use An Informational Interview to Learn About the Industry

Unless you are particularly talented or are well connected, it will clearly be more difficult to compete with others who have industry experience if you have none. Before you jump off the deep end and end up in a pile of frustration, let me suggest you test the waters. Here's how to do it:

- Use your contacts to network to someone in that industry. (*Hint*: Try a fellow member of your professional association who already works in the industry.)
- Arrange an introduction to the functional head for whom you would work if you were employed by that company.
- Call this individual, using your referral's name, and ask for a lunch meeting. You'll buy!
- Tell this contact that you would like to learn something about the industry.
- Keep the call general; don't even hint that you might be looking for a job.

During the subsequent luncheon, ask some penetrating questions to get a feel for how well you might like the industry and whether you have the necessary qualifications to compete for a job in this function. When it comes to the matter of competition, be realistic. Do you honestly have the necessary qualifications to realistically compete with others for a position in this company and industry? If so, go for it!

When meeting with this networking contact, don't make the mistake of asking the contact whether you are qualified to work in their industry. Because a fellow employee referred you, many will simply say "yes," just to be polite and not offensive; but when the rubber meets the road, they wouldn't hire you on a bet!

You are better off asking questions of a less sensitive nature that will get you the information you need. Here are a few:

- When you hire people for your department, what do you look for?
- What qualifications do you feel are most valuable?
- What skills, in particular, do you feel are important to success in your function?
- Is industry experience important to you when hiring?
- Why do you feel this experience is important?
- In what way does this help you?

As you can see, it will take some time and effort to make this assessment. But if you really don't stand a ghost of a chance to compete for a spot in this industry, why put yourself through the frustration? Fall back on what you know and where you are most able to compete.

Industry Reference Sources

If you want to stimulate your thinking about the types of industries for which your interests and background may be a fit, I suggest you go to the Occupational Safety & Health Administration Web site at www.osha.gov/pls/imis/sic_manual.html. Here you will find a standard list of industrial classifications, with 10 major industry categories and some 99 industries (many with subcategories). By clicking on any of the 99 industries, you will find a short description of the industry and its products or services.

Also, try FirstResearch.com, an online Web site that lists more than 150 industries, divided into 11 categories. Hopefully between this and the OSHA Web site, it will stimulate your thinking and help you identify some target industries that might be of interest.

Industry Listings

If you don't have access to a computer, table 8.1 is a somewhat shorter list of industry categories that may be of some help.

Table 8.1: Industry Categories

Accounting	Energy	Non-profit
Advertising & PR	Entertainment & Sports	Paper
Aerospace & Defense	Financial Services	Petrochemical
Agricultural Products	Food	Printing & Publishing
Automotive	Forestry & Fishing	Real Estate

Biotech & Pharmaceuticals	Furniture	Retail Trade
Chemical	Government Services	Rubber
Commercial Banking	Health Care	Security Services
Communications	Hospitality & Tourism	Social Services
Computer Hardware	Human Resources	Telecommunication
Computer Software	Insurance	Transportation
Construction	Internet	Textile
Consulting	Investment Banking	Transportation
Consumer Electronics	Journalism & Publishing	Travel
Consumer Products	Legal Services	Utilities
Culinary	Manufacturing	Venture Capital
Education	Metal	Wholesale Trade
Electronics	Mining	

Identify Target Companies

Now that you have defined your target geography and settled on a target industry or two, your next step will be to identify target companies that have operations in the geographical area you have chosen. Remember, you are not simply looking for a total list of companies within your selective industry grouping, but rather only those companies that have operations within your geographical target.

Here are some ways you can create such a list of target companies.

Google Search

Try an online Google search by inserting the type of company and locations you are targeting, in the search box on Google's homepage (www.google.com).

For example, I typed "paper companies in Mississippi", and instantly got some encouraging results. The first hit was entitled Paper Manufacturers, followed by a short description of the site ("Find Paper Manufacturers and Converters—Search Locally by State and Zip Code").

By clicking on this listing, I was immediately transported to the Web site ThomasNet.com. Here I selected the state of Mississippi and hit the "go" button, instantly generating a list of 16 Mississippi paper companies, along with addresses, phone numbers, and brief company overviews. This page also contained a link that took me directly to each company's own Web site (which included a complete listing of functional executives). This entire search took all of about two to three minutes, at most.

In addition to the ThomasNet.com site, my Google search turned up the "ministore" Web site, offering to sell me a hard copy of the Mississippi manufacturer's directory (3,804 firms) for only $86, as well as a searchable CD for $323. By searching these (either hard copy or CD version), I could easily identify a comprehensive listing of paper companies (my target industry) within the state of Mississippi (my target geography).

ThomasNet.com

ThomasNet.com is an online directory produced by the *Thomas Register*, which has long been the mainstay product directory and reference source used by procurement professionals for more than 100 years. Each annual edition contains more than 20 volumes. It can be used to identify essentially all companies that manufacture any given product. Thus, ThomasNet.com is the ideal online reference source for identifying manufacturing companies of almost any type, by both target industry and geographical preference. And, best of all, it's free!

Industry/Trade Directories

Almost all industries have a trade directory of some sort that lists hundreds of member firms. These directories are published either by the trade association itself or by an outside publishing house. Many trade associations now also have searchable, online databases (or CD-ROMs) listing their entire membership, as well as each member company's multiple locations. Additionally, many online association directories are linked directly to the member company's Web site, much like ThomasNet.com, so you can go directly there to get the names of target managers for networking purposes.

If you are unsure whether your target industry has a trade association, the best source for finding out is the *Encyclopedia of Associations,* which you can access online or find a hard copy at most libraries. (Some libraries may also have free access to the online version.) This encyclopedia lists more than 22,200 associations in the U.S., and is searchable by industry or trade. Using the index to look up your target industry will normally yield a list of all trade associations connected to that industry, along with a page reference number for each. By using the encyclopedia to look up each industry-related association, you will find an address and phone number, as well as a brief description of the association. Then, with a quick phone call to the association's headquarters, you can get information on available membership directories: their content, structure, and price.

> **Tip:** Look for directories that provide geographical listings of their member companies and provide the names of key executives as well. These will save you some time.

I should mention that some of these membership directories can get pretty pricey. So, if this is the case, and you want to save some money, find a member company located near you and see whether you can borrow a copy for a couple of days. Perhaps this will also provide you with an opportunity to apply your newly learned networking skills, and may lead to further opportunities to discuss possible employment as well.

Use *Directories in Print* as a cross-reference against the *Encyclopedia of Associations* to identify any additional membership directories. *Directories in Print* lists more than 15,500 membership rosters, and can be searched for specific industry membership directories or rosters by using the index. There is also an online version of this directory. You can usually find hard copies at your local or county library.

> **Tip:** There is usually a fee for most of these directories. Although many are moderately priced, some can be quite expensive. To save money, remember to borrow copies from a local member company or, of course, check your local or county library, where usage is free. If you're using the library, don't forget to ask whether they have free access to an online version.

The National Trade and Professional Association Directory also provides a listing of more than 7,500 trade associations, professional societies, technical organizations, and labor organizations in the United States. It is similar to the *Encyclopedia of Associations*, but is more modestly priced at $189.

And finally, check out the *Yahoo! Business and Economics* section, which provides a free listing of many trade associations, along with links to their Web sites. This one is free.

Don't Forget Career Services at Your Alma Mater

Try calling the career services center at your alma mater. Any college or university career services center worth its salt will have free online versions of many of these directories, and would be more than happy to help a graduate. Many university career services centers now also provide job search services to alumni; so don't feel embarrassed to call them.

And, while you're there, remember to pick up a copy of your alumni directory, which is an excellent networking source. Also, check to see whether the school has a searchable online directory of alumni. Searching this online alumni directory for employees of your target companies will give you a huge advantage when you start your networking campaign. These contacts are invaluable.

Using the reference sources covered in this section, you can almost always get exactly what you are looking for. Many of these directories contain the names of key functional managers as well. This can help you quickly build your list of target company managers with whom you will want to network.

Identify Target Functions

By the term "functions," I am referring to traditional business functions. In a manufacturing company, for example, these would likely be the following:

Marketing	Information Technology
Sales	Accounting
Operations	Finance
Engineering	Human Resources
Research	Public Affairs
Logistics	Legal

Non-manufacturing industries, although having most of the preceding administrative functions, have additional functional areas related to the type of company they are. Insurance companies, for example, have additional functions such as underwriting, claims investigation, claims adjusting, and the like.

If you are targeting an industry with which you are unfamiliar, I would suggest networking into an industry member company (through friends, relatives, and business associates) and see whether you can lay your hands on a copy of its organization chart, showing the company's organization by functional area. Because this might be somewhat difficult, depending on how security-conscious the company is, simply try asking a knowledgeable employee to list the company's functions for you and describe those with which you are not familiar.

Once you have defined these functions, determine which functions are the best match for your specific skill and knowledge profile. If you are not familiar with some of these functions, you might want to again network your way into one of the target companies and see whether you can get an informational meeting set up through your contacts.

Get the Names of Target Managers

I have already provided a partial answer to this question in the previous section, as I dealt with the subject of target companies. As you will recall, many manager's names and titles are readily available in association membership directories. While going through these same directories, then, you will likely be able to identify the names and titles of many of the target managers for whom you are searching. In this section, however, I discuss some additional ways to identify these names.

Infiltrating Professional Associations

Many of the managers you want to target belong to professional associations related to the business function or profession in which they work. Some examples are the American Marketing Association, the Society for Human Resource Management, the Society of Women Engineers, the National Lawyers Association, the American Purchasing Society, the American Society of Mechanical Engineers, and so forth.

Start by making a list of the professional associations to which your target manager is most likely to belong. If you are unsure, again consult the *Encyclopedia of Associations*, which not only lists trade associations to which companies belong, but also lists professional societies and associations to which individual professionals belong. Here again, a brief visit to the encyclopedia's index using the name of the profession will yield a number of appropriate associations to which your target manager might belong.

> **Tip:** Pick associations that are larger as well as those that have some sort of connection to your target industries, where this exists.

Once again, you will want to contact the association headquarters office to inquire about their membership directories—whether they are available to the general public and their cost. Several of these professional associations now have online membership directories, which are searchable (by company name and location) for the target managers on your networking list. This type of resource is perfect for your purposes because it will save considerable time and eliminate the need to go through numerous printed pages of the directory looking for your target group.

Although generally modestly priced, some membership directories can be expensive, or not even made available to the general public. If either is an issue, consider joining the association. Sometimes membership is cheaper than the price of the directory, and as a member you usually get the membership directory (and access to the online version) free with your membership. Besides, joining one or two of the association's regional chapters and attending their monthly meetings provides an ideal forum for building personal relationships and presents tons of networking opportunities. You will also want to be alert to the fact that many of these professional associations publish lists of job openings, specific to the profession, in their newsletters and also on their Web sites.

If you are on a tight budget and can't afford to join the association or purchase its membership directory, consider taking the following tack. Find out from the association's office the names of the presidents and membership directors of local area chapters on the basis that you are considering the possibility of joining the association. Then, call these local officers to see whether you can attend their next meeting as a guest, explaining that you would like to see what they do. Most will be delighted to host you.

While at the meeting, take the opportunity to do some networking, but also see whether someone with whom you establish rapport might be willing to let you borrow a copy of the membership directory. You will want to be tactful in making this request; however, if you ask in the right way, most people will be happy to lend you a copy.

Also consider that a fellow employee or professional colleague might already be a member of the association, and willing to loan you their copy or even help you gain access to the association's online, searchable membership directory.

Researching Company Web Sites

An obvious tactic for finding names of target company managers is to visit the company's Web site. The Web site usually includes a list of the company's officers as well as members of its board of directors. Finding this information for each target company might take you a little time, depending on the size of your company target list; however, it costs nothing and the information is readily available. This technique, however, typically provides only the names of top executives, which might not be advantageous if you are looking for a lower-level management position or as a nonmanagerial professional. In such cases, your target executives will hold management positions at a lower level in the organization, so you will need to dig more deeply using the strategies already described.

Calling the Company Directly

Another tactic for finding names is to simply call the company directly and ask for the name of the person who holds your target manager's position. Although this can work, some companies are tight-lipped about providing names to unknown callers via the phone. This is a tactic used by many employment agencies and search firms that want to recruit away valuable employees. So, don't be surprised if your phone call is quickly routed to the human resources department, where you will be politely told that their policy does not allow this information to be given over the phone. As an alternative tactic, sometimes a call to the public affairs/public relations department may provide the name you are seeking.

> **Note:** Although it can be extremely time-consuming, another way to find managers' names is to search the Internet for news feeds that may yield the name for which you are searching. This is not a recommended strategy, however, if you are trying to keep your job search to a reasonable time frame.

Expensive but Productive Sources

If money is not an obstacle, and you want to quickly identify target companies and executives within your area of geographical preference, consider the following sources. A caution about these sources, however: In addition to their cost, these sources have somewhat limited capability to identify functional executives much below the vice president and director level. Thus, if you need to target managers at a lower level in the organization, these are not the ideal sources to use.

- **Hoover's Pro:** Hoover's is a Dun & Bradstreet company, offering a huge array of online databases for use in researching companies. Its "Pro" version allows you to build targeted company and executive lists from its database of three million small and medium-sized companies and 290,000 large, international firms. It is also searchable by geography as well. The basic subscription price, however, is $2,495. Although it's unlikely that they will have it, you might want to check with your local and county libraries, as well the career services center of your college or university, to see whether it is available free.

- **D&B's Million Dollar Database:** This online database has essentially the same functionality as Hoover's Pro, but has options to access only selected regions of the country. Depending on which regions you select, the price for online regional access ranges anywhere from a current low of $200 to a high of $1,200. You can obtain a specific price list for your region(s) by calling (800) 888-5900 or contacting the company via its Web site at www.dnbmdd.com. When ordering, make sure that the names of company executives are provided at the organizational level required for your networking purposes.

Other Well-Known Reference Books

If you are in your local or county library, check to see whether they have any of the following reference books, which are good resources for use in identifying target companies and key executives:

- *Million Dollar Directory:* Published by Dun & Bradstreet, covers 100,000 of the largest U.S. corporations, providing addresses, phone numbers, products, sales volume, number of employees, and a list of top officers.

- *Ward's Business Directory:* Published by Gale Group, this directory provides brief data for both public and large private companies arranged alphabetically, geographically, and by sales volume.

Planning the Networking Process

Now that the research process is out of the way, and you have identified your list of target companies and managers, the next step is to plan your networking calls. The process begins with identifying your level 1 contacts—the people you know personally.

As you will recall, the glue that holds the entire networking process together is personal referral. It is the personal referral that creates a sense of obligation to respond to your request for assistance with your job search. This glue is exceptionally strong, and, if you network correctly, will help you smoothly navigate the networking chain with ease and considerable success.

This chain begins with your own personal contacts. Once identified, you can prioritize these contacts on the basis of their ability to rapidly lead you to your list of target managers. Unless you carefully prioritize these calls, you will waste considerable time and the process will become unwieldy.

Don't Waste Time—Go for the Bull's-Eye!

Over the years, networking has sometimes gotten a bad rap as a long and laborious process. Consequently, many job seekers put it off (or don't do it at all), feeling they just don't have the time to do it. This is especially true if they are currently employed and have only minimal time to devote to their job search.

But, networking doesn't have to be difficult or time-consuming. If you have done the research to identify target managers, you are more than halfway there. Now, it's just a matter of identifying the shortest route to these managers (your target's bull's-eye). And typically, the shortest route is to network through your contacts who are directly affiliated with the industry you have targeted.

Unfortunately, networking got its bad reputation as being difficult and time-consuming as a result of poor training by some of the nation's major outplacement firms. Many of these firms have long advocated a more obtuse, nonfocused process—advising the job seeker to simply start with a list of all people they know (regardless of whether they have a connection with the job seeker's target industry), and then laboriously network through these contacts to eventually make contact with key hiring managers.

Although it has been proven that this kind of indirect, non-focused approach does work, the process can be exhausting and can take considerably longer to land a job. It is far better to have clearly defined your target right from the beginning, and planned the most efficient and expeditious route for getting there. Should this approach fail (which is quite doubtful), you can always resort to a less focused process later in your job search. This, however, should be you fallback position, and certainly not your primary strategy.

Identifying Level 1: Target Industry Contacts

The place to start network planning is with your primary or level 1 contacts. These are the people with whom you already have some connection or relationship. Moreover, you will want to select individuals who are in some way connected with the target industry (or industries) you have chosen.

At first you might feel that your industry contacts are somewhat limited. However, through the process of association, you are likely to find that you have many more contacts then you first imagined.

When using this process, start by identifying common groups to which many of your contacts belong. In particular, think broadly about those groups of people who are connected with your target industry. By first identifying these groups or categories, through association, you will likely remember many people who you know and would not have otherwise remembered.

These target industry-connected groups include the following:

- Vendors
- Contractors
- Consultants
- Analysts
- Bankers
- Attorneys
- Trade association members and officers

- Co-workers (current and past)
- Past bosses
- Industry colleagues and acquaintances
- Target industry professional society—members and officers

The following pages contain forms for use in recording the names and phone numbers of people you know who fit these categories. You might find vendor company phone directories and association membership directories helpful in remembering people with whom you have had professional contact, but whose names you might have forgotten.

Target Industry Contractors, Vendors, and Consultants		
Name	**Phone Number**	**Networking Priority**

(continued)

(continued)

Name	Phone Number	Networking Priority

Target Industry: Analysts, Bankers, and Attorneys

Name	Phone Number	Networking Priority

Name	Phone Number	Networking Priority

Target Industry: Trade Association Officers and Members

Name	Phone Number	Networking Priority

(continued)

(continued)

Name	Phone Number	Networking Priority

Target Industry Co-workers and Bosses (Past and Present)		
Name	Phone Number	Networking Priority

Name	Phone Number	Networking Priority

Target Industry Colleagues and Acquaintances

Name	Phone Number	Networking Priority

(continued)

(continued)

Name	Phone Number	Networking Priority

Target Industry Professional Society Members and Officers

Name	Phone Number	Networking Priority

Name	Phone Number	Networking Priority

Assigning Priority Ratings to Contacts

To further increase your efficiency and shorten networking time, assign a priority rating to each contact's name, based on that individual's potential for introducing you directly to one of your target managers. The following rating system may prove helpful in accomplishing this:

Priority Rating	Rating Definition
#1	High probability of direct relationship with target manager(s)
#2	Reasonable probability of direct relationship with target manager(s)
#3	Limited direct access to target manager(s), but may know some
#4	No direct relationships, but knows others who can make introductions to target manager(s)

When assigning a priority rating to each contact, consider the following:

- What is the level and type of work they do?
- Does this level and type of work require direct contact with target manager(s)?
- How frequent is such contact? (Seldom? Occasionally? Frequently?)
- By virtue of the level and type of work done, is contact likely through others?
- Does this allow some direct contact, or is all contact through others?
- How well is this person likely to know your target managers?
- How wide is this relationship? (One or two managers, or several?)
- Is there a special or personal relationship with any of these managers?
- How well do you know this networking contact? (Barely? Somewhat? Well?)

Obviously, where a networking contact is known to have direct relationships with a number of these target managers, and where you have an established relationship with that individual, this contact would be rated as a #1. Conversely, someone who deals with these target managers only through others, and with whom you have only a mere acquaintance, should receive a priority rating of #4.

Clearly this is not a very scientific approach to ranking these contacts, but it should be of some help in separating these networking contacts in order of their importance. It certainly beats a random approach, and should serve to help you to more productively use your time.

Identifying Level 2: Non-Industry Contacts (Fallback Strategy)

Should your list of level-1 target industry contacts be somewhat limited, you may want to expand your networking contact list to include others not known to have links to your target industry. These are known as level-2 contacts.

Although such relationships are not apparent, with some careful probing, you might be quite surprised to learn that your least likely contact has some powerful connections you would never have thought possible. So don't overlook someone who might at first glance, not appear a likely networking contact.

To get the process rolling, simply ask yourself, "Who do I know?" This might be a good time to pull out your Christmas card list, your Rolodex or electronic address book, that stack of old business cards in your bottom desk drawer, and other organized (or disorganized) lists of social, business, and community contacts.

You will generally find that most of your personal contacts fall into one of 10 categories. These are the following:

- Relatives
- General business contacts (non-target industry)
- Friends
- Community leaders
- Neighbors
- Church members
- Friends of friends (acquaintances)
- Education contacts
- Social club members
- Alumni contacts

I have provided a simple form to help you collect and assign a priority ranking to each of these level-2 contacts. Spend some time filling in these lists so that you will have a good foundation on which to build your networking process. If you get stuck, call other members of your group to help you remember the names of additional people, and to solicit their assistance in helping you identify individuals who have strong business and social networking contacts.

In this case, a simple priority rating of level-2 contacts might be as follows:

Priority Rating	Definition
#5	Strong business network, with many business connections
#6	Strong social network, with some business connections
#7	Some networking contacts (business or social)
#8	Unlikely to have many (if any) networking contacts

As with level-1 contacts, you will assign higher priority ratings to those people most likely to be able to provide you with valuable contacts. Individuals with large networks, both business and social, are more likely to be able to make worthwhile contacts than those whose contacts are limited.

Relatives		
Name	Phone Number	Networking Priority

Friends and Neighbors		
Name	Phone Number	Networking Priority

Friends of Friends (Acquaintances) and Social Club Members		
Name	Phone Number	Networking Priority

General Business Contacts (Non-target Industry)		
Name	Phone Number	Networking Priority

Community Leaders and Church Members		
Name	Phone Number	Networking Priority

Education and Alumni Contacts		
Name	Phone Number	Networking Priority

Index Calling Cards

Now that you have identified and prioritized your networking contacts, you will need to organize them so that the highest-priority contacts are always at the top of your call list. This will give you some control over the process, so that you are not wasting time calling the least valuable contacts first.

To simplify the process, list each contact, along with appropriate information, on a 4″ × 6″ index card. Each card should contain a priority number, based on the priority rating system described earlier in this chapter. This way, by simply shuffling the cards once a day, or periodically throughout the day, you can continuously move the highest-priority calls to the top of the deck. Doing so enables you to maximize your overall efficiency and greatly reduce networking time.

An Example Card

Figure 8.3 is an example of an index calling card. It contains all of the pertinent information you will need when making a call. It includes space for recording the contact priority rating at the top-right of the card. It also contains a "Referral Source" section as a quick reminder of the person who provided the referral, as well as the relationship between this person and the contact you will be calling. This is all critical information you will need at your fingertips as you make each networking call.

Don't forget that this is a dynamic process. Each time you make a networking call and come away with new contacts, you will need to assign a priority rating and fill out a new index card for each new contact. If you fail to manage this process right from the start, it will quickly bury you.

Remember, this is also an exponential process, which multiplies itself quickly. You could soon be dealing with well over a hundred contacts, each at a different stage of the process.

> **Tip:** Before you make a networking call, it is important to set some objectives and priorities. Without doing so, you will waste considerable time and often come away with little information or meaningful assistance. When laying out your networking index cards, include a section for establishing three to four networking priorities.

Managing Your Contacts

In order to control this process and ensure that it does not get out of hand, I would also suggest creating a simple system, filing each contact's card into three separate categories based on the stage of the call process that the contact is in. These categories are

- To Call
- Will Call Back
- Completed

(Last Name) (First Name) (Middle Initial) (Priority #)

Personal Data

Address: _____
Phone: Work: _____ Cell: _____ Home: _____
E-mail: _____
Employer: _____ Location: _____ Job Title: _____

Referral Source

Referred By: _____
Nature of Relationship: _____

Networking Objectives/Priorities

1. _____
2. _____
3. _____

New Referrals

Name: _____ Phone: _____ Relationship: _____
Name: _____ Phone: _____ Relationship: _____
Name: _____ Phone: _____ Relationship: _____

Figure 8.3: Sample index calling card.

The "To Call" category contains index cards for new contact calls that you have not yet made. These cards should be filed by their preassigned priority number, with those calls to which you have assigned the highest priority rating arranged at the front of the deck. This is your working deck of cards from which you will be making your calls. Thus, by frequently shuffling the deck based on priority, you ensure that you are efficient and focused on the calls that show the greatest promise for success. Such organization and focus is likely to cut serious time off your job search and bring you promising job leads much faster.

> **Note:** When making a networking call, it is very important to not only get the names of new contacts, but to also understand the relationship between the current contact and the person to whom they are referring you. As you will see in chapter 9, this information is vital to establishing rapport with the new contact quickly, and is an important part of the networking glue that holds the whole process together.

As you might have guessed, the "Will Call Back" section is for filing the index cards of those contacts whom you could not reach, and for whom you have left a phone message. File these cards alphabetically, by last name, so that you can retrieve them quickly when the contact calls you back.

Finally, as I'm sure you surmised, the "Completed" section of your filing system is for those calls that you have completed, and where no further action is required by you.

> **Tip:** If you are computer oriented and don't want to deal with a manual system, you might want to invest in one of the many automation software products used by sales professionals in managing a contact database. You can easily adapt these for networking purposes. Two of the more popular programs are Goldmine and ACT!.

Print up several index cards containing the following information:

- The contact's personal information (name, address, phone numbers, and e-mail address)
- Networking priority rating
- Contact's employment (company, title, location)
- Referral source (the person who referred you to the contact)
- Referral relationship (how the referral source and contact know each other)
- Networking call priorities (the type of assistance the contact is most likely able to provide)
- New referrals (names, phone numbers, e-mail addresses, employers, job titles)
- Nature of relationship (how the contact knows the new referral)

- Place for notes (provide space to write notes—probably the back of the index card)

These index cards should be filed alphabetically using the contact's last name. Therefore, the card should be designed accordingly, showing the last name of the networking contact first, followed by first name and middle initial.

Chapter Summary

Networking is known to be one of the most productive of all employment sources, accounting for from an average of about 25 percent to a high of more than 90 percent of all jobs found (depending on the job seeker's job level). The more senior the position you seek, the more important networking becomes in landing employment. Therefore, networking needs to be a major component of your overall job search plan. Key points to remember when preparing your networking plan are the following:

- The referral process is the "glue" that holds the networking process together and accounts for its enormous success.

- The best, most satisfying jobs are found through networking.

- Networking enables you to access the "hidden job market" and can reduce your competition for a job to zero.

- Networking can sometimes create jobs that didn't exist before the networking call.

- Through effective networking techniques, you can multiply your personal contacts many fold, and quickly recruit a large army of allies ready and willing to help with your job search.

- If planned carefully, you can reach almost anyone you target with only six networking phone calls.

- You can cut considerable time from your job search and realize results from networking much faster by prioritizing and planning each networking call.

- Advanced research to identify your target managers can shorten networking time considerably and get you to the right decision-makers faster than most other employment techniques.

- Having an effective system in place to manage the networking process is essential to keep you focused and efficient in quickly reaching your job search goals.

CHAPTER 9

Making Networking Work: How to Make Networking Calls

At the heart of the networking process is the networking phone call. Unless you are skilled at making these calls, you can waste considerable time and have little to show for your effort.

In this chapter, I provide you with both basic and advanced techniques that will enable you to capitalize on this important process. You will learn effective strategies and tactics that can cut precious time off your job search and connect you with great job opportunities very early in the process. By following this advice, you will also discover that networking can be fun, and not nearly as difficult as you might think.

How to Plan a Networking Call

Taking a brief moment or two to plan each networking call, before picking up the phone, will greatly impact your effectiveness and ensure a much higher level of success than going into the conversation cold. When planning the call, there are a couple of key points to keep in mind.

Approach and Positioning

First, you need to understand the vast majority of networking contacts will be quite willing to lend you a hand if you approach them in the right way. I have witnessed hundreds of networking calls, and can assure you this is the case. If the conversation is well planned and choreographed, it is extremely unusual for a contact to be rude, abrupt, or unwilling to help. So, put aside any fear of rejection.

Second, how you go about positioning the call will have significant impact on its outcome. In particular, how you introduce the call can create a positive atmosphere, which encourages the contact to be of assistance to you. When you plan the objectives of a given call, therefore, ask yourself two simple questions:

- Considering this person's position and background, what type of assistance is he or she most likely able to provide?
- In what secondary areas might he or she also be helpful?

Taking a moment or so to establish some clear-cut objectives, based on the answers to these questions, will definitely get the conservation off on the right foot.

An important point to think about is that, by targeting your request for assistance to those things the contact is most likely able to provide, the networking contact will feel more comfortable because you are asking for something they are able to deliver. This often gets them into the mode of helping you, and serves to create a more friendly and congenial atmosphere. It also allows you the opportunity to establish some personal rapport with the individual, which sets the stage for some of your more specific requests later in the conversation.

Don't Ask for a Job

Believe it or not, the last thing you will want to do is ask a contact for a job or job lead. Novice networkers often have considerable trouble grasping this concept and understanding the underlying subtleties. But a little reflective thinking can help you see the light.

Just think about it for a moment. What happens when you ask someone for a favor they are unable to grant? Yes, they feel somewhat awkward and embarrassed that they cannot grant your request, and this typically puts a slight strain on the conversation. The same thing happens during a networking call. If you ask someone for a job or a job lead at the beginning of the conversation, and they are unable to deliver it, there can be an awkward moment or two of silence, following which the conversation will be somewhat strained. The reality is, the contact is slightly embarrassed that he or she cannot respond positively. The net result is a desire to end the conversation at the earliest possible moment, without being offensive, and move on to something else. This is not the outcome you seek.

Moreover, asking for a job or job lead early in the networking phone conversation can be seen as over-aggressiveness. The contact hasn't even had a chance to get to know you, and here you are asking them for a job, job lead, or introduction to an important contact. Don't you agree this seems a bit forward or pushy? Wouldn't you like to get to know the person a bit better before passing along a job lead or providing the names of valued contacts? Obviously!

As the saying goes, "All things in good time." You need to first establish some personal rapport with your contact before moving on to these more privileged topics. Your contact needs to know more about you, your background, your skills, and your personality before feeling comfortable about providing meaningful help and valuable introductions.

I will cover the best tactics for beginning your networking call and establishing rapport a little later in this chapter, but let's first close the loop on planning the call.

Things Contacts Can Deliver

At some point, early in the networking call, you will want to approach your contact with a request for assistance. As stated earlier, this should begin with something the contact, by virtue of his or her background and position, is most likely able to provide. This will help the conversation get off to a smooth start, and set the stage for a productive discussion. Furthermore, it provides a psychologically positive environment in which the contact very naturally gets into the mode of helping you.

What are some of the "deliverables" you might want to ask a contact for (by virtue of who they are), early in the call? Here is a list to get you thinking. This list starts with the least threatening topics, and gradually transitions to those topics of a more delicate or privileged nature.

- General job search advice
  - Thoughts/ideas for conducting an effective job search
  - Productive sources for finding a job
  - Effective job-hunting strategies and techniques
  - Key employment agencies and search firms
  - Key advertising sources: newspapers, trade journals, job boards, and so on
  - Career and industry alternatives
  - Resume format and content
- Target industry observations/trends (what they know)
  - Observations and trends affecting your target industry's job market
  - High-growth companies
  - Companies that are retracting
  - New industry trends
  - Key moves: acquisitions/divestitures
  - Companies rumored to be expanding and hiring
- Target industry contacts (who they know)
  - Industry leaders
  - Officers and members of trade associations
  - People who are well networked
  - Target industry executives
  - Target company executives

- Employees of target companies
- Key vendors and suppliers (especially those with good contacts)
- Well-established consultants
- Former employees now working for competitors
- Current company employees who are well networked
- Well-known academic contacts at key schools
  - Job leads (possible opportunities for job openings)
    - Recent promotions
    - Company transfers
    - Retirements
    - Resignations
    - Planned or current expansions

Figure 9.1 shows the recommended progression (by topic) of a networking phone call. As this "funnel approach" shows, it is best to begin by making general requests (for example, ideas and advice) of your contact, and then later proceed to specific requests (contacts and job leads). This approach allows sufficient time to establish trust and rapport with the contact before zeroing in on what are thought to be the more sensitive and privileged requests, such as key introductions and job leads. You will find your tact and patience pays off, as you win the trust and confidence of the networking contact.

Once you have established the order of topics you want to cover with your networking contact, record these topics, in order of their importance, in the objectives section of your networking index card (see chapter 8 for more on how to create a networking card). This will serve as an instant reminder if the networking contact returns your call at a time you are least expecting it.

Getting Past Bulldog Gatekeepers

Job seekers who are new to networking soon discover that being prepared for a discussion with the networking contact is not enough. To get to your targeted contact, you must first get past determined and conscientious administrative assistants who are responsible for guarding their boss's time. Some are particularly tenacious and will do their best to screen you out and send you packing.

Here are some typical screening questions you must be prepared to address if you are going to be successful in reaching your networking contact:

"Ms. Carey is particularly busy right now and will be unable to take your call. May I ask what this is in reference to?"

"Is this a personal call? Why are you calling?"

"Mr. Thornton is tied up at the moment. I would be glad to take a message. May I ask why you are calling?"

171

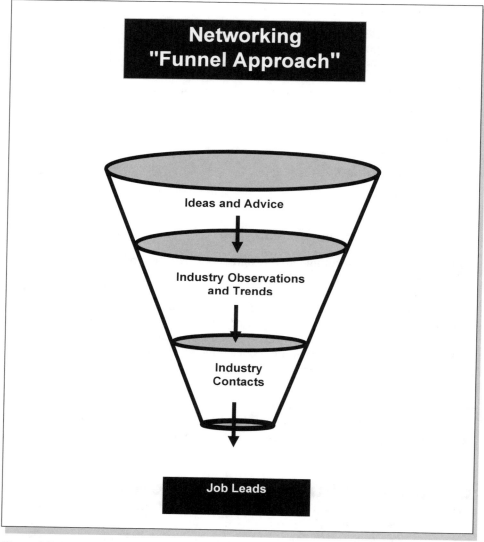

Figure 9.1: Recommended progression of a networking phone call.

To penetrate this fortress, you will need some ammunition. Your best weapon in this case is the name of the person who referred you to the gatekeeper's boss. Here's how to use it:

> "I appreciate that Ms. Carey is busy, and I really don't want to take up her time. Please tell her I was referred by Barbara Davies and really only need a minute or two. If this is inconvenient, please ask her when a good time would be to reach her."

"Yes, this is a personal call. Please tell Mr. Thomas I was referred by Jennifer Schmidt, and only need a few short minutes of his time."

"Yes, I was referred to Mr. Thornton by Linda Wilson, and would like to speak with him on a personal matter. If he is tied up, perhaps there might be a better time for me to call. What would you suggest?"

As you can see from these examples, using the referral's name is a fairly potent weapon for penetrating this particular armor. Personal referrals usually warrant courteous treatment and are usually sufficient reason for facilitating contact with the boss. Certainly if you state that you are calling regarding a "personal matter," few administrative assistants will push the matter much further.

If you are told the boss is busy, always be respectful of their time. Offer to call back, and ask for advice or help in setting up a second call at a time that would be more convenient.

Voice Mail (The Big Black Hole)

In this day and age, unless you are networking at very senior levels, few networking contacts have administrative assistants who answer their phones. In most cases, therefore, you will need to leave a voice-mail message in what is sometimes referred to as "the big black hole."

If your networking contact is very busy (and most are today), you are unlikely to get a callback quickly; and, in some cases, perhaps they won't call you at all. Therefore, a lot is riding on the message you leave. Keep it simple and to the point. Here are a couple that work:

"Hello, Kim! My name is Phil Rogers. Dave Ferguson suggested I give you a call. I need only a minute or two of your time. Can you please give me a call at (669) 430-9821? Thanks! Look forward to your call."

"Harold, this is Wilma Heidrich calling. Kay Dunkin referred me to you. She felt you would be a good person for me to talk with. I only need a couple minutes. Can you please give me a call? My number is (609) 477-5297. Thanks!"

A cursory scan of these sample messages reveals that there are two common elements. These are use of the referral's name and a statement suggesting you will be brief (in other words, respectful of their time).

How to Structure an Effective Networking Call

Having trained and observed hundreds of job seekers making networking calls has led me to realize that there is a certain logical structure to an effective call. Figure 9.2 illustrates this structure and its various components.

To help you structure a call that gets the results you need, I will briefly explain each of these components and the role they play in effective networking. Each explanation is followed by a sample networking call, which demonstrates how these various elements come into play in ensuring a productive networking call.

Once you have structured your own call, I would suggest a few dry runs followed by some feedback from a spouse or friend. You will want to get comfortable with the process so that it is spontaneous and feels quite natural to you. Use this opportunity to get most of the bugs out before you go live.

Then, when you have fine-tuned your approach, try some actual networking calls, followed by a brief self-critique. See how effectively you have used your training and the specific techniques you have learned. Make sure, however, that your first few calls are made to those individuals who have the lowest priority ranking. You don't want to still be wearing your training wheels when calling your very best prospects.

Step 1: Introduction and Referral Statement

The introduction and referral statement is comprised of three basic elements. These are the greeting, the positioning of the referral connection, and small talk (usually related to the connection between the referring source and the networking contacts). Here are a couple of examples:

Example 1

> *Greeting:* "Good morning, Brenda, this is Carla Baker calling."
>
> *Referral Connection:* "I'm calling you at the suggestion of Sandra London. I understand the two of you were team members during the recent A.M.A. session."
>
> *Small Talk:* "I just joined the A.M.A. this past November and attended my first session two weeks ago in Princeton. It was very interesting. How long have you been a member?"

Example 2

> *Greeting:* "Hello, David."
>
> *Referral Connection:* "Martin Gossberg suggested I give you a call. Martin and I have known each other for about five years, and play in the same golf league together."
>
> *Small Talk:* "He tells me that you're tough competition on the links and carry a four handicap. That's really impressive! How long have you been playing?"

Example 3

> *Greeting:* "Good evening, Michele. How are you? This is Steve Baker calling."

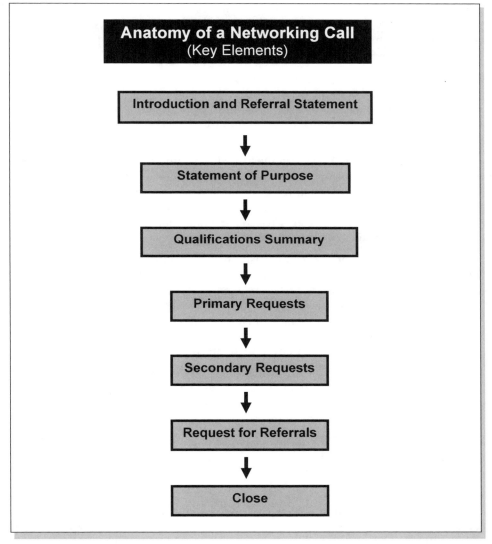

Anatomy of a Networking Call
(Key Elements)

Introduction and Referral Statement

↓

Statement of Purpose

↓

Qualifications Summary

↓

Primary Requests

↓

Secondary Requests

↓

Request for Referrals

↓

Close

Figure 9.2: The anatomy of a networking call.

Referral Connection: *"I was referred to you by Ellen Haywood, a good friend of mine."*

Small Talk: *"Ellen was telling me how the two of you used to work at Traxlers together between your junior and senior years at Princeton. Traxlers was always a fun place to work, and I remember some great times I had while waitressing there during summer vacations in Ocean City. It's funny we never ran into one another. Out of curiosity, how did you come to work there?"*

The preceding introductions are classic examples of how to position your referral and get the networking discussion off to a smooth start. This is especially true of Example 3, in which small talk plays a vital role in helping to set a very friendly tone for the conversation.

Naming your referral right at the beginning of the conversation helps establish that important glue that keeps the networking process together and makes it work. The very fact that someone referred you, whom the contact knows, creates an immediate sense of social or personal obligation to treat you cordially and to offer whatever assistance they can.

The use of small talk, as effectively illustrated in Example 3, can enhance this feeling of obligation because it leaves the networking contact with the feeling that there is more than just a casual relationship between you and the person making the referral. You can see the reinforcing effect that small talk can have. If you were on the receiving end of this call, I feel relatively certain you would respond in a positive and responsive way. Do you agree?

Thus, small talk, used properly and positioned early in the conversation, can be a powerful networking tool. It establishes a friendly, informal tone to the discussion, which encourages the contact to feel relaxed and comfortable, to "let their hair down" a bit, and to share more of an insider's perspective with you. This informality can lead to the sort of friendly openness whereby the contact begins to share such important tidbits as confidential information, personal insights about people or organizations, or prized and coveted contacts, and might even express a willingness to make personal calls and introductions on your behalf.

For some networkers, small talk might not come easily. This is especially true when you are at the fourth or fifth level in the networking chain and don't personally know the person who made the referral.

So, you might wonder, "How do I engage in small talk when I have absolutely no connection to the person who has made the referral and, furthermore, know nothing about the relationship between this person and the contact with whom I will be speaking?"

The answer to this question rests with how you handle the conversation with the original referral source. To set the stage for small talk and provide you with the ammunition needed to make it work, you will obviously need to know more about the relationship between the person making the referral (the referral source) and the contact you are about to call. So, in the conversation with the referral source, when provided with the name and contact information for your target contact, ask a few questions about the relationship between these two parties. Here are some questions you might try:

- How long have you known Sandra, and how did you get to know her?
- What is your relationship with Jim? How do you know him?
- Have you known Carolyn very long? Where did you meet her?
- Do you see David very often? How did you come to meet him?

Don't forget to make a note of this relationship on your call index card, so that this information is readily available when you make your networking call to the new contact. A quick reference to this person's relationship with your referral source is good fodder for small talk, and will help cement your relationship with the person you will be calling.

Step 2: Statement of Purpose

Because you have a number of networking calls to make, and don't want to lose momentum, you will need to smoothly transition the conversation from small talk to the purpose for your call. This needs to happen as early as can be comfortably done. Be careful, however, not to be abrupt or to lose the friendly tone you have worked so hard to establish. Once small talk begins to lapse, however, and you can comfortably make the shift, you will want to do so. To accomplish this, I suggest a fairly direct approach.

Here are a couple of typical transitional statements you might use, each with a slightly different slant.

Example 1

> *Transition:* "*Peggy, I am in the process of making a career transition, and Linda felt you might be a good person to speak with. She said you recently went through a career transition of your own about a year ago, and might have some good ideas and suggestions for me.*"

Example 2

> *Transition:* "*Lyle, I am considering making a career transition, and Jim felt you would be a good person with whom to speak. He said you have some good contacts in the food industry, and might be able to provide some insight and offer some good advice.*"

Example 3

> *Transition:* "*Wanda, I am in the process of a career transition and, at Tim Bradford's suggestion, I am calling for some information and advice. Tim seems to feel, as a result of your position on the board of the American Marketing Association, you might have some interesting perspectives and observations that might be helpful to me in connection with my job search.*"

Example 4

> *Transition:* "*Pete, I am considering leaving my current position as accounting manager at Wilson Corporation for a more challenging opportunity. I know from talking with Chris Mackey that you have been very active as an officer in the paper industry trade association. Because this is one of my target industries, Chris felt you could provide me with some insight and perhaps suggest a contact or two. I would be really appreciative of your help.*"

When structuring your transition statement, there are certain basic principles or guidelines worth following. Review the preceding sample transition statements to see how these principles are applied.

- Never volunteer that you are unemployed (even if you are).
- Always use the referral's name when positioning requests for assistance.
- Ask first for "deliverables"—things the contact can easily provide (ideas, advice, and so on).
- Never, ever ask for a job or job lead!

Don't Volunteer Your Employment Status

If you are unemployed or have recently left your company, never volunteer this information while making your transition statement. Many job seekers feel compelled to offer up this information, even when it is totally unnecessary to do so.

Volunteering this information can raise unnecessary doubts and concerns in the mind of the networking contact. "Why did you leave? Did you quit in a huff? Were you fired? If not fired, were you caught in a layoff? If laid off, why were you chosen? Was it for performance reasons? Were you one of the less-valued employees? Are your skills sub-par?" These are but a few of the "red flags" now circulating in the contact's head, and you can bet that he or she is going to approach the rest of your conversation with a much greater sense of caution. This could get in the way of drawing out this person's best information and most valuable contacts. So, clearly, there is nothing to gain by volunteering this information. Conversely, there may be a lot to lose.

As you can see from some of the preceding sample transition statements, the best way to avoid this entire issue is to simply state that you are "in the process of a career transition." This is a rather benign way of describing your status and doesn't lead to the doubts and concerns that might otherwise surface. Moreover, the fact is that the contact really has no need to know your current employment status in order to render job search advice or provide a referral. So, why volunteer it?

Use the Referral's Name

When reviewing the preceding transition statements, you will note how the networker positions the name of the referral source. Making this personal connection, simultaneously with a request for assistance, heightens the contact's sense of obligation to respond in a positive way. This personal connection with the referral source is the glue that holds the networking process together and compels the networking contact to respond appropriately.

Furthermore, when the contact is told that the source of the referral felt he or she "is a good or excellent person to talk with," this is complimentary and suggests that the contact is someone who is respected for their knowledge, skills, or position. This serves to heighten the contact's need to respond in a positive manner.

Ask for "Deliverables"—Not Job Leads

Job seekers often avoid networking because of the perceived need to ask others for jobs or job leads. This makes them feel vulnerable and might, in turn, elicit feelings of awkwardness and embarrassment. Somehow, in our society, not having a job or needing to ask for one is something to be ashamed of. Yet, the irony is that most people undergo an estimated seven to eight job transitions during their career lifetimes.

Well, if you share these concerns, the good news is that networking does not require asking for a job or job leads. In fact, as any good networker will tell you, asking a contact for a job or a job lead can cause "instant death" on what otherwise would have been a very productive networking call. There are several reasons for this.

As pointed out earlier in this chapter, asking for job leads right out of the box will likely catch your networking contact completely off guard. If your contact is unable to think of any, he or she is bound to feel awkward and embarrassed by his or her inability to respond. The natural tendency, at this point, then, is for the contact to want to end the conversation and get off the phone as soon as possible. This is not what you want!

Moreover, at this point in the conversation, the contact knows little or nothing about you. How could they possibly feel comfortable about suggesting an appropriate job opening or arranging an introduction to a valued contact?

To make matters worse, they might view your directness as aggressive, pushy, or presumptuous. Your lack of tact and sensitivity might be seen as inappropriate behavior, and could cause your contact to have serious reservations about providing the names of valued colleagues and important contacts. Certainly, this is not the impression you want to make.

Good networking protocol requires that you rarely ask for a job or job lead, and especially not during the early stages of a networking call. It is important to understand that by applying good networking techniques, you will almost never have to ask for a job or job lead during a networking call. In most cases, leads will automatically be provided, without the need for you to ask for them.

So, when structuring your networking call transition statement, avoid asking for a job or job leads and instead focus on deliverables. Asking for such general information as ideas, advice, observations, and trends will work far better. This will give you an opportunity to engage the person in meaningful dialogue and get them to open up with thoughts and ideas that they feel might be helpful to you.

As this dialogue continues, some of the initial barriers begin to break down, and a basic level of rapport is established between you and the contact, as he or she becomes more actively engaged in helping you.

Step 3: Qualifications Summary

Once you have established the reason for your call, it's typical for the networking contact to inquire about your qualifications, experience, and job interest.

179

Therefore, you need to be prepared to present a brief synopsis of your professional background and career interests. In career consulting circles, this career summary is often referred to as the "two-minute drill."

The two-minute drill is designed to provide a concise summary of your education, your relevant skills and experience, as well as your job and career interests. It needs to be sufficiently detailed to enable the contact to make appropriate recommendations concerning job opportunities; however, it shouldn't be so long that it ends up boring the contact to death. As suggested by the name, this drill should be no more than two minutes in duration.

When preparing your two-minute drill, write and rewrite it again and again until it will fit on a 4" × 6" index card (both sides). This exercise will force you to be concise, and reduce your presentation to only "need-to-know," relevant facts. Moreover, it provides a welcome visual crutch for your use in making those first few networking calls.

Here are some examples of qualifications summaries:

Example 1

"Barbara, my background includes nearly 16 years in accounting management with major companies in the chemical process industry. Following graduation from Penn State with a B.S. in Accounting, I went to work with General Chemicals in their Fine Chemicals Division, where I advanced to the position of manager of cost accounting. In 1997 I resigned to accept the job of accounting manager for Davidson Chemical in Greenville, Texas. Davidson, as you may know, Barbara, is a $200 million manufacturer of agricultural chemicals and chemical intermediates. Some key contributions at Davidson eventually led to a promotion to the position of corporate controller and later to the company's chief financial officer. In 2004, Dow recruited me to my current position as financial vice president for its Polymers Group, which is a $1.8 million operation. I am now looking to further my career and am seeking a position as the top financial officer at another major chemical company."

Example 2

"Bill, I am a 1994 graduate of the University of Maryland, where I earned a bachelor's degree in Mechanical Engineering. Following graduation, I went to work as a project engineer for Fort James Corporation in the Tissue Department of its Pennington, Alabama, plant. For the next four years, I handled major paper machine rebuild projects with a focus on wet end design, installation, and start-up. In 1997, I was promoted to senior project engineer, and then moved to converting engineering manager for the mill site in 2001. Since then, Bill, I have been managing a team of six engineers successfully leading over $50 million in converting-equipment capital projects. I am now looking for an engineering management position at the corporate level,

where I can expand my management responsibilities and work toward a senior management position with the firm. I would also consider similar positions with an engineering consulting firm or equipment manufacturer, provided that the position is challenging and there are comparable growth opportunities."

Example 3

"Willa, I have been a senior accounts payable clerk with the Martin Company for the last three years. This requires my review, approval, and accurate processing of over $3 million in vendor invoices weekly. I enjoy an excellent reputation for work volume and accuracy, and have received top performance evaluations from management for all three years. Prior to Martin Company, Willa, I worked in the Accounts Payable Department of Baxter Corporation as an accounts payable clerk. My education consists of an associate's degree in Accounting from Wilson College, where I was an academic scholarship recipient. I am now looking for a position as an accounts payable supervisor or manager with either a manufacturing or service company."

As you can see from these examples, the qualifications summary needs to be concise and to the point. It provides the networking contact with only the bare essentials required to understand your basic qualifications and job search objectives. Avoid long-winded, detailed recitations, as these can be distracting and cause your contact to "turn you off," quickly losing both attention and interest.

Steps 4 and 5: Primary and Secondary Requests

As I pointed out earlier in this chapter, your immediate objective when placing a networking call is to get information, advice, and referrals to others in the contact's network, not to ask for a job or a job lead. Prematurely asking for a job or job leads can strain the relationship, cause feelings of awkwardness, and lead to an abbreviated and nonproductive call. If you are using proper networking techniques and avoid such a direct approach, you will almost never have to ask for these items. To the contrary, the contact will willingly volunteer job leads as a natural outcome of the networking conversation.

To get the process underway, then, you need to take a more obtuse, indirect approach to networking. Begin the conversation by asking your contact for such deliverables as information, advice, ideas, suggestions, and the like. These are all things the contact can (and will be willing to) provide. This softer approach puts the contact at ease and encourages an open, friendly dialogue, which will later prove beneficial to your underlying needs.

Having successfully navigated the social warm-up period and established some rapport and trust with your networking contact, you are now in a position to be more specific with your requests for assistance. The specific nature of these primary and secondary requests will vary with the contact's background and position. This is where some prior planning comes into play. Reviewing the various topical areas presented earlier in this chapter (see "Things Contacts Can Deliver") will enable you to tailor your requests accordingly.

For example, trade association officers are uniquely qualified to provide broad observations about the general state of the industry, current industry trends, company expansions that could spell job openings, and valuable industry contacts. Target company employees, on the other hand, can provide such valuable information as an insider's perspective of the company, what it's like to work there, current issues and problems (which might suggest job opportunities), economic expansion or contraction, recent retirements or transfers, introductions to key personnel, and the like. As you can see, you can directly tailor each informational request to what your contact knows and what he or she can realistically provide. This kind of advance planning and tailoring of your requests can have a huge payoff, and is far superior to an unplanned cold call.

So, take time to define your primary and secondary requests prior to making the networking call, so that they are tailored to the "deliverables" of the networking contact. This will get you job leads and vital information much more quickly.

The following are a few examples of how a networker might tailor his or her conversation and request for assistance to the background and position of the networking contact.

Example 1

"Joan, as an executive in the food industry, I would value your perspective concerning some of the current trends and events that might impact my job search. I'm thinking here about your knowledge of such things as company expansions and contractions, new product rollouts, expanding or contracting market segments, new problems and challenges, and the like. Where do you see the greatest opportunity for someone with my skill set? I would greatly appreciate your thoughts and ideas on this subject."

Example 2

"Tim, Debra shared with me that you recently underwent a similar career transition to my own. I'd be interested in hearing about what you learned from this experience. In particular, I'd be interested in hearing about your approach to job hunting. What seemed to work for you, and what didn't work so well? What have been your most productive sources, and is there anyone who was especially helpful? This information would be very helpful to me, and I would very much appreciate your advice."

Example 3

"Linda, as an association board member, you may be privy to a number of key moves in the industry. Through your close association with others in the industry, are you aware of any personnel changes that

could suggest key management openings in the manufacturing arena? Have you heard of any recent changes such as promotions, transfers, resignations, or other personnel moves of which I should be aware? This information could be particularly helpful to me."

Example 4

"During a conversation with Barry Saunders, he told me that you recently were successful in changing career direction from chemical manufacturing to the environmental field. This is of interest to me since I have been thinking about a similar career change. Making a dramatic industry shift such as this is generally difficult to do. I am interested in learning how you were able to do this, and whether you could provide me with some advice that would be helpful. I would greatly appreciate your insight."

Example 5

"Sharon, as an experienced human resources manager with several years in the field, I'm sure you have a great deal of insight about those specialties that offer the greatest career growth opportunity. As someone just entering the profession, I would greatly appreciate your insight and advice on this subject. If you were starting all over again, where would you place your emphasis?"

Example 6

"Carol tells me you are responsible for much of the engineering hiring at the Gilbert Company. I'm sure, as a result, you have read your share of resumes. I have just finished writing a rough-draft resume for a project engineering position and was wondering whether you would be kind enough to take a look at it. I would really appreciate having it reviewed by an experienced eye such as yours. Would you have a minute or two to look it over? I would greatly value your suggestions because it's been a while since I wrote my last resume."

Reviewing these examples should illustrate just how easy it is to tailor your information requests to the various backgrounds and specific areas of knowledge of the networking contacts on your target list. It should also be evident, with a little imagination and forethought, just how effective a networking call can be in providing valuable information and advice that can both cut valuable time off your job search and help you identify interesting career opportunities much earlier in the game. Placing a cold call and asking your contact for job leads is simply not going to do it.

Step 6: Getting Referrals

When planning networking calls, your initial, primary objective should be to request general information and advice from the networking contact. As the conversation moves along, however, you will want to skillfully transition the focus to topics more directly related to your target industry and the target executives whom you want to reach. Obviously, referral or direct introduction to these executives is the ultimate objective of making these networking calls.

To keep the networking process alive and reach your final destination, it is imperative that you continuously get new referrals with every networking call. Ideally, you should shoot to get an average of two to four new referrals with each call you make. It is also important that you focus on getting meaningful referrals—those that can help you penetrate your target companies as early in the networking process as possible.

This is the reason I strongly recommend assigning a priority rating to each new referral. You will always want to keep high-priority calls (those that are most directly connected to your target companies and target managers) at the very top of your networking call list. Doing so will enable you to penetrate these target companies much sooner, and cut significant time off your job search. Lack of such prioritization and focus is sure to add unnecessary weeks, if not months, to the time it takes to land an attractive career opportunity.

Here is where the "six degrees of separation" concept comes into play. It has been effectively demonstrated that you can reach almost anyone in the world, through intelligent networking, by using your personal contacts and making no more than six well-placed phone calls. I have seen this validated time and again by those who use their personal contacts to network intelligently. There is no reason why this should not be the case with you as well.

There is no subtle or indirect way to ask for referrals. This is a fairly direct and deliberate process. It is for this reason that this request is best delayed until the later part of your networking call. By then, chances are you have successfully navigated through the social warm-up period and established some level of personal rapport with your networking contact. When the timing is right, however, you will definitely want to ask your contact for referral to others.

Here are some examples of how you can do this:

Example 1

> *"Sandra, as you probably already know, the key to finding new career opportunities is networking. It is often who you know, and their introductions to others, that lands most jobs in this market. As you know, I have targeted the food industry and am looking to penetrate some of the key players such as Kraft Foods, General Mills, and Hershey. With all your contacts in the food industry, do you know anyone at these companies—or, for that matter, other major food companies—who might be helpful? I'm not expecting them to provide me with job leads, but I am interested in gaining some inside perspective on their companies."*

Example 2

"Mike, as you know, the key to finding a job in this market is networking. With this in mind, are there people whom you know who, like you, are well networked in the consumer electronics industry?"

Example 3

"Peggy, I know from conversations with Margaret that you have been very active in the American Marketing Association, and have attended many of their conferences. I'm sure by now you have established a fairly good network. As you think about others you have met at these conferences and elsewhere who appear to be very active and well networked, are there some names that come to mind as good general networking contacts?"

Example 4

"John, two of my target companies, in which I have a great deal of interest, are Kimberly Clark and Fort James Paper Company. Do you know anyone who works for either company, whom I might contact?"

There may be times that your networking contact might hit a blank wall. They might be unable to come up with appropriate names, especially of specific employees who work for your target companies. This might be perfectly legitimate, and will happen from time to time. In such cases, ask for "secondary" contacts. These are contacts that, although not employed at your target company, might know others who are. Some examples of these secondary or indirect contacts include the following:

- Vendors
- Consultants
- Trade association officers or members
- Professional association officers or members
- Trainers or educators with close industry ties

Should your networking contact hit a blank wall when it comes to providing key contacts at your target companies, you might consider using the "laundry-list" approach. Here is how it works:

"Marge, I know you don't personally know any employees at my two target companies, but you might know others who do. For example, who are some of the vendors or consultants who call on you and who might have contacts at these firms? Also, how about fellow trade association members or trainers that cater to the industry who may have possible connections there? Some of these individuals could prove very helpful."

As shown in this example, when using the laundry-list technique, ask for the names of "secondary contacts" (those not employed at your target companies but who, by virtue of their profession, are likely to know others who are). By providing your networking contact with a laundry list of such categories of people, your contact will often come up with valuable names they would never have considered. Some of these "secondary referrals" might have excellent connections at your target companies, and might be quite willing to pave the way to some key introductions. At least you won't be coming away from the networking call empty-handed!

When getting a new referral from a networking source, be sure to get the new contact's telephone numbers and, if available, his or her e-mail address. Also make sure you understand the relationship between the new contact and the referral source. This will provide you with the ammunition you'll need later to engage the new contact in small talk and establish some personal rapport. Furthermore, be sure to ask the referral source for permission to use their name during your phone introduction to the new contact.

Make sure the referring source understands that you are simply asking to use his or her name as a means to making your initial introduction, and are not asking them to serve as a reference. Nearly all referral sources will willingly allow use of their name, and some will even tell you to say "hello" to the networking contact. This adds a nice personal touch to any new networking introduction.

Step 7: Closing the Networking Call

A simple "thank you" is always appreciated when someone goes out of his or her way to help you. Be sure, then, to take a moment or two to thank your contact for helping you. Although you will not have time to write to all the people who have taken some time out of a busy workday to provide assistance, make sure you do so in those cases where the contact has truly gone out of their way to lend a hand.

Certainly, when anyone takes the time to get actively involved in your job search and goes the extra mile (such as making phone calls and arranging personal introductions on your behalf), a thank-you letter and some follow-up conversation is clearly warranted. Be sure to e-mail or call this contact from time to time to update them on your job search status and advise them of the outcome of their referrals and introductions.

The Networking Meeting: Let's Do Lunch!

Although networking lunch meetings can sometimes prove to be extremely beneficial, especially if they result in introductions to key people, be careful not to waste time in meetings that offer low probability for meaningful results. You could end up with little to show for your effort except a larger waistline and a thinner wallet. The rule of thumb is, "Only feed those who will feed you." Pick and choose these meetings carefully.

Moreover, be careful not to use the opportunity for a networking meeting as an excuse to avoid sitting at your desk and making networking calls. Some job seekers have an aversion to networking, and look for every opportunity to avoid it. This is especially true when they lack the necessary skills and training to network effectively. If you have carefully read the preceding two chapters, you should definitely not fall into this category.

Certainly, if a person is one of your target managers, is a key person employed by one of your target companies, or is otherwise in a position to offer you a job or open an important door for you, by all means, take him or her to lunch! And you pick up the tab!

When the contact is well connected and in a position to be of major assistance, there is nothing that beats a personal meeting. When two people meet eyeball-to-eyeball, especially for this type of meeting, the networking contact is bound to come away from the meeting with a much more visible commitment to helping you than had this conversation taken place over the telephone.

Countering Networking Objections

Although a rarity, when you are making dozens of networking phone calls, you are bound to occasionally run into that one individual who is outrightly rude and is unwilling to lend a hand. Typically they will present one of a small handful of networking objections intended to shorten their conversation with you and get off of the telephone.

Unless you're prepared for these moments and equipped with good counter-strategies, you might scuttle one of your most promising networking opportunities. In this case, a little persistence can sometimes have a great payoff.

Here are some typical networking barriers and some effective counter-strategies.

I Don't Have Time to Talk

Contact: *"I'm sorry, I'm very busy right now and don't have time for this call."*

Networker: *"Gee, John, I'm sorry to interrupt you at such a busy time. Perhaps I could call at a later time that is more convenient. When would you suggest?"*

I Don't Have Time to Meet

Contact *"I'm sorry Mary; although I would normally be willing to meet with you, my current schedule is really hectic, and I simply don't have time at the moment."*

Networker: *"No problem, Barbara. I can appreciate that you have a very busy schedule and a number of demands on your time. Perhaps, then, we might discuss this matter briefly by phone, rather than in person. Is this a good time to talk, or would you prefer that I call back at a more convenient time?"*

I'm Not Aware of Opportunities

Contact: "I'm not really in touch with the job market and am not aware of any job opportunities for you."

Networker: "Not a problem Karen, I didn't expect you to provide job leads. I was really calling more for some general thoughts and ideas you might have that would be helpful to me. I would be particularly interested in learning more about some of the newer developments in the use of sales force automation software. This appears to be a high-growth area, and is an area of career interest to me. Connie says that you have become quite an expert in this field."

I Can't Think of Any Contacts

Contact: "Sorry, Dick; I'm just drawing a blank. I really can't think of anyone who might be looking for someone with your background."

Networker: "Debra, that's okay. I really appreciate your trying. Actually, though, I wasn't just thinking of people who might have a job opportunity for me. Instead, I'd also be interested in knowing about others you have met who might have connections with the consumer electronics industry. For example, this might include vendors who sell to the industry, consultants, or people you have met at trade or professional society meetings. Really, anyone you can think of who has connections to the industry."

I Don't Think I Can Help

Contact: "Don, although I would like to be of assistance, I'm not sure I can help you."

Networker: "Bob, although on the surface this might appear to be the case, there are some areas where I feel your knowledge and advice could be particularly beneficial to me. For example, Stacy tells me you are very active in the American Marketing Association and know a lot of executives at both companies and consulting firms. Are there specific marketing people who you know from your professional affiliations that appear well connected in the metals industry?"

I Really Don't Know You

Contact: "I really don't know you, so I am reluctant to provide you with the names of any of my contacts. I don't feel they would appreciate being hounded for job leads by someone they don't even know."

Networker: "Mike, I can certainly understand your feelings. I would likely feel the same way as you do, and calls of this type are very difficult for me to make. Mike, Perhaps if I sent you my resume, it would *give you an opportunity to become familiar with me and my background. I'm sure you know that Mildred Fleming would never have suggested I call you if she had any reservations about me or my credentials. I know she would be glad to give you a call and fill you in on both my background and professional reputation, if that would be helpful. In the meantime, I would be grateful for any suggestions you might have for improving my resume. I have just completed my first draft."*

I Don't Take Calls of This Type During Office Hours

Contact: "I'm sorry, I don't take personal calls of this type during office hours."

Networker: "I apologize, Marian; I was not aware of your policy. I hope I have not caused a problem for you. I would be more than happy to call you at home during non-business hours if that would be acceptable to you. When would you suggest I call?"

How Did You Get Past My Administrative Assistant?

Contact: "How did you get by my assistant? He knows I never take calls of this type!"

Networker: "I'm really not sure how my call got through to you. I just called, and you happened to pick up. I apologize, but I had no way of knowing you don't take calls of this nature. In my discussions with Mary Turner, she never mentioned this to me. She seemed to feel you would be someone with whom I should talk, and suggested I call you. She was very complimentary, and said you are a good friend and colleague. I hope I have not imposed in any way."

You Need to Talk to Human Resources

Contact: "Carla, you need to contact John Dawson, our human resources manager. He handles all employment matters. Let me get John's extension for you."

Networker: "Yes, I appreciate the referral, and will certainly give John a call. Thank you. Dave, my intent, however, was not to call you for a specific job lead or an employment application. Instead, I was calling at the suggestion of Karen Washington, to get some general career advice. Karen seemed to feel you would be an excellent person to talk with, in a general sense, about the feasibility of making a career transition to the petrochemical industry. Would you mind taking a few minutes to answer a couple of basic questions?"

I Have No Suggestions or Ideas

Contact: "Jeff, I'd really like to help you, but right now I just simply can't come up with any creative ideas or suggestions concerning your job search. I'm sorry!"

Networker: "That's certainly not a problem, Andrea. I know if you were to think of something appropriate, you would be happy to share it with me. Perhaps, however, we could shift our focus to another area. As you know, this is a rather difficult labor market, and job-hunting success is very much dependent on personal referral and networking. Andrea, as you think of various people you know in the steel industry, through trade or professional association connections, are there key persons who seem to have a lot of industry contacts who I should consider calling? Also, can you think of any key vendors or consultants who are also well networked in the industry?"

Just Send Me Your Resume

Contact: "Look, Susan, why don't you send me your resume and I'll see what I can do."

Networker: "I'd be happy to, and really appreciate your willingness to help out. I'll plan to give you a follow-up call in a couple of weeks, to see whether anything has turned up. Also, John, if in the meantime you could give some thought to some good industry contacts who you feel would be worth giving a call, I would very much appreciate it. I'll plan to give you a call around the 15th. Again, I appreciate your willingness to help out. Thank you."

I Have No Reason to Help You

Contact: "Quite frankly, Daren, I have no reason to help you. I don't even know you!"

Networker: "I realize sometimes this kind of call can be an annoyance. This is especially true when you don't know the person calling. I can appreciate your feelings. But in this kind of labor market, when jobs are difficult to find, sometimes there's no other option but to network through contacts. Quite frankly, the reason I'm calling is that Sharon Baxter encouraged me to give you a call. She felt you could be very helpful to me. I would certainly appreciate anything you could do to lend me a hand."

Despite all of the potential networking barriers I've cited, I want to reassure you that most contacts will be very cordial and, if approached properly, more than willing to help you. It's all in how you go about asking for assistance, and how facile you become at redirecting the conversation when you hit a dead end. You will rarely, if ever, encounter anyone who is outright rude. However, should you call that one-in-a-million "stinker," at least you will have some idea of how to handle the situation.

A Sample Networking Call

The following is an example of a typical networking conversation. It employs most of the strategies and techniques covered in this chapter, and should give you a good feel for the natural ebb and flow of an effective networking call.

Contact: "*Good morning, this is Cornell Wilkins. How can I help you?*"

Networker: "*Good morning, Cornell, this is Janet Morse calling. I'm calling at the suggestion of David Beasley. David and I are tennis partners at the Fair Oaks Tennis Club.*"

Contact: "*Oh, so you're a tennis player also. Any good?*"

Networker: "*Some days are better than others, but you'd have to ask David that one.*"

Contact: "*I think you are a bit modest. If you're David's partner, I'm sure you've got to be good! Janet, what can I do for you?*"

Networker: "*Cornell, I am in the process of a career transition and David felt you are someone with whom I should be talking.*"

Contact: "*Why is that? What is your background?*"

Networker: "*I have a bachelor's degree in life sciences, and a little over four years as a sales representative for Bio Pharmaceuticals in the Philadelphia region. I have done well, and exceeded sales quota during three of my four years with Bio; however, I don't see much opportunity for career advancement in the near future and feel I'm ready for my first management assignment as a district or regional manager. I would like to stay in the pharmaceutical field, but would prefer a more progressive company with more new products in the pipeline. David said you have been very active with Sales and Marketing Executives International, both nationally and at the local level. He felt you might have a pulse on the market and might be in a position to make a few key introductions. In any event, I would appreciate any thoughts or advice you may have for me.*"

Contact: "*Do you have a resume?*"

Networker: "*Absolutely! Would you like me to e-mail it to you?*"

Contact: "*That would be great. My e-mail address is Cornellwilk@yahoo.com. I'll take a look at it and see what I can do.*"

Networker: "Much appreciated, thank you. Cornell, while I have you on the line, who is the current membership chairperson for the association's Philadelphia region? I would love to make contact and see if I can buy or borrow a copy of the regional membership listing for networking purposes. I am also interested in the names of other regional officers. I would think with their connections, I might be able to come up with a potential job lead or two. Would you happen to have their names and phone numbers handy?"

Contact: "Sure, give me a moment and I will look them up for you."

Networker: "Outstanding! I sure appreciate your help. Would you mind if I were to tell them I got their names from you?"

Contact: "Not at all; feel free!"

Networker: "Thanks! Cornell, while we're on the subject of names, are there any sales managers or executives who belong to the association and who work in the pharma industry? I'd be particularly interested in any who appear well tuned in to what is happening in the market and seem to be well connected and networked locally."

Contact: "Yes, there are two who come to mind. One is Jimmy Halliard, director of sales and marketing for Brackston Pharmaceutical, and the other is Sally Dawson of Chemtron Pharma. I'm not sure on Sally's title, but she seems to be liked and well connected in the local pharma market. Both would be excellent contacts for you."

Networker: "Gee, Cornell, that's really great! Do you happen to have contact information for them, and would you mind if I told them you suggested I call? Also, do you know either of them very well?"

Contact: "Sure, here are their numbers, and feel free to use my name when you call. In answer to your other questions, I have known Jimmy for about six years now. He's really a nice guy. Been very active in a number of area charities, and serves on the board of the local chapter of the American Cancer Society. Unfortunately, his wife passed away from cancer about four years ago. It was quite a blow for Jimmy, but he seems to be doing well. Oh, I also know he's quite a tennis player. Perhaps you've run into him on the courts."

Networker: "Not really, but I think I have heard his name mentioned. Sounds like we have something in common."

Contact: "Listen, Janet, I've got to run. But before I do, here are the names and phone numbers of the association officers I promised you. I'm sure they would be happy to talk with you. Perhaps they might even talk you into becoming a new member. By the way, I'll be looking forward to getting your resume."

Networker: "Cornell, you've been a great help! I really appreciate the time you've taken with me this morning. Thanks so much for the names and contact information. Perhaps you'll see me at one of your upcoming association meetings. Who knows, I might just join."

Contact: "You're quite welcome, and I would look forward to seeing you there."

Hopefully this sample call has enabled you to see just how productive a networking call can be. This call went very smoothly, and Janet was able to use quite successfully some of the networking techniques we have discussed. These resulted in at least four to five excellent networking contacts, as well as Cornell's permission to use his name when making future networking calls. This should serve to effectively illustrate how a job seeker, with some advanced thought, can tailor his or her networking call to the contact's position and background. Janet took full advantage of Cornell's position as a board member of Sales and Marketing Executives International, and it had a major payoff for her.

If you use the various strategies and techniques I have described in the last two chapters, I am confident that you will realize the same kind of success as Janet did. As a coach and professional career transition consultant, I have trained and coached *hundreds* of job seekers in these techniques and watched them land excellent career opportunities through effective networking, time and time again.

Chapter Summary

Networking is a top source for finding jobs. It should therefore be a principal component and major focal point of much of your Ultimate Job Search strategy. When placing a networking call, key points to remember are the following:

- Plan your call in advance. Have firm objectives.
- Have a good system for managing, tracking, and controlling the networking process so that it doesn't get out of hand.
- Prepare and practice your "two-minute drill."
- Use small talk to set a less formal tone for your networking conversation, thus establishing early rapport.
- Use the name of the referral source to create a personal bond and sense of obligation to respond to your requests for assistance.
- Never ask for a job or job leads.
- Do not volunteer that you have left your past employer. It can raise unnecessary concerns.
- Tailor your requests for job search assistance to things your networking contact can deliver.

(continued)

(continued)

- Ask for general advice and ideas first. Save requests for networking referrals until later in the conversation, when you have established rapport and trust.

- Use the "laundry-list" approach to help your networking contact come up with the names of additional valuable referrals.

- Establish the nature of the relationship between your networking contact and his or her referrals.

- Ask for permission to use the referral source's name when introducing yourself to the person to whom you are being referred. It will make the next call much easier, and is the glue that makes networking work.

- Take time to send a thank-you e-mail or note to those who have gone out of their way to help you, and keep them apprised of your progress.

Effective networking doesn't just happen. It requires good planning and practice. But the rewards are well worth the effort!

CHAPTER 10

Conducting a Targeted Direct-Mail Campaign

Many other sources of employment are much easier and less expensive to use than mass mailing your resume directly to employers. A general broadcast mailing can be both time-consuming and relatively expensive; however, it can sometimes produce interesting results.

The value of this type of mass mailing, provided that it is addressed to your target managers, is that it can hit at just the opportune time, when the manager is just beginning to contemplate the need to hire someone. In some cases, it can actually serve as the catalyst, sparking the manager to make a definite decision and give you a call. It can also serve to pave the way for a follow-up phone call and, if there is no need for someone with your skill set, it can provide some valuable networking contacts that could prove beneficial.

Mailings of this type are generally not as productive as other strategies presented in this book, and should therefore be seen as a secondary part of your Ultimate Job Search strategy. However, if you are looking to launch a comprehensive, "all-out" job-hunting campaign, you will want to consider using this approach.

The Rules for a Successful Direct-Mail Campaign

If you are contemplating making such a mailing, there are some basic rules to ensure best results. These are as follow:

- Never mail an unsolicited resume directly to the human resources or staffing department.

- Always target your resume mailing to the top functional manager or director who heads the business unit or function in which you would be employed.

- Follow your mailing with a follow-up networking phone call (rather than a straight employment inquiry).

This chapter explores each of these rules as well as the logic behind them. I also give recommendations for following these rules most effectively.

Never Mail an Unsolicited Resume to the Human Resources or Staffing Department

Unless you are responding directly to a job advertisement or Internet job listing, there is little point in sending your resume directly to either the human resources department or the staffing department. If you e-mail or snail mail your unsolicited resume to either of these two departments, it is likely to receive little if any attention and will likely be automatically entered into the company's electronic resume database—along with about a "gazillion" other resumes.

Although there is always the possibility that your resume might be identified for a future search opportunity, the odds are not particularly in your favor. In addition, if you send your resume to the firm via snail mail, it is likely to sit around with several thousand other unsolicited resumes until someone can find the time to scan it into the company's resume database.

> **Note:** Sending an unsolicited resume to either of these two areas is not an effective use of your time and money. There are far more effective things you can do with your time to target specific openings for which you are qualified, and thereby increase the probability of employment. These include networking, using Internet job boards, using job aggregators, and using an automated mass e-mailing of your resume to search firms. See earlier chapters in this book for details on these other methods.

Send Your Resume to Target Executives

If you are going to make an unsolicited mailing to target companies, it's best to send your resume directly to the functional head of the department in which you would be working. There are several reasons for doing this.

First, assuming that there is sufficient budget, this functional head has the authority to hire you, whereas the human resources function does not. Human resources is typically aware of only those positions that have been formally approved through the new hire requisition process and have been turned over to the company's staffing function to be filled. They are not normally aware of events dynamically occurring within your target function that might call for someone with your skill set.

Sometimes hiring decisions can be very spontaneous and immediate, and can arise in response to myriad factors affecting current business plans and operating conditions. As a former staffing executive for a major corporation, I have seen this occur on numerous occasions. Here are some of the circumstances that can lead to such spontaneous employment needs:

- **Responding to an unexpected job vacancy:** There are occasions when a function or business head suddenly becomes aware of an unexpected job vacancy and feels there is a need to move quickly to fill the position. This vacancy could occur due to a sudden resignation, retirement decision, or critical health issue of an existing employee. If the functional manager becomes aware of a well-qualified candidate before this need is communicated to human resources,, he or she might decide to move quickly to hire this individual before the need has been formally communicated to human resources or an employment requisition has been officially approved.

- **Expansion of function and increased workload:** Sometimes a senior-level management decision, such as the approval of a major capital project or the decision to enter a new market, might suddenly give rise to an increased workload and the need to expand staff. In such case, before these needs are specifically identified or hiring requisitions are completed, the functional head might become aware of a well-qualified candidate and elect to bring this person in for interviews. A resume hitting the functional manager's desk at just the right time can, under these circumstances, be just the catalyst to prompt an interview and subsequent job offer.

- **Employee performance issue:** If a current employee has had a habitual performance issue and the functional head is about to take action, contact from the right employment candidate can sometimes provide the impetus that sparks the decision to separate the poor performer from the business and hire the newly identified employment candidate.

- **Addressing key problems and issues:** There can be times when a functional leader has been wrestling with a major, long-standing problem or issue that needs resolution, and he or she receives the resume of a qualified person who has had a history of successfully solving such problems. This might suddenly lead to an interview and hiring decision.

- **New strategic initiatives:** Sometimes shifts in business strategy can lead to the sudden need for people with entirely new skill sets because none of the existing employees have the needed qualifications. Should an appropriately qualified individual surface, either through resume submittal or networking contact, it is quite possible that a new job could be created to accommodate this individual.

So, as you can see from these examples, a direct-mail campaign targeting these functional heads can sometimes prove quite effective as a means of surfacing hidden employment opportunities that have not yet materialized in the formal sense. The beauty of a direct-mail strategy, of course, is the fact that these positions have not yet been available to the general public through normal employment channels. This has the potential to literally eliminate all competition, assuming your resume hits at just the right time and an appropriate opportunity exists.

> **Note:** In order to implement a direct-mail campaign, you will need to identify the firms you want to target as well as the names and titles of the function or business heads who lead the business functions in which you would work. The research process for accomplishing this is thoroughly described in chapter 8.

Follow Up with a Phone Call

This type of mailing works best when followed by a networking phone call. When calling, reference your letter as the reason for the call. Express strong interest in working for the company, but leave the door open for other suggestions or ideas the employer might have.

When you call, there is either an appropriate opening or not. Hopefully your cover letter and resume arrived at a time when an opportunity exists, or is just materializing. If there is clearly no opportunity for employment at the time of your call, however, you might then want to take advantage of this opportunity to do a little networking. Here is an example of how you might do this:

> *You: "Barbara, I really appreciated the opportunity to speak with you this morning, and I am disappointed to learn that you do not foresee anything developing for me at Manning Paper Company in the immediate future. I am wondering, however, if you might be able to help me in another way. Do you have any suggestions of people who you feel would be good for me to talk with? I am thinking of people working outside of Manning Paper, who are well networked in the industry and might be aware of opportunities—for example, colleagues you might know through your trade association, industry consultants, vendors, or others. I would really appreciate any ideas you might have."*

As you can see, this type of conversation can open the door to other key introductions that you can use for networking purposes. So, despite the fact that there were no openings at Manning, at least you have taken full advantage of this opportunity to develop other important industry contacts.

The Target Mailing Cover Letter

In order to implement a direct-mail campaign, you will need a basic cover letter to send with your resume. Figure 10.1 is a sample cover letter. In reviewing this sample cover letter, you will note the following features:

- The letter is brief, concise, and to the point.
- Use of white space and short paragraphs makes the letter easy to read, which invites and encourages readership.
- The first paragraph briefly and succinctly states the reason for writing, including the level and type of position sought as well as an expression of interest in working for the company.

August 15, 2007

Ms. Barbara M. Moore
Engineering Manager
Manning Paper Company
122 River Road
Marionette, MI 23719

Dear Ms. Moore:

I am writing to express interest in working for your company in the capacity of Senior Project Engineer in central engineering or at one of your plant locations.

I hold a B.S.M.E. degree from the University of Wisconsin and have eight years of engineering experience in the paper industry with Wisconsin Paper Company. Core skills and competencies include the following:

Paper Mill Engineering

- Led team of engineers and technicians in the rebuild of the #4 paper machine (a $60 million capital project)—completed on time and 3 percent below budget.

- Lead engineer in rebuild of dryer section of #6 paper machine, replacing Yankee dryer and after-dyers (an $18 million capital project)—completed on time and within budget.

- Led design team responsible for total redesign of pulp preparation area for #7 paper machine.

- Project engineer on numerous other paper mill engineering projects.

Finishing & Converting Engineering

- Managed design, installation, and successful startup of Super Soft tissue converting line to include converting, finishing, and packaging operations ($12 million capital project).

- Lead engineer in the design and installation of the Soft Cloud packaging and distribution line, including poly wrap, boxing, sealing, and conveyor equipment. ($4 million capital project).

I have solid engineering skills and have been a strong contributor at Wisconsin Paper. I also enjoy an excellent reputation for delivering projects on time, and at or below budget.

I will plan to call you shortly to explore the possibility of employment with your company. Thank you for your consideration, and I look forward to speaking with you.

Sincerely,

Michael B. Johnston

Figure 10.1: A sample cover letter.

- The second paragraph provides a simple, one- or two-sentence overview of education and job-relevant experience.

- The center, and focal point of the letter, highlights two to three core skill areas with related accomplishments in each.

- The second-to-last paragraph highlights some job-relevant skills known to be important to success in the targeted position.

- The final paragraph is intended to pave the way for a phone conversation and possible job interview.

Although this letter is fairly basic, it is designed to encourage an employer to read it. The use of short one- and two-sentence paragraphs, combined with ample white space, certainly makes it very easy to read. Because of this simple and efficient design, the letter can be easily read in a matter of seconds and still have strong impact on the reader.

The center area is the heart of the cover letter and focuses on two to three key skill or competency categories, which are then followed by accomplishment statements. When choosing skill areas to highlight, select those two to three areas that will be universally recognized, within the profession, as most critical to successful performance of your target position. Following this same logic, when selecting key accomplishments, choose those that speak to your ability to deliver important results and demonstrate your value as an important contributor.

Chapter Summary

When planning a direct-mail campaign and sending your resume to many employers, keep the following key points in mind:

- Never send your resume to the human resources or staffing departments. They are not always aware of new or potential hiring requirements.

- Direct your mailing to your target managers, those for whom you would work if you were hired.

- Your resume can sometimes serve as the catalyst that prompts a target manager to move ahead and fill a position, especially if its arrival happens to coincide with the sudden development of an unplanned or unexpected business need.

- Follow up your mailing with a direct call to the target manager.

- If no need exists for your skills, convert your call to a networking call that can yield some valuable new contacts.

CHAPTER 11

Interview Preparation: Great Ways to Stack the Deck in Your Favor

When preparing for a job interview, there are a number of things you can do in advance to gain a competitive advantage and walk away with a job offer. Unfortunately, many job seekers elect to fly by the seat of their pants and end up walking away naked. Unless you are an exceptionally fleet-footed, silver-tongued devil, this is not a strategy for winning the interview game.

Modern interviewing has come a long way in recent years. Companies have become far more sophisticated and skilled at the interview process than a few years back. Much of the focus now is on "behavior-based interviewing," where the employer probes the candidate's knowledge and skills far more deeply than before. Good advance interview preparation is the only way to survive and excel in today's interview process. Relying on on-the-spot thinking and your gift-of-gab, in most cases, is simply not going to get you through.

Fortunately, if you are willing to invest a little time and effort to prepare for the interview process, there is much you can do to dramatically improve your effectiveness and positively affect the outcome. This chapter will help you systematically plan an interview strategy that will provide you with a distinct advantage and all but guarantee a positive result.

Think Like an Employer

If you want to gain important insight, you need to think like the employer. Put yourself in the employer's shoes. What are the principal accountabilities of the job, and what is needed for successful performance? What knowledge, skills, and personal attributes are essential to performance success? These are the questions you must answer before you can expect to formulate a winning interview strategy.

Can You Get Results?

The lion's share of interview time is devoted to exploring the candidate or job seeker's ability to get specific results. The successful candidate must be able to demonstrate, during the course of the interview, that he or she has the necessary knowledge, skills, and abilities to tackle the key challenges and problems of the job and get the results the employer desires.

Figure 11.1 illustrates the major focal points of most job interviews. Employers use the interview to determine whether you have the necessary skills to arrive at good solutions that will yield the key results expected of the job. For example, you are applying for the position of project engineer; do you have the knowledge and skills to solve certain design problems and come up with a practical, efficient, and cost-effective design?

You might be presented with certain design problems you would encounter in the job, and then asked what you would do. The employer will be interested in finding out whether you understand and apply certain design principles and can come up with a good design solution. The members of the interview team will then measure the quality of your solution on the basis of whether the design is sound, practical, efficient, and cost-effective. This is the end result of good engineering design, and the end result by which you will be measured.

So, as you can see from this example, the basis for an employer's interview design is to determine whether you have specific technical skills (in this case, engineering design) and can effectively apply them to achieve a specific desired end result (in this case, a solution that is sound, practical, efficient, and cost-effective).

Do You Have the Necessary Skills?

When interviewing, you will quickly discover that much of the employment interview centers on what I call a job's "technical skill" requirements. It is this skill requirement area that most employers will zero in on for the bulk of the interview. In fact, if I had to put a number on it, I would estimate that as much as 80 to 90 percent of the interview will be focused on exploring this technical skill set, and whether you can apply these skills and deliver the key results expected of the position. Therefore, you must focus much of your interview preparation on this area. What are the technical skills required by the job, and what are the key results expected of the job incumbent?

So that you don't get the wrong idea, let me pause for a moment to define what I mean by "technical skills." In using this term, I am not referring to science, engineering, or math skills (although this could be the case if you are an engineer or scientist). Instead, when I use the word "technical" in this context, I am referring to the "specialized knowledge and skills" required for successful performance of a given job. These are the skills or skill areas often also referred to as "hard skills." They are the skills that can easily be measured during a job interview.

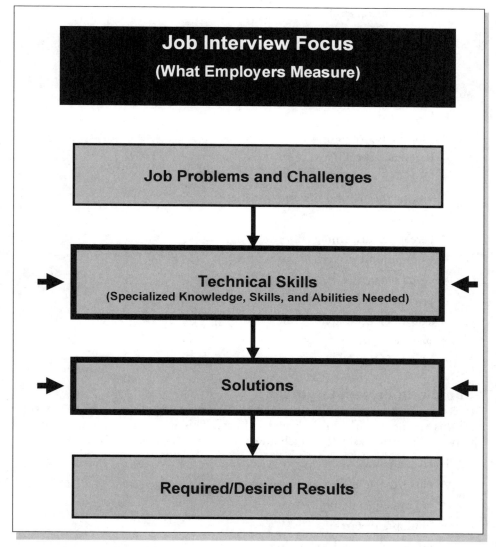

Figure 11.1: Job interview focus.

On the other hand, jobs also have "soft skill" requirements. Soft skills are the personal attributes and qualities the employer feels to be essential to good job performance. Let me cite an example or two, of both "hard" and "soft" skills, so you get the idea.

Example A: Employment Manager/Recruiter

Most people are reasonably familiar with the job of recruiting manager or recruiter, so it is probably a good example to choose. The following is a sampling of both the hard and soft skills required to be good at recruiting.

- Hard (technical) skills
  - Candidate identification
  - Employment source utilization
  - Resume screening
  - Candidate screening
  - Interviewing
  - Candidate evaluation
  - Reference checking
  - Job offer formulation
- Soft skills (personal traits and qualities)
  - Persuasive
  - Perceptive/discerning
  - Communicator (verbal and written)
  - Good listener
  - Friendly/affable
  - Thorough/accurate
  - Well-organized
  - Multitasking

Example B: Project Engineer

Project engineer is another position with which many people are familiar. Assume that this engineer works in the paper industry. This will give you a better feel for the type of specific skills for which an employer might look.

- Hard (technical) skills
  - Paper machine design
  - Machine installation
  - Equipment start-up
  - Engineering troubleshooting
  - Machine wet-end design
  - Control system applications
  - Motor controls and power
  - Project planning
  - Construction supervision
  - Cost control

- Soft skills (personal traits and qualities)
  - Hands-on personality
  - Organized planner
  - Analytical
  - Thorough/accurate
  - Team player
  - Resourceful/creative
  - Responsive/timely
  - Self-motivated

As you can see from these examples, hard skills, for the most part, are pretty easy to identify and can be fairly objectively measured during the course of a job interview. On the other hand, soft skills fall primarily into the subjective category. They cannot normally be measured as finitely as hard skills, and are much more dependent on the personal opinion of the interviewer. Soft skills are usually certain traits, personal qualities, and behaviors the employer is looking for and attempting to evaluate throughout the course of the interview by simply observing the candidate's behavior.

Moreover, hard skills are fairly standard and universal. Except for some minor tweaking to reflect industry specialization, they are fairly uniform from employer to employer. A project engineer, for example, must be capable of engineering design. A recruiter, regardless of industry, must be skilled at interviewing and evaluating employment candidates. As the above examples show, certain soft skills can also be fairly standard and universal from employer to employer. For example, it would be pretty hard to be a good engineer if you were not thorough and accurate. Likewise, most recruiters must be friendly, affable, and persuasive if they are to be effective at establishing relationships with candidates and persuading them to come to work for their company.

Other soft skills, however, are not universal from employer to employer and might instead be specific to the company environment in which the work is performed. For example, in an open-system culture, which performs much of its work through team collaboration, traits such as being aggressive or confrontational might not be seen as desirable qualities. On the other hand, in a work environment that feels confrontation is important to good decision-making, the company actually values a candidate who is aggressive and confrontational. So if you are to win a job offer, you will need to understand not only the universal technical skills and personal qualities required for job performance, but also the work environment or culture in which the job will be performed.

What Is a Behavioral Interview?

I mentioned at the beginning of this chapter that most employers today use some form of behavior-based interview to evaluate employment candidates. So, what is a behavior-based interview, and why is it important for you to know about it?

The behavior-based interview is an interview process based on the concept that "the best predictor of future behavior is present or past behavior." This concept has a scientific basis. Psychologists have been able to conclusively demonstrate, during the course of a career lifetime, that most people really don't change their stripes. If, up until now, they have always looked and behaved like a striped zebra, they aren't very likely to now suddenly become a spotted giraffe. There is high likelihood that their behavior will remain essentially the same.

If an individual has been energetic, well-motivated, highly productive, and results-oriented in past jobs and past work environments, assuming the new job and work culture are substantially similar, the likelihood is high that the individual will continue to behave the same way. If you change the job or culture substantially, however, all bets are off, and things become far less predictable.

Therefore, the focus of the behavior-based interview design is to examine your past work behavior. The employer will explore your past work experience to determine how you behaved and what you did. For example, they will ask "What were the problems and challenges you faced? What did you do, and what were the end results?" In other words, they will attempt to discover how you have behaved and what you did in the past as the basis for predicting how you will behave and what you will do if hired into the position they have to offer.

Employers will use your answers to these types of questions, as well as their behavioral observations during the interview, to compare you with other candidates, and to predict the probability of success in the position they are offering. They will use the job interview to look for "evidence" of the behavioral qualities they desire as well as the results and accomplishments they consider essential to job success. This will be the focal point of the interview.

To prepare for the interview, your job will be to essentially mimic the employer's approach. You will need to first define the hard (technical) as well as soft skills required by the job, and then prepare to cite evidence that you possess these skills and can achieve the results for which the employer is looking.

For each of the key hard-skill areas you identify through this process, you need to prepare to eloquently describe the problems or challenges you faced, the specific actions you took, and the results you achieved. In this way, you can effectively provide concrete "evidence" that you not only have the requisite skills, but can also apply them to achieve the results the employer desires. If you can do this convincingly, there is a high likelihood that a job offer will be coming your way.

One commonly used form of the behavioral interview, which you are likely to encounter, is called the "situational interview." Instead of simply measuring past behavior, the situational interview is intended to examine candidate behavior on a "real-time," present basis.

When using this approach, the employer simply poses a real problem or challenge you will face in the new position and then asks what you would do. By doing this, the employer can actually observe your behavior. Are you knowledgeable? Can you think on your feet? Are you thorough and logical in your analysis of the problem? Were you thorough in gathering all the facts and clearly defining the problem? How creative were you in exploring alternative approaches and solutions? Were the conclusions you drew logical and sound? Was it a good solution? How about your communications skills? Were you articulate, concise, and convincing?

As you can see from this description, employers can use the situational interview to measure much more than just your technical skills. They can use it to more accurately assess the soft skills they feel are important to successful job performance.

> **Note:** As a form of the behavioral interview, the situational interview is used by the employer to observe and assess your current behavior. Thus, it can be used to fairly accurately predict how you are likely to behave in the future if hired for the position in question.

Predicting What the Interviewer Will Ask

It is believed that with a little advance forethought and planning, most job seekers will be able to anticipate and predict, with a high degree of accuracy, about 80 to 90 percent of the questions they will face during a typical job interview. This is like having access to the test questions in advance of the exam. There are several practical tools and techniques that will enable you to do just that.

Look at the Job Description and Employment Ad

The first such tool is the job description. Contact the company recruiter or hiring manager who invited you for a job interview and ask him or her whether they can e-mail or fax a copy of the job description to you. Most will be more than happy to do so. While you are at it, ask if they would also please send a copy of the company's most recent annual report. This will be helpful to your interview preparation process.

> **Tip:** In addition to helping you prepare for the interview, asking for the job description in advance shows that you have a solid interest in the position for which you will be interviewed, and that you are the kind of person who likes to be prepared. Most employers will be favorably impressed by your thoroughness and diligence.

The job description is typically an excellent source for identifying functional responsibilities for which you would be accountable, as well as key results expected of the position. It also often describes particular challenges and problems faced by the person in the position. Chances are this description was authored by the hiring manager and emphasizes the aspects of the job that this manager believes are most important. You will therefore want to read this document very carefully to see what the main focus of the position is and those aspects of the job that receive particular attention and emphasis.

Moreover, if the position was advertised on an Internet job board or in a newspaper, also pull a copy of the ad, so that you can compare it to the job description. You don't have to be a skilled detective to see common themes and trends in these two documents. In analyzing the two, ask yourself the following questions:

- What are the principal accountabilities of the position?
- What are the principal challenges and problems faced?
- What specialized knowledge and skills are required to address these?
- What are the "deliverables"—the end results expected?

> **Tip:** Although both documents are important to your analysis, I recommend putting slightly more emphasis on the ad than on the job description. Although the job description will help you zero in on many of the job's principal, ongoing responsibilities and challenges, the ad is probably more predictive of the issues and qualifications that are currently on the hiring manager's mind.

To help you with this analysis, I have provided Skills Profile Analysis worksheets for you to record this information for both the job description and the employment advertisement. Fill in these forms as you complete your analysis of each document.

Skills Profile Analysis: Job Description

Principal duties and accountabilities of this job:

_____

_____

_____

_____

_____

Principal problems and challenges faced by this job:

_____

_____

_____

_____

_____

Key results required of this job:

_____

_____

_____

_____

_____

Important education, skills, competencies, and personal qualities:

_____

_____

_____

_____

_____

Skills Profile Analysis: Employment Advertisement

Principal duties and accountabilities of this job:

_____

_____

_____

_____

_____

Principal problems and challenges faced by this job:

_____

_____

_____

_____

_____

Key results required of this job:

_____

_____

_____

_____

(continued)

(continued)

_____

_____

Important education, skills, competencies, and personal qualities:

_____

_____

_____

_____

_____

When writing an ad for a job, managers frequently tend to stress their most current, critical problems and needs, and to also describe the personal attributes they feel are most important to job success. You will seldom find the latter in the typical job description. You can pretty much bet the skills and personal qualities mentioned in the ad will be the same ones the hiring manager will elect to focus on during the interview. So, put them on your analysis sheet and mark them with an asterisk.

Moreover, when scrutinizing employment ads, pay particular attention to the language they use. What seem to be the "hot buttons," the things this hiring manager is emphasizing as especially important? Following are some key words and phrases to which you need to be particularly alert. This can provide major clues to the hiring manager's preferences and priorities:

- Must have the ability to....
- Prefer someone who....
- Key responsibilities include....
- A _____ is highly desirable.
- Seeks someone who can....

While reading both the ad and the job description, use a marker to highlight those functions, problems, challenges, results, and personal qualities that the employer appears to emphasize.

When performing your analysis, don't ignore the soft skills the company is seeking. Be sure to note any personal qualities or traits the employer appears to emphasize, and record them on your analysis sheet. Think about how the employer will likely measure these soft skills during the interview meeting. Will it simply be through observation, or are you likely to get some direct questions? If asked directly, how will you describe your personal qualities? How will you respond if asked how others would describe you? Also, can you describe what you have done in a way that will highlight these important qualities and personal attributes?

For example, if the employer emphasizes strong team leader skills in the employment advertisement, how can you provide evidence of your strong leadership skills during the course of the interview? Perhaps you led and motivated a team that achieved some significant result of interest to the employer. In describing this experience, you might therefore want to describe how you selected and organized the team, and what you did to develop, lead, and motivate them to achieve this outstanding accomplishment.

Compare Ads from Different Employers

Another good technique for identifying both the hard (technical) skills and job-relevant soft skills that are most likely to be targeted by employers during interviews, is to compare ads of several different employers for the same type of position. To accomplish this, use the newspaper or one of the major Internet job boards to find a number of these ads. Then lay them side by side, systematically analyzing each ad to determine the universal set of skills, competencies, and personal qualities most employers are seeking. Score these skill areas by putting a checkmark behind each one as it is specifically mentioned in each of the ads you review.

You can use the following worksheet to systematically collect and analyze this comparative data.

Skills Profile Analysis: Multiple Employer Ad Comparison

Principal duties and accountabilities of this job:

_____

_____

_____

_____

_____

Principal problems and challenges faced by this job:

_____

_____

_____

_____

Key results required of this job:

_____

_____

(continued)

(continued)

_____

_____

_____

_____

Important education, skills, competencies, and personal qualities:

_____

_____

_____

_____

_____

Pay particular attention to the number of checkmarks recorded. This will give you a good idea of which topics are most likely to be major focal points during your forthcoming job interviews.

What will emerge from this simple analysis is a universal list of hard (technical) skills and personal qualities most employers would agree are essential qualifications for effective performance of this type of work. This is an excellent "skills profile" on which to focus when preparing for a job interview in the field you have chosen.

Check the Internet

The Internet, as we all know, is a fantastic resource for researching almost any topic known to man. Job-specific core skills and competencies are no exception. Someone out there is bound to have looked at the skills and competencies pertaining to the position you are seeking and published an article on this subject.

So, using a search engine or two, try typing the title of the position you are seeking along with various combinations of the following words, and see what pops up.

- Skills
- Competencies
- Skills and Competencies
- Core Skills and Competencies
- Skills Profile

With a little imagination and persistence, you are unlikely to come up empty-handed.

Now record your findings on the following Skills Analysis worksheet.

Skills Profile Analysis: Internet Research on Core Skills and Competencies

Technical skills (specialized knowledge, skills, and abilities)

_____

_____

_____

_____

_____

_____

_____

_____

_____

_____

_____

_____

Personal traits and qualities

_____

_____

_____

_____

_____

_____

_____

_____

_____

_____

Look to Professional Associations

Another source for researching and preparing a universal list of core skills and competencies for your target position may be a professional association. Because these organizations exist primarily for the purpose of fostering the professional development of their membership, you might find they have already done the work for you.

A quick call to the association's corporate offices, or a visit to its Web site, might produce exactly what you are looking for. You can oftentimes find a beneficial list of the knowledge, skills, abilities, and personal qualities thought to be important to successful performance as a professional in your target field.

Record this information on the following Skills Profile Analysis form.

Skills Profile Analysis: Professional Association Research on Core Skills and Competencies

Technical skills (specialized knowledge, skills, and abilities)

_____

_____

_____

_____

_____

_____

_____

_____

_____

_____

_____

_____

Personal traits and qualities

_____

_____

_____

_____

_____

_____

_____

_____

_____

Your Consolidated Skills Summary

You have now gathered relevant data on both the hard (technical) skills and soft skills thought to be required for successful performance of your target position from five reliable sources.

The next step is to compare the Skills Profile Analyses you developed from these five sources and consolidate them into one final core skills and competencies set. Record this set on the Consolidated Skills Profile worksheet below. As you can see, this form is divided into two distinct categories:

- Hard (technical) skills: specialized knowledge and skill areas
- Soft skills: personal traits and qualities

Although the total list may have a tendency to get rather long, try paring it down to a more workable number of skills and competencies. Try to get down to a truly "core" list of no more then 8 to 10 key skills areas for each of these two main categories. Thus, your final competency profile should contain no more than 20 competencies in total.

In listing these core skills and competencies on the consolidated form, also record them in order of their importance or priority. Those skills and competencies that were most often listed first by the five research resources you used, or those that were especially emphasized by these sources, are likely those universally thought to be most important to successful job performance. List these first, and then follow with those of lower importance.

Consolidated Skills Profile: Hard/Technical Skills

Hard/Technical Skill:

_____

_____

_____

_____

Hard/Technical Skill:

_____

(continued)

(continued)

_____

_____

_____

_____

Hard/Technical Skill:

_____

_____

_____

_____

Hard/Technical Skill:

_____

_____

_____

_____

Hard/Technical Skill:

_____

_____

_____

_____

Hard/Technical Skill:

_____

_____

_____

_____

Hard/Technical Skill:

_____

_____

_____

_____

_____

Hard/Technical Skill:

_____

_____

_____

_____

_____

Hard/Technical Skill:

_____

_____

_____

_____

_____

Hard/Technical Skill:

_____

_____

_____

_____

_____

Consolidated Skills Profile: Soft Skills—Personal Traits and Qualities

Soft skill:

_____

_____

(continued)

(continued)

_____

_____

_____

Soft skill:

_____

_____

_____

_____

Soft skill:

_____

_____

_____

_____

Soft skill:

_____

_____

_____

_____

Soft skill:

_____

_____

_____

_____

Soft skill:

_____

_____

_____

_____

Soft skill:

_____

_____

_____

_____

Soft skill:

_____

_____

_____

_____

Soft skill:

_____

_____

_____

_____

Soft skill:

_____

_____

_____

_____

Connecting Skills with Results

The final step in preparing for your job interview is to link your consolidated list of core skills and competencies with specific results you have achieved. This is the most important part of interview preparation, so take your time and do it well.

If you need some extra motivation to complete this final phase of preparation, just remember: This will be the employer's principal focus throughout the job interview. In each of these key skill areas, the employer will want to know, "How did you use this skill, and what results did you get?" Remember, the employer is not going to hire you simply because you say you possess certain skills. Instead, they will want to see "evidence" that you can effectively apply these skills to get the results for which they are looking.

During this final phase of interview preparation, you are providing the very evidence the employer will be searching for during the entire course of the interview process. Don't wait until you are in the interview to try and make this connection. Doing it now will give you a huge competitive advantage in the interview.

Being able to quickly cite examples of how you have used these important skills and competencies to drive results and bring continuous improvement to past employers will be enough to excite any employer's interest in your employment candidacy. Doing this well throughout the interview will be most impressive, and is likely to win you that important job offer for which you are searching.

Chapter Summary

With a little time and some rather simple analysis, you can take much of the guesswork out of the interview process and identify, with reasonable accuracy, those areas that will likely be the major focal points of your upcoming job interviews. It is believed, through this analysis, you can predict upwards of 80 to 90 percent of the interview in advance, before you even head off to your first job interview.

In order to adequately prepare for an interview, you need to think like the employer. You first need to identify both the "hard" and "soft" skills required by the position. Second, you need to be well prepared to demonstrate proficiency in these core skills and competency areas by citing specific results you have achieved.

Systematic analysis using the following sources should enable you to accurately identify this universal set of core skills and competencies and give you a decided competitive advantage in the interview itself:

- Employer's job description
- Employer's job advertisement
- Multiple employer job advertisements (same position)
- Internet search for core skill and competency set (same position)
- Professional association competency models (same position)

CHAPTER 12

The Interview Day: Turning an Interview into an Offer

Turning an interview into a job offer is obviously your primary objective on the day of the interview. Because the job interview is essentially a process by which the employer is going to scrutinize nearly every inch of your background and qualifications, this is no easy task. It takes clever strategy combined with a few tricks and techniques—as well as a small dose of detective work. So, it's now time for a bit of fine-tuning.

In chapter 11, you saw how, with some focused research and a little analysis, you can predict the core skills and competencies the employer will most likely focus on during the job interview. You are also aware, from careful review of both the job description and recruitment ad, what the hiring manager's hot buttons are, and which of your skill sets are likely to be of greatest interest. This advanced preparation should already have helped you establish a reasonable level of confidence and self-assurance because you are now at least better prepared for what lies ahead.

If you've done your homework, as outlined in the preceding chapter, you are also fully prepared to cite several examples of results and achievements, providing the employer with strong evidence of your skills and capabilities in the qualification areas that are bound to be of greatest interest to the company. You are fully prepared to meet the interview head-on, and already know you'll do more than just survive. You are already halfway there, and clearly have a leg up on much of your competition.

But then there's that matter of competition! It would be foolhardy to assume that some of the others with whom you will compete are not equally or perhaps even better prepared at this stage of the battle. These are hopefully in the minority, but they are likely there, lurking in the wings. So, what else can you do to set yourself apart from these worthy opponents and ensure victory in the end? This chapter explores techniques you can use to triumph over the competition and win the offer.

Be a Private Eye

It's time for a bit of detective work on your part. So, get out your magnifying glass, your plaid hat, and your pipe and get to work. At this point it would be extremely helpful, from a competitive standpoint, to get some insider information.

What You Want to Find Out

It would be very advantageous for you to know a number of things in advance of the interview. Here are a few:

- Why is the position open?
- Who had the job previously, and why did they leave?
- Were they promoted, transferred, fired—or did they resign?
- If they were fired, why?
- If they were fired for performance, what were the issues? Where did the person fall short?
- If they resigned, why did they do so? What caused their dissatisfaction?
- What are the major problems and challenges currently facing the department?
- What are some of the objectives and goals—things the hiring manager is emphasizing?
- What is the boss's management style?
- What does she or he seem to emphasize from a performance standpoint?

Certainly, answers to some or all of these questions would be extremely helpful to formulating a winning interview strategy and securing a competitive advantage over others who go into the interview cold. This kind of information will surely provide the inside track, and you will have the advantage of focusing much of your conversation on topics that you know, in advance, are of great interest to the hiring manager. For example, by knowing about key problems and challenges in advance, you have the opportunity to think about solutions you might bring and value you can add to the organization. How would you feel, as the hiring manager, if the candidate you were interviewing appeared to have some good solutions or great ideas concerning major problems or challenges currently facing you? This would pique your interest, wouldn't it?

Additionally, if you knew in advance that this same manager had just fired the previous job incumbent because his or her engineering designs were impractical and not cost-effective, you would have a definite advantage. Knowing this ahead of time would allow you to emphasize your design skills during the job interview, citing examples of equipment designs that were both practical and very cost-effective.

Clearly, these are skills the hiring manager is particularly sensitive to and will be looking for in the replacement candidate.

So, as you can see, having the right kind of insider information in advance of the interview can prove very beneficial. You would have a definite head start and decided advantage over others who are entering the same job interview without the benefit of such valuable advanced information.

How Do You Get the Information You Need?

But, how do you get this kind of information? You really don't have to be a detective to uncover it. You only need to be an average to slightly above-average networker. Here is how you can do it.

Start by finding someone who currently works for this company and see whether you can convince your contact to introduce you to someone who works in the department for which you will be interviewing. Shoot for someone who would be a peer and is currently working at the same level as you would be. It is important, however, that this contact person work in the same group or at least with another group that works very closely with your target department.

If all else fails and your personal contact draws a blank, call a peer who is now working for the company and is a fellow member of your professional association. At least you have something in common that can be used as an icebreaker.

Here is an example of how to handle this kind of networking call. This can be used by you as a guideline for handling similar calls:

Caller: "Good morning, John, this is Mary Copperfield calling. I was referred to you by Michele Goodperson. She seemed to feel you would be a good person to talk with, and you might share some helpful information with me."

Contact: "Sure, what kind of information do you need?"

Caller: "John, I am going to be interviewing this Friday with William Belcher for the position of technical recruiter, and thought it might be helpful to learn a little more about the job and work environment prior to my interview. Would you mind sharing some information with me?"

Contact: "I guess not. What would you like to know?"

Caller: "By the way, John, before we start, I want you to know that anything we discuss here will be strictly confidential. I am simply trying to get some basic information that will help me make a good employment decision. Obviously a good decision for me will also be a good decision for the company as well. I'm sure you can appreciate this."

Contact: "Sure, Mary, what would you like to know?"

Caller: "Well there are a number of things. First, do you know why the position is open?"

Contact: "Yes, the person who was in the job was let go."

Caller: "Do you know why they were let go?"

Contact: "I believe it had something to do with not getting enough jobs filled. I know some of the department heads in central engineering were complaining that it was taking too long, and it was delaying some projects."

Caller: "John, were there any other issues besides this that you are aware of?"

Contact: "Well I'm not really sure, but I think there were some complaints of bringing in unqualified candidates and wasting managers' time."

Caller: "Thanks, John, that's helpful. I appreciate your sharing that with me. Let me shift gears a bit. What do you feel are some of the department's biggest problems and challenges right now? What do you feel Mr. Belcher is most concerned with at the moment?"

Contact: "Well, he has really been on the warpath quite a bit about budgets. We are over budget by about 20 percent, and I know he is getting some heat from up above."

Caller: "What's causing the budget overrun?"

Contact: "Well, I know hiring volume is up a bit, but he seems concerned that we are spending entirely too much on employment agency fees. He's been after us on this one."

Caller: "Why are agency fees up?"

Contact: "It's certainly partially explained by the increased hiring volume. After all, when you hire more people, and the pressure is on to get jobs filled faster, there is a tendency to rely too much on agencies rather than advertising or direct sourcing. There just isn't enough time!"

Caller: "Yeah, John, that's a tough one. Are you using RSS news feeds, Web spiders, and other Web technology to try and identify candidates? I know this can cut down on the time it takes to find qualified candidates, and it sure cuts down on hiring costs!"

Contact: "No, none of us has been trained in this area. Have you had much experience using these? Is it worth it?"

Caller: "Yes, I had a great course a couple of years ago, and it really helped. Close to half the jobs I now fill are with passive candidates. I have also been able to cut hiring-cycle time nearly in half, and our expenses are down at least 20 percent."

Contact: "Sounds like something you might want to mention to Mr. Belcher during your interview. I think he would be very interested in *that. By the way, what was the name of the course you took? Sounds as though it was really helpful."*

Caller: *"It was a course called "Using the Internet to Find Passive Candidates," and it was offered by the Human Resources Institute in Boston."*

Contact: *"Sounds like a course I should look into! Listen, Mary, I need to run. A candidate is waiting to see me. Perhaps I'll get to see you on Friday."*

Caller: *"I'll make a point of stopping by. Thanks for your time, John, I really appreciate it."*

Contact: *"You're welcome, Mary, I'll look forward to meeting you. Who knows, Mr. Belcher may be putting me on the interview schedule. He often does that, but sometimes he waits until the last minute. Well, I need to take off. Good to talk with you. See you."*

Caller: *"Likewise. See you Friday."*

This example is not atypical of what can occur in a networking call of this type. If approached properly, a high percentage of people will be very cordial and willing to share important information that can be of enormous benefit to you.

You can see what a dynamite call this was. Think how helpful this call was for Mary. Can you guess what her interview strategy is going to be? It sounds like her Internet recruiting skills are just what the doctor ordered. I would venture to say that Mr. Belcher is going to be quite impressed. Mary brings skills and abilities that could quickly resolve many of his most immediate and serious concerns. And, she knows it! Think of the huge competitive advantage Mary has over other candidates as she walks into this interview.

I strongly recommend that you follow a similar strategy. You might not get everything you are looking for, but you know that old saying, "Nothing ventured, nothing gained." What do you have to lose? Why not give it a try?

Strategies for the Day of the Interview
Now let's move to the actual day of the interview and some effective interview strategies you might use to gain a significant advantage and encourage the employer to make you a job offer.

Finding Out What the Employer Is Looking For
All job seekers would like to know exactly what qualifications the hiring manager is looking for in the perfect candidate. Knowing this would make the job of interviewing a lot easier and greatly increase the candidate's chances. So, how can you find this out?

Well, you could ask, and you might be surprised that the hiring manager actually answers. If that's the case, you should consider yourself very lucky. You now have a huge advantage in the interview and need to take full advantage of it. Chances are, however, that if the hiring manager has any interviewing experience, she or he will politely decline to answer your question. Instead, she or he will say something to the effect of, "Bob I'd be very happy to answer your question a little later, but not at this point in the interview. Instead, I think it is important for me to get to know you first. I will be glad to answer your question a little later, however."

As you can see, this kind of direct, up-front question can often lead nowhere fast. Moreover, the hiring manager is now onto your game, and is going to be extra guarded. Your motives are just a bit transparent. Some managers might even feel a little insulted or agitated that you would think them so naive as to answer such a question. If so, you've lost the battle right then and there.

There is a much more subtle way of getting the answers you need by reframing the same basic question in an entirely different way. Here is how you might ask it:

> *"John, as you consider people who have really thrived and done well in your group, what is it that caused them to stand out?"*

or

> *"John, what do you feel a candidate coming into this job needs to do to stand out? What, in your mind, is important to success in this position?"*

Both of these questions are really the "perfect candidate" question in disguise. You can see that this is a much more subtle, indirect way of getting at the same information. It is far less obvious and transparent and will almost always get a response.

The Value-Added Strategy

Another very effective interview strategy that can excite hiring managers and win job offers is the value-added strategy. Hiring managers are always looking for that one outstanding candidate who can add real value to their function and make the manager, as well as the new hire, look particularly good. A goal of your interview strategy should therefore be to find a way to cast yourself in this image. In order to do this, however, you first need to know where the hiring manager, and his or her department, needs the most help.

Here are some questions you might try in order to define these significant improvement opportunity areas:

> *"Vicki, as you think about this department as a whole, what do you feel are the most important opportunities to improve and increase its value to the organization?"*

or

> *"What are the greatest problems and challenges currently faced by this group, and what would you like to see happen in these areas?"*

or

> *"As others in the organization view this department, what do you feel they might suggest as areas where overall contribution to the business could be improved? How do you feel about this observation? Do you feel they have a valid point? What is your opinion?"*

As these examples illustrate, it is quite possible to get some quick insight into major opportunities for organizational improvement. Further, these are the improvement needs as defined by the person who will be hiring you, and to whom you would report. These are areas that are extremely important to the organization's reputation and to the hiring manager's professional reputation.

If you have ideas for helping this manager bring about significant improvement to the organization in these critical areas, you will want to share them. Few things will excite the manager more, and provide a real incentive to make you a job offer, than this kind of value. Few candidates will even think to ask the question, let alone present possible solutions.

The Job-Improvement Strategy

Another interview strategy you might consider using is the job-improvement strategy. Here, you find out what the hiring manager would like to see in the way of improvement in the position for which you are being interviewed. Then, having established this, you can offer some ideas for bringing about improvement in these very areas.

Here are some questions that will help you lead into this strategy:

> *"Carolyn, what do you see as some of the opportunities for improvement with regard to this position? What type of improvement would you feel would be helpful?"*

or

> *"As you think of this position, what changes and improvements would you most like to see?"*

or

> *"As far as the position currently stands, where do you feel things could be most improved? In this regard, what do you consider the opportunities for greatest improvement?"*

Think about it for a moment. If you were a hiring manager on the receiving end of these questions, what would your impression of this candidate be? I think you would agree that your feelings would be quite positive. Questions of this type clearly begin to separate the "run-of-the-mill" candidates from the superstar.

Not only is this candidate interested in the basic job, but he or she is already thinking about bringing major improvement in the way it is performed.

What Are the Hiring Manager's Priorities?

Most hiring managers have a list of priorities, things they want to get done. If you could help this manager with these priories, do you think this would heighten his or her interest in you? Of course it would!

Here are some questions you might consider using to define what these priorities are:

> *"Phil, what are some of your priories—things you want to get done here?"*

or

> *"Linda, what are your most important priorities during the next year or so? What do you feel will be most important to accomplish?"*

or

> *"Bob, I'm sure you have some organizational priorities for this department. What are they, and which do you feel are most important?"*

Here again are some significant clues for creating interest and excitement about your candidacy. If you can come up with some ideas for helping the hiring manager to accomplish his or her goals, you will be miles ahead of the average candidate who simply comes in and waits to be asked questions.

Taking Control of the Interview

As you can see, by employing many of the interview strategies covered in this chapter, you have an opportunity to take full control of the interview, and you should! Some people might argue that this is not a good idea, but I disagree.

Although many companies have now become more sophisticated in their interview practices, and might want to control the job interview, there is still plenty of opportunity for some give-and-take and a better balance in the flow of information between the parties. After all, not only is the company interviewing you, but you also need to interview the company.

If you are a shrinking violet and sit back and wait your turn, it might not come. If you are not sufficiently assertive, you can become an interview victim rather than a victor. Most of us would prefer the latter. So, get your oar in the water early and often. You need to steer this process in your direction.

Moreover, the strategies I have discussed in this chapter require you to get answers early in the interview process. In doing so, you'll have a much better understanding of the hiring manager's needs, and sufficient time to demonstrate that you can not only meet them, but can also help drive significant improvement in the organization. What more could an employer want?

Sure, you'll need to pause from time to time to give the interviewer a shot. There are some important things they will need to know about you in order to make their decision. But, don't let them dominate the interview. Make sure they understand that although you are quite willing to answer their questions, they are not the only ones in the room needing to make a decision. You need to make one too.

So test the waters. What do you have to lose? Get your questions out on the table early in the game so that you have the opportunity to unfurl your winning interview strategy and come away with a job offer. Most interviewers will never know what hit them!

Using Feedback to Your Advantage

When it comes to the job interview, feedback goes both ways. At the end of the interview, the employer needs to know whether you are interested in the job, and you need to know whether the company has an interest in you.

In my previous life as a corporate employment manager for a Fortune 100 company, I was always impressed, at the end of the interview day, when the candidate would return to my office and enthusiastically express interest in the position. Such enthusiasm is contagious and it does rub off on members of the interview team.

I can recall specific instances when we were attempting to decide between two equally qualified candidates, and one seemed more excited and interested in the opportunity than the other. Guess which one got the job offer?

So, at the end of the interview day, and before leaving the hiring manager, if you are interested in the job, say so! Additionally, at the same time, express your confidence in being able to bring some real value to the organization. This helps to reinforce the positive impressions the hiring manager might already have about your ability to contribute.

How to Show Interest in the Job

Here are some ways to express job interest and simultaneously reinforce the positive image of you as a contributor. Also, when making your closing statement, don't forget your manners. Thank your host for the time he or she spent with you. It will be appreciated.

> "Pearl, thanks for the opportunity to be here today. I appreciated the chance to meet you and the other members of the interview team. The job is very interesting, and I would enjoy working with the group I met. Pearl, I am especially excited about the opportunity to help you with implementation of the SAP program. As you know, I have been through this before, and know that I can help you get over some of the current hurdles you are facing."

> "Pearl, I'm curious. How did things go from your standpoint? What were your impressions, and where do we go from here?"

As you can see, this is a powerful way to close the interview. You have expressed strong interest in the position and also in working as a member of the team. You have further reinforced your value to the department as someone who can help them overcome some significant hurdles they are currently facing with their SAP program implementation. This is a pretty strong and positive way to close.

Importantly, as illustrated, you have also asked for feedback in a fairly direct fashion. It will be hard for the hiring manager to sidestep this one. They are either interested, or they are not. Either way, it's okay, as long as you know where you stand.

Yes, No, or Maybe?

When you ask for feedback in this fashion, you will likely get one of four answers:

1. **The "Yes":** "Things went well. We have a lot of interest in your background and hope to make an offer to you shortly."

2. **The "Maybe":** "Sally, we were pretty pleased with what we saw, but still have a few more candidates to interview before making a decision."

3. **The "Probably Not":** "Although you have many of the skills we are searching for, we are a little concerned about your lack of experience with _____."

4. **The "Kiss of Death":** "Dave, we very much appreciated your spending time with us today. Although you certainly have some fine qualifications, we have interviewed some other candidates who we feel are a better match for our specific requirements."

Reversing a Negative Decision

My years as a corporate employment professional tell me that answer 4 is an absolute dead end. There is nothing short of sheer bribery that will change the employer's mind. It's time to say "thank you," head out the door, and move on to the next job opportunity. This one is final!

Answer 3 is probably a long shot. Unless the interview team has misjudged your qualifications in the areas singled out as your shortfall, it is unlikely you will be seeing an employment offer. In this case, however, it is worth finding out more specifics. Here are some follow-up questions you might want to ask:

> *"Mildred, when you say I lack experience in SAP implementation, what do you mean? Can you be more specific? I have occasionally worked part time with some of the SAP implementation project team during the planning phase, and pretty much understand what is required. Additionally, I have had considerable project implementation experience with other complex IT software installations. Can you please share with me the specific areas of concern?"*

Although you may or may not be able to turn around this decision, in asking these kinds of follow-up questions, you are at least giving it a good try, and this kind of persistence can sometimes pay off.

Many times, due to the time constraints of an employment interview, there may be insufficient time to fully probe a candidate's qualifications in a given area. Consequently, the interview team might come away with some uncertainty (or a false impression), feeling that the job seeker lacks the depth of knowledge or experience required for successful job performance in a given area.

Under these circumstances, unless you ask for further details, the interview is lost and you will go away empty-handed. However, in a number of cases, I have seen an interview pulled completely out of the fire and interest in the job seeker's candidacy revived through use of such tactics. By asking this kind of probing, follow-up question, I have seen some job seekers buy the necessary time to provide sufficient additional information about their qualifications in the area of concern. Consequently, they were successful in totally flipping the employer's initial impression, and ended up with a job offer and the job.

Although this might be a bit of a long shot, the door is still slightly ajar. Unless you open it, it will shut completely. So my advice is, go ahead and ask your follow-up questions. See if you can pinpoint the specific area of concern, and then counter with a last-ditch effort to reverse the initial decision. You never know what might happen.

Tip: Another bonus of getting more details on your perceived deficiencies is that what you learn could help you prepare better for future interviews.

The alternative is to accept the employer's initial decision and walk away defeated, with your tail between your legs. I suggest you go for the gold. The worst thing that can happen is that the employer still says no. I have never seen an employment candidate die from being turned down for employment.

Don't Be a Stalking Horse

When the employer tells you they were pleased with the interview, have some interest in your candidacy, but need to interview other candidates before they can arrive at a decision, things are likely to slide downhill from there. This is what I call being a "stalking horse."

What is really going on, in this case, is that the employer considers you a "maybe," someone they will make a job offer to unless they find a candidate who they feel has better qualifications. You have now become the benchmark (the stalking horse) against whom all other candidates will be measured. Maybe they will find a better candidate, and maybe they won't. If they don't, you'll be getting a job offer.

Experience has shown that the longer the time lapse since your job interview and the employer's eventual decision, the higher the probability that you will not get a job offer. This is what I call "the law of diminishing interest." It's simply a matter of numbers. The greater the time lapse, the more candidates interviewed by the employer. The more candidates interviewed, the higher the probability the employer will find someone they like better. Besides, with the passage of time, the employer's memory becomes clouded. Due to the time lapse and additional candidates interviewed, the employer's memory of you and your qualifications begins to fade, and so does the probability of a job offer.

So, what should you do when this happens? The answer is simple. Don't allow it to happen! If the employer says they are interested, but have additional candidates to interview, simply tell them that's fine, but they need to know that you are "actively pursuing other opportunities and expect to be in a position of needing to make a decision shortly." Also, ask them for a deadline by which they will give you a final decision. Here is an example of how to say this:

> *"Gee, Arthur, I was hoping that we might have a fairly quick decision within the next few days or so. Quite frankly, I am actively considering other opportunities and expect to be in the position of needing to make a decision shortly. How quickly do you feel you will have a final decision for me?"*

This is a very effective way of forcing a decision. They obviously like you, or they wouldn't have told you so. So, by using this tactic, you are putting them somewhat "under the gun." If they fool around and waste time, they might lose you. Additionally, you have given them the message that others feel you are worthwhile and are interested in you. Moreover, you have put the pressure on and forced them to commit to a definite time frame. They cannot afford to dilly-dally.

By employing this technique, your chances are 50-50 or better. And, psychologically, you are better off knowing the outcome sooner rather than later. So, what do you have to lose? Nothing, except the job offer, if you elect to wait and let the employer dictate the time frame!

So, at this point, you are ready to go forth and slay the dragon. You now have a number of strategic weapons in your arsenal that can turn the tide of battle substantially in your favor. Try some of the techniques recommended in this chapter, and I know you will be surprised and impressed by just how much you impact interview results and walk away with job offers in your pocket.

Chapter Summary

There is much you can do to significantly impact the outcome of a job interview and stack the deck in your favor. Some key pointers are

- Use networking to get key "insider" information in advance of the job interview.
- Helpful advance information includes
  - Reason(s) why the position is available
  - The hiring department's biggest problems and challenges

- Possible causes of these problems and challenges
- The hiring manager's major priorities and concerns

- Formulate a strategy for addressing these major problems and challenges in advance of the interview.

- Be assertive during the interview. Ask key questions of the hiring manager to "zero in" on those areas of greatest interest to him or her.

- Don't waste time dwelling on subjects of little or no interest to the hiring manager. Focus on the hiring manager's greatest concerns and priorities, and the improvements you can bring in these areas.

- Take control of the interview; don't let the interview control you.

- Use interview feedback to your advantage by addressing any perceived shortcomings before the interview is over.

- Don't let the employment decision drag on and on. Force the issue with the employer by implying you have other opportunities developing and will require an answer shortly.

- When the employer stalls on their decision, ask for a definitive "drop-dead" date. Don't allow yourself to become a "stalking horse."

CHAPTER 13

Interview Questions: Practicing Your Interview Skills

In the preceding two chapters, I provided a number of overall strategies and techniques designed to both prepare you for the job interview and provide you with a competitive edge. Now, how about the interview itself? What kinds of interview questions will you get, and how should you answer them?

Although on the surface it appears that there are literally hundreds of questions you might encounter during the course of the job interview, the reality is that once you move away from the "technical" side of the job interview, most interview questions fall into a limited number of core categories. So many interview questions are really quite similar and are principally variations of these same basic core themes.

Job seekers seldom have difficulty with the "technical skills" side of the interview. Most are relatively comfortable discussing their professional knowledge and skills, and the things they have accomplished. Where many interviews fall apart, however, is on the "soft skills" side. Candidates are often far less comfortable when discussing their personal traits and characteristics. They are simply not accustomed to talking about themselves in this way, and it is awkward for them to do so. Yet, some of the job interview is bound to focus on soft skills. So it is wise to practice and become proficient at discussing your soft skill qualifications well in advance of the actual interview.

This chapter discusses these core soft skill categories and recommends some strategies for effectively handling them. Where appropriate, a list of commonly asked interview questions follows each such discussion. These questions will provide you with an opportunity to practice what you have just learned.

You can use this chapter as a practical test of your interview readiness. After first studying the chapter, you might test your interview skills by then flipping through it, randomly selecting questions from any of the pages, and then practicing what you have learned. This practice will help bolster your overall interviewing skills and ensure your readiness to perform in the live interview, when you are on the firing line.

After some practice, go back through the interview questions and highlight those questions you feel are the toughest to handle. Then using the recommended strategies for the relevant core interview category, formulate carefully crafted answers with which you feel comfortable. Having done this, you can practice providing these answers until you can easily do so convincingly and without hesitation. Once you learn to handle these "tougher" questions with ease, your confidence level will increase dramatically and the rest of the interview will seem like a breeze.

Soft Skills (Personal Qualities, Traits, and Characteristics)

As discussed in earlier chapters, the job interview can be broken down into two main areas of focus. The first is the "technical" area (the specialized knowledge and skills required for successful job performance), sometimes called the "hard skills" area. The second is the "soft skills" area (the personal traits and characteristics required for job success). This chapter focuses on soft skills, which is the area with which job seekers struggle the most.

Interview questions employers use to probe these soft skill areas are designed to help them better understand your personal profile—that combination of personal qualities, traits, characteristics, and behaviors that makes you uniquely you.

When employers focus on these soft skill areas, what are they really after? What are they really attempting to measure, and why?

Why Employers Measure Soft Skills

There are two primary reasons why employers are interested in a candidate's soft skills. They use them to measure "job fit" and "cultural fit." I will discuss each of these separately.

Job Fit

When measuring job fit, the employer is interested in knowing whether the candidate has the personal qualities essential to successful performance of the job. These are what are known as the "job-relevant" soft skills. They are the job-related personal traits and characteristics required by the nature of the work itself.

So that you have a better understanding of this concept, the following is an example of job-relevant soft skills for the position of accountant. These are personal traits and characteristics that are absolutely essential for successful performance of accounting work. No one can expect to be a successful accountant without possessing these essential personal characteristics.

Accountant: Job-Relevant Soft Skills

- Thorough
- Accurate

- Timely
- Organized
- Objective

As an additional example, here are some of the job-relevant soft skills required of someone working as a sales representative:

Sales Representative—Job-Relevant Soft Skills

- Persuasive
- Articulate
- Confident
- Persistent
- Resilient

One cannot imagine a successful sales representative who doesn't have these personal qualities. They are essential to the process of selling. The nature of the work absolutely demands this skill set.

Cultural Fit

On the other hand, certain personal traits and characteristics are important to fitting into the work environment or culture of a particular organization. These personal qualities are referred to as "culture-relevant" soft skills. Because organizational cultures and work environments can vary significantly from company to company, so can the personal qualities and traits organizations seek in their ideal candidate.

There are a number of variables that affect organizational culture and therefore determine the specific traits and characteristics an organization seeks in employment candidates. The principal ones include the following:

- Economic state of the business
- Organizational values
- Organizational beliefs
- Management philosophy
- Strategic initiatives

The culture of an organization is driven by its beliefs. You might therefore visualize organizational culture as "a commonly held set of values and beliefs" to which the organization subscribes. These values and beliefs are universally held by both management and employees, and are believed to be essential to the success of the organization as a whole.

Employees who share the organization's beliefs will respond and behave in a certain way that reflects the organization's common belief system. Their behaviors reflect the organization's "valued behaviors." Employees who align well with these values exhibit certain traits and characteristics that are compatible with the organization's culture. These people are said to "fit in."

On the other hand, those who do not share this common set of values and beliefs, and behave differently, are seen as incompatible with the culture of the organization. They exhibit personal traits, characteristics, and behaviors that do not fit well with that of the organization, and are often seen as renegades or outcasts. They are employees who simply do not fit in.

Therefore, organizations often use a portion of the job interview to determine whether there is a good match with its culture. They are interested in learning about the job seeker's personal traits, characteristics, and behaviors as a way of determining whether the candidate aligns well with the common set of values and beliefs—those criteria that the firm feels are important to its overall success.

From an interview strategy standpoint, therefore, it is extremely important to understand a company's culture before you can expect to interview successfully. Specifically, you need to know what personal traits, characteristics, and behaviors the company values in order to prepare and implement a winning interview strategy.

Let's take a look at two entirely different organizational cultures so that you can see how an organization's culture can dramatically affect the soft skills profile being sought.

Profile 1

This company values employee participation. It makes extensive use of teams in making decisions and in carrying out the work. It therefore fosters democratic decision-making and heavy employee involvement in all facets of its business.

When filling a management job, therefore, this company would likely seek candidates with a soft skills profile similar to the following:

- Open/friendly
- Flexible/adaptive
- Team vs. individual focus
- A facilitator/enabler of others
- Collaborative
- Consensus builder
- Empowers and develops others
- Manages through others
- Encourages diversity of opinion

These soft skills are compatible with the company's values, beliefs, and general business philosophy. It is firmly believed this is the management skill set that is important to the overall success of the company.

Profile 2

This is a company that is tightly controlled and run by a small group of top managers. It firmly believes that business success requires hard-nosed, decisive managers who are fiercely independent and can make quick decisions on their own. It believes that senior management should make most if not all decisions, and the principal role of employees is to efficiently carry out the orders of senior management.

In this case, the soft skills profile sought in the ideal management candidate would likely resemble the following:

- Decisive/quick acting
- Independent minded
- Strong-willed/tough
- Aggressive/a driver
- High energy
- Demanding
- Controlling
- Results-focused

So, as you can clearly see from these two illustrations, despite the fact that both companies are seeking management candidates, the soft skills profile each seeks is very different. In fact, one is the absolute antithesis of the other. These are two different companies with polar opposite views about those personal traits and characteristics required for success of the organization. They are two very different cultures.

You can now appreciate just how important it truly is to understand the culture of the organization with which you will be interviewing. Without this insight, it would be extremely difficult to interview successfully, and your chances of winning a job offer would be slim to none.

Interview Questions: Job-Relevant Soft Skills

Let's now have a look at some of the soft skill interview questions commonly used by employers to size up your personal profile and identify your most prevalent traits, characteristics, and behaviors. I first discuss job-relevant soft skills, and then follow this with a discussion of culture-relevant soft skills.

Here is a typical collection of interview questions often used by employers to measure job fit.

- "From a work perspective, what adjectives best describe you?"
- "What do you consider to be your strongest personal qualities? How have these qualities benefited you?"

- "What adjectives would your peers use to describe your personal style? On which of these qualities would they most likely agree?"

- "What do you feel your peers would agree is your strongest personal trait or attribute?"

- "If we asked your peers to agree on two personal traits or characteristics that could most be improved, what would they choose? Why?"

- "How would your boss describe you? Based on your work performance, what adjectives would he or she use?"

- "How would your friends describe you? What adjectives would they use?"

- "Which of your personal qualities have most contributed to your job success? In what ways have these been helpful?"

- "Which work-related personal qualities do you feel need further refinement or development? Why have you chosen these? In what ways have they inhibited your job performance and/or career growth?"

- "Tell me about your personal style and how it impacts your job performance."

- "If there were something you might like to change about your personality, from a work perspective, what would it be and in what way would you like to change it?"

- "What personal traits and characteristics do you feel are most important to success in this job? Why do you feel these are important?"

  - "Which of these do you consider to be your greatest strengths?"

  - "Which of these are most in need of improvement?"

How you answer these questions will obviously have significant impact on the outcome of the job interview. You either have the personal qualities essential to job success or you don't. Unless you have done the necessary homework to identify job-relevant soft skills in advance of the interview, you will be in serious trouble and grasping at straws in your effort to make a positive impression and find the right combination.

So, in order to field these questions successfully, you need to understand which personal qualities, traits, and characteristics employers universally see as being absolutely essential to job success.

In chapter 11, you already did this basic analysis and should have a well-defined profile of the soft skills required for the type job you are seeking. These were summarized on the "Consolidated Skills Profile," which you completed at the end of the chapter. Pull out this skills summary and review it. It highlights those key soft skills essential to job success. Now use this profile summary to formulate answers to the preceding questions, and you are well on your way to having a successful interview.

If you have not already completed the "Consolidated Skills Profile" in chapter 11, this would be an excellent time to do so. In the absence of this, however, you will at least want to perform some basic job analysis in an attempt to ferret out these important soft skills. Here then is a shortcut version of job analysis:

- Define why the job exists. What is its main reason for being?
- What is the principal result expected of this job?
- Define the major functional accountabilities of the job. What functions does the job manage and/or perform?
- For each of these functional accountabilities, what is the expected result?
- Now, considering these expected results, what are the principal personal qualities, traits, characteristics, and behaviors essential to successfully achieving these results?

A comprehensive list of common personal traits, characteristics, and behaviors has been provided in table 13.1 to assist you with this analysis.

Table 13.1: Soft Skills: Personal Traits, Qualities, Characteristics, and Attributes

Accountable	Counselor	Impactful	Profit-oriented
Accurate	Courageous	Independent	Resilient
Adaptive	Creative	Influential	Responsible
Affable	Creator	Innovative	Resourceful
Aggressive	Decisive	Intelligent	Self-assured
Analytical	Dedicated	Intuitive	Self-confident
Animated	Detailed	Kind	Self-motivated
Approachable	Determined	Knowledgeable	Self-reliant
Arbitrator	Developer	Leader	Sensitive
Articulate	Diplomatic	Logical	Sociable
Assertive	Direct	Loyal	Strategic
Astute	Disciplined	Mentor	Supporting
Balanced	Diverse	Methodical	Systematic
Brief	Encouraging	Meticulous	Sympathetic
Builder	Energetic	Motivated	Tactful
Calculating	Efficient	Motivator	Teacher
Change Agent	Expressive	Networker	Team-focused

Charismatic	Extrovert	Objective	Tenacious
Coach	Facilitator	Open	Timely
Compelling	Fearless	Organized	Thorough
Composed	Flexible	Outgoing	Thoughtful
Conceptual	Focused	Perceptive	Tolerant
Concise	Forthright	Persuasive	Tough
Confident	Friendly	Persistent	Trustworthy
Convincing	Goal-oriented	Positive	Understanding
Collaborative	Hardworking	Precise	Visionary
Cooperative	Honest	Principled	Warm

If, after using this shortcut method, you continue to experience difficulty in defining job-relevant soft skills, return to chapter 11 and complete the exercises provided there. These are simple to complete and I am sure you will quickly appreciate the value of doing so.

Interview Questions: Culture-Related Soft Skills

When attempting to identify culture-related soft skills in advance of the job interview, you are faced with a far more difficult challenge. Unlike job-relevant skills, these soft skills are not universal; instead, they vary significantly from company to company. However, identifying these skills before (or during the early stages of) the interview is absolutely essential to interview success.

Unless you are already intimately familiar with the organization's culture, you cannot use simple logic to deduce which soft skills the employer is seeking. Absent any kind of "insider" knowledge, you will be totally in the dark. There are therefore only two practical ways to obtain this insider perspective. A description of each follows.

Networking Approach

When networking, you will want to use a combination of personal and professional contacts to attempt to network into the company. In order to get reliable information, however, you will need to penetrate the department in which you would work. Specifically, you need to use your contacts to arrange introductions to future peers who are currently working in the function for which you will be interviewing. General information about company culture acquired from other company employees working outside of your target function, although helpful, still leaves some significant knowledge gaps about the culture within the hiring department itself.

Although there is a universal set of values and beliefs held by the overall company (the company culture), there are also specific values and beliefs held by each individual workgroup within the organization (the workgroup culture). For example,

241

the values and beliefs by which employees in a sales organization operate—and which they see as important to success—can be quite different from those of employees working in a research organization. So, where a sales organization might value risk taking and the ability to "wing it" as essential characteristics, the research organization would not value these attributes at all.

Obviously the values and beliefs of the manager who manages the function in which you will work pretty much drive and set the tone for workgroup culture. This manager has definite beliefs about the personal traits and characteristics that are important to the success of the function, and therefore tends to reward and favor those employees who exhibit the preferred profile.

For example, a functional manager who is "hard driving and results-oriented" might prefer employees who are "decisive, quick, and action-oriented." Another functional manager who takes pride in being "strategic, analytical, and methodical," however, might instead prefer employees who have similar characteristics to his or her own. This second manager might therefore see candidates who are "decisive, quick, and action-oriented" as being "impulsive" or "slipshod."

As this example emphatically demonstrates, if you are going to experience a successful interview, you will need to determine the personal qualities most valued by the functional manager for whom you will be working. It is important therefore that you use your networking contacts to penetrate the immediate workgroup and define these personal attributes in advance of the job interview.

Here are some questions you might consider using with future peers for this purpose:

- "What is it like to work here? How would you describe the culture and work environment?"

- "How is this culture or work environment different from other places you have worked?"

- "What do you like most about this work environment?"

- "What do you least like about working in this environment?"

- "What personal qualities do you feel are most important to fitting in and being successful in this environment?"

- "What is different or unique about the culture or work environment of this department versus the rest of the organization? Is there anything that differentiates you?"

- "What personal traits and characteristics do you feel are most important to success in this workgroup?"

- "What personal traits and characteristics do you feel your boss prefers—the kinds of behaviors he or she tends to recognize and reward?"

Interview Approach

If you are unable to network to these future colleagues in advance of the interview, you will then need to wait until the interview itself in order to gain insight into both organizational and workgroup cultures. Should this happen, you will need to ask some key questions of your future colleagues early in the interview discussion in order to get a handle on organizational and workgroup culture. In such a case, here are some questions that should prove helpful:

- "How would you describe the culture or work environment here at XYZ Company? How does it differ from other places you have worked?"
- "As you think of the culture here, what are some of the personal traits and characteristics you feel are most important to success at this company?"
- "What are some of the personal traits and characteristics you feel are most important to fitting in and working well in this workgroup?"
- "What do you feel are the principal qualities important to success in the position for which I am interviewing?"
- "When you think about persons who have previously held this position and have done particularly well, what personal traits and characteristics do you feel most accounted for their success?"
- "What do you consider to be most important for success in this position?"

As you can see, answers to questions of this type should enable you to gain great insight into the culture of both the organization and the workgroup. These answers should enable you to determine the preferred personal profile of the "ideal candidate" and enable you to package your responses to interview questions accordingly. By acquiring and skillfully using this information during the interview, you will enjoy a huge competitive advantage over other candidates who have no clue about the organization's culture and are "flying blind" in the interview.

Strengths and Weaknesses

A favorite interview category of many employers is the infamous "strengths and weaknesses" category. This is always a tricky area that requires some careful advance planning on your part.

Here are some typical "strength and weakness" questions you might run into during the course of an interview. Take the time to practice answering these questions well in advance of the job interview, and rehearse exactly what you are going to say when the time arrives.

- "What do you consider to be your greatest strengths—your greatest assets?"
- "What are some of your shortcomings—those areas where you most need to improve?"
- "If I were to talk with your boss, what would he or she say are your greatest assets?"

- "If I were to ask your boss to be critical of your performance, in what areas would he or she say you most need to improve?"

- Tell me about your last performance review. In what areas was you boss particularly complimentary?"

- During your last performance evaluation, what areas did your boss suggest for improvement or development?

- "What steps are you currently taking to improve your overall performance?"

- "What has been your greatest failure? Why did it occur, and what did you learn from it?"

- "What has been your greatest success? Why were you successful? What did you do?"

Clearly, your answers to these questions will greatly influence interview results. Being articulate about one's strengths and assets is key to making the sale and convincing the employer you have what it takes to be a top performer. On the other hand, if you stumble through questions of this nature, employer interest will quickly wane and you are likely to walk away empty-handed.

The following guidelines are offered to help you successfully field these types of interview questions.

Guidelines for Fielding "Strength" Questions

When asked about your areas of strength:

- Be prepared to cite four to six "technical" strengths (areas of specialized knowledge and skills in which you excel).

- Be prepared to cite at least two or more accomplishments or results you've achieved in each of these "technical" skill areas.

- Prepare to cite at least four to six personal qualities (soft skills) that you feel are your strongest personal traits and characteristics.

- Be prepared to provide some examples of how these personal qualities have enhanced your job performance.

Being prepared to not only cite your strengths, but also offer up examples of how you have successfully used them, is a foolproof strategy for interview success. Such examples provide the employer with concrete "evidence" of your skill proficiency, and add considerable credibility to your candidacy.

Guidelines for Fielding "Weakness" Questions

When asked to cite weakness, or areas where you need to improve:

- Select areas that are least critical (that have minimal impact) to job performance success.

- Preferably, also select areas where you have demonstrated improvement and can describe steps you have taken to improve.

> **Note:** Employers are often favorably impressed when a candidate can demonstrate that they have taken the initiative to improve themselves.

This is, perhaps, the most difficult portion of the interview for most job seekers to handle. It is always difficult to be self-critical and share your weaknesses with others. This is especially true in a job interview, when you are attempting to put your best foot forward. Yet, failure to effectively handle this type interview question will probably scuttle an otherwise good interview faster than any other factor, and quickly negate any possibility of a job offer.

Obviously, no candidate is perfect, and employers realistically don't expect to see perfection. If you say you have never made a mistake or had a failure, the employer will know you are lying. Everyone has areas in which they can improve, and this is expected. When it comes to the job interview, however, success depends on what weaknesses you choose to highlight and how you choose to position this disclosure with the employer.

When disclosing areas of "weakness" (improvement needs) to employers, there are some very effective strategies you can employ that will minimize the potential damage that could otherwise be incurred. The following sections include a brief description of each of these strategies.

Cite a Low-Impact Skill Area

Obviously, when an employer asks you to disclose areas in which you could improve, you cannot deny that you have some faults. The key, however, is to select specific skills or attributes that have minimal impact on overall job performance. You will also want to choose a skill deficit that can also be viewed as a "strength" as well.

For example, if you were interviewing for the position of project engineer, you might choose to admit that sometimes you are a bit impatient. Here is how you might present this fact:

> *"There are times when* perhaps *I could be a little more patient. I tend to be results-focused, so I am* sometimes *impatient with fellow team members when they don't deliver what they are supposed to deliver on time. This is especially true when their lateness impacts my ability to meet my own deadlines."*

Obviously, this trait can be seen as both a strength and a weakness, especially in the context of this example. Timely delivery of projects is important to success as a project engineer. It is therefore understandable that a project engineering candidate might be impatient with others if their delay impacts negatively the candidate's own performance. So, in this example, impatience is both a vice and a virtue.

The overall effect on the interview is fairly neutral and, in many cases, might actually be seen as a positive.

Another example of an attribute that can be seen as both a positive and negative quality is that of being "overly detailed." Here is an example of how you can present this:

> *"My boss might tell you I tend to* sometimes *be a bit overly detailed, but at the same time, I think she would tell you she appreciates my thoroughness and accuracy."*

Here again, you can see how picking an improvement area that is both a vice and a virtue can be to your distinct advantage. It's all in what you pick to disclose and how you choose to describe it. In this case, being thorough and accurate is probably much more important than "sometimes" being overly detailed.

You will also note key words that I have highlighted in these examples. Use of the word "sometimes" suggests to the employer that that the negative characteristic is only an occasional problem rather than a continuous one. This tends to mitigate the seriousness of the problem. Moreover, using the word "perhaps" is also intentional because it suggests that the weakness is of minor consequence and is even doubtful. The effect of using specific words such as these can greatly reduce the negative impact of your disclosure to the point that it is essentially neutralized. Where it is comfortable for you to do so, therefore, you will want to practice using these words to have a similar neutralizing effect.

So, in advance of your job interview, creatively think about similar examples of weakness that can also be viewed as strengths. A good way to accomplish this is to begin by making a list of your actual weaknesses. Once this list is complete, select one or two weaknesses that are relatively unimportant and have least impact on job success. Now, think creatively about ways to shift the paradigm and also describe these same qualities as strengths.

Then, practice articulating your answers to these "weakness" questions until you are totally comfortable and confident in answering them. In doing so, you are now prepared to answer perhaps the toughest of all interview questions.

Not an Issue—Minor Impact

When sharing a "skills deficit" with an employer, you might choose to minimize the potential negative effect by simply telling the employer that it is not really an issue and has had very little impact on your overall performance. Here is an example of how you might do this:

> *"There are times when* perhaps *I could be a* little better *organized than others. This is especially true when I am under a tight deadline. Although occasionally brought up as an improvement area,* **it has never been cited as a major problem.** *In fact, my boss has been very complimentary of my overall performance, and* **this has never really been an issue.** *I know she appreciates my promptness in getting things done."*

Also, as in previous examples, note the use of words such as "perhaps" and a "little better." Using these words tends to minimize the impact of this negative information. Using the word "perhaps," in fact, suggests that it might or might not be true. Using the words "little better" also tends to minimize the degree or seriousness of the problem. You will also note how the candidate quickly shifts the employer's focus away from the negative attribute to a positive quality. This can be a very effective technique.

In this example, it is understandable that a candidate can sometimes be a little disorganized when under tight deadlines. This is certainly not uncommon. But, as the employer, it's also good to know that this has never been a major performance issue. Also, knowing that the job seeker's overall performance is good is clearly an offsetting factor that puts the issue in context and relegates it to being relatively unimportant in the overall scheme of things. This is a great way to neutralize what might otherwise have been seen as a serious objection.

Using Historical Context as Your Ally

If you are pushed to the wall by a seasoned interviewer and are forced to disclose that you and your former boss didn't get along, or that there was a performance issue, putting the issue into historical context can sometimes serve to either neutralize or eliminate the issue entirely. Here is an example of how you can accomplish this:

> "If you talked with my boss, he might say he feels I could somewhat improve my interpersonal skills. Unfortunately, I believe his perception stems from an argument I had with a co-worker. Although it is true we did have some differences and were both rather vocal, the truth of the matter is, with this one exception, I have always enjoyed excellent relationships with co-workers. In fact, I would be pleased to provide you with names and contact information for several of my peers, both current and past, and would strongly encourage you to contact them. I am sure they would be quite complimentary of my interpersonal skills and tell you they enjoyed working with me."

As you can see, putting a current performance issue into historical context may eliminate or neutralize its effect and remove it as a potential "knock-out factor." To do so, however, you must be able to demonstrate that it has never previously been an issue. Offering references to confirm this fact can be a very convincing tactic.

Work Motivation

It's one thing to have the needed skills essential to job performance, yet another to be motivated to actually do the work. Employers are aware of this distinction, and refer to this phenomenon as "can do" versus "will do." So, many employers will attempt to assess not only if you have the skills to do the job, but also whether you are sufficiently motivated by the work to perform well.

To evaluate this factor, interviewers will typically ask a series of questions focused on determining the type of work you most enjoy and the type of work you find less satisfying. Obviously, when asking questions of this type, the employer is attempting to evaluate whether the type of work you most enjoy performing has similar characteristics to the type of work they have to offer. Clearly there is a high degree of correlation between the type of work an individual enjoys doing and his or her motivation to perform that type of work.

Questions an Employer Might Ask to Determine Work Motivation

Here are some interview questions an employer might ask to measure your work motivation:

- "Of the positions you have held, which did you enjoy most?"
- "What was there about this job that caused you to like it?"
- "Of the various positions you have held, which did you least enjoy?"
- "What was there about this position that caused you to dislike it?"
- "What aspects of this job most interest you?"
- "What aspects of this job hold the least amount of interest for you? Why?"
- "What type of work do you most enjoy?"
- "What type of work do you least enjoy?"
- "How would you describe the perfect or ideal job?"
- "What aspects of your current job do you most enjoy?"
- "What aspects of your current job do you least enjoy?"

Obviously, if you are planning on receiving a job offer, you don't want to tell the employer that the job you least enjoyed was the one most similar to the position the employer has to offer. This is clearly not a winning strategy. Your strategy therefore needs to be to describe work that you most enjoyed as being the positions that most closely approximate the job the employer has to offer you.

Winning the job offer is one thing, but landing a job you dislike is clearly another. Obviously, you don't want to distort the truth to the extent that you end up accepting a position that will make you unhappy. Most such unhappy employment marriages end up in quick divorce.

So, give some careful advance thought to this category of interview question and prepare your responses accordingly.

Other Indicators of Motivation

In addition to using interview questions to judge a candidate's job motivation, employers will often look for other signs of this motivation. Body language, for example, can speak volumes about your degree of interest and motivation to perform the work. So, you need to pay particular attention to your body language when discussing the job and its responsibilities.

For maximum effectiveness, therefore, you will want to appear alert, interested, and relatively enthusiastic throughout the interview process. Sit up relatively straight in the chair. Good posture conveys a sense of positive energy and increased level of interest compared to someone who is laid back or slouching in their chair. Acknowledge key points made by your host with a nod, smile, or other appropriate gesture. This physically telegraphs your interest and attentiveness. Maintain good eye contact throughout your discussion as well.

Moreover, during the course of the job interview, be alert for opportunities to demonstrate your motivation and confirm your interest in the position. Be sure to verbally express your interest and demonstrate your enthusiasm. Here are some key statements and phrases that can help accomplish this objective:

- "That sounds very interesting!"
- "I have always liked doing _____."
- "That sounds exciting and challenging!"
- "I think I could be of some real help in that area."
- "I have ideas on how to address that issue."
- "That's something I faced at XYZ Company. I think I could help you with that."
- "That's an area that I really enjoy!"

As you can see, statements and expressions of this type can go a long way toward telegraphing a high level of motivation and interest in the position.

Chapter Summary

Effective interviewing requires you to both anticipate and practice answering the "tough" interview questions. Although most job seekers are comfortable answering questions about their "technical" or "professional" knowledge and skills, many are unprepared to effectively field interview questions designed to probe their "soft" skills (i.e., their personal qualities, traits, and characteristics). This is where many job offers are lost.

When preparing to answer soft skill questions, keep the following key points in mind:

- Employers routinely use soft skill questions to measure both the candidate's job fit and fit with organizational culture.
- Job-relevant soft skills are those personal traits and characteristics essential to successful job performance. Such skills can be readily identified through simple job analysis using a job description. (A more comprehensive approach is presented in chapter 12.)

(continued)

(continued)

- Because organizational culture varies from company to company, so too does the soft skills profile they seek. You can define these culture-relevant soft skills by asking a combination of networking and interview questions during the course of the job interview.

- Interview success requires you to understand both the job-relevant and culture-relevant soft skills sought by the employer with whom you are interviewing. Without this knowledge, it is difficult to win in the interview.

- Be prepared to answer questions concerning your major strengths and weaknesses. Choose weaknesses that have minor impact on performance or where you can demonstrate improvement. Where appropriate, also state that the weakness you cited has had "minimal effect" on your overall performance.

- Employers seek evidence of motivation to perform the work. Demonstrate your interest and motivation through a combination of physical and verbal indicators. Sit straight, look the employer in the eye, ask questions, show interest, and be enthusiastic. Tell the employer that you are "interested and excited" about the work they have to offer.

- Use the interview questions in this chapter to practice what you have learned. Particularly focus on those questions you find most difficult to answer. It will build confidence, and the rest of the interview will be a breeze.

CHAPTER 14

Making the "Right" Employment Decision

The goal of all job-hunting campaigns is, of course, not just to find a job, but also to make the "right" employment decision. Clearly, we spend too many of our waking hours engaged in work-related activities not to get it right.

If you stop to think, most professionals and managers spend an estimated 50 to 60 hours or more each week either directly working or doing something related to their job. Considering that the average person sleeps approximately 8 hours a night and is awake the other 16, this means the typical manager or professional is spending approximately 45 to 50 percent of his or her waking hours working. If you don't like your boss, the work that you do, or the environment in which you work, this means you are spending nearly half of your conscious life in a state of dissatisfaction and unhappiness.

Unfortunately, such unhappiness is not simply left behind at the workplace at the end of the day, waiting behind a closed door for your return. Instead, it goes right along home with you, and has a way of spilling over into your personal life, dragging down your spirit, and coloring the way you feel about a lot of things. It affects your general outlook, your disposition, your overall sense of well-being, and your relationships with those around you.

Not only can a poor employment decision affect your state of mind, but it can also have serious physical implications as well. Much research has been done on the connection between mental attitude and physical well-being. Studies have shown that job-related stress and anxiety can have dire consequences from a health standpoint, and in some cases can be a key contributor to chronic illnesses and even death.

Yes, you can pay a very, very dear price for making a poor employment decision. The really sad part, however, is that in most cases, all of this is avoidable.

This chapter will help you more objectively evaluate employment opportunities, and your final employment decision, so that you have the best chance of experiencing a high level of job satisfaction and happiness with your job, your new boss, and the overall work environment.

Revisiting Your Ultimate Job Profile

This is a good time to dust off that "ideal job" profile that you worked so hard on in chapter 2. This can be an extremely valuable tool, and now you will see how effective it is in making the "right" employment decision.

For those of you who skipped chapter 2, take heart. I will provide a little extra help along the way. To get the full benefit of this chapter, however, you might want to revisit chapter 2 and take an hour or so to go through the self-assessment exercises presented there. I think you will find them useful in better understanding yourself as well as those aspects of work life that can have considerable impact on your level of job and career satisfaction.

When we strip it down to the basics, making a good employment decision is dependent on having a good match in three fundamental areas. These are the following:

- Job Content
- Compatibility with Organizational Culture
- Compatibility with Your Boss

It's no surprise that all three of these elements play a critical role in career success and happiness.

To make an intelligent employment decision, therefore, the selection process requires close and systematic assessment of all three of these important components. When evaluating a given employment opportunity, you will need to systematically collect data on each of these three areas so that you have the information needed to make an objective and intelligent final decision.

If well planned, the employment decision process will allow you to construct a valid job and "organizational profile" of the target opportunity and predict, with a reasonably high degree of accuracy, whether this profile is a good match for your personal profile as well. So, this boils down to a simple comparison process, whereby you compare your own personal profile with that of the organization in the three critical areas of job fit, boss compatibility, and organizational compatibility. In doing so, you can take a lot of the guesswork out of the employment decision process because you are making a more objective evaluation of those factors known to be most important to personal success and career satisfaction.

The Two Components of Job Fit

The question of job fit has to do with whether you have the knowledge, skills, and motivation to perform the job. When you assess a new job, therefore, the two important areas to focus on are the following:

- Core knowledge and skills
- Motivation to perform

Having the basic knowledge and skills to perform a job is one thing; however, motivation to perform is something different entirely. However, both of the elements must be solidly in place if there is to be reasonable expectation of performance success and personal contentment. To assist in the evaluation of these two important components, therefore, I have provided some practical exercises that should prove helpful.

Start by taking a clean sheet of paper and drawing a large circle, labeling it "*Job Profile.*" As you complete the following exercises, you will want to transfer certain descriptive information about the job and work environment to this circle, constructing the first section of the *organizational profile*.

It is important to understand, at this juncture, that you will not have much of the information needed to complete this process until after your interview with the company. You will want to review these exercises in advance of the interview, however, so that you are prepared to thoroughly probe each of the key areas during the course of the interview itself.

Required Core Knowledge and Skills

It stands to reason that the first element of the job you will need to evaluate is that of core knowledge and skills. Do you have the knowledge and skills required to perform the job? Will you be able to perform the various tasks required by the position, solve the key problems you will face, and achieve the results expected? These are all key questions you will need to answer honestly and objectively if you want to be sure that this is the job for you.

To assist you in this process, I have formulated some basic questions you will need to answer in order to define this important aspect of the job profile:

- Why does the job exist (in other words, what is its principal role in the organization)?
- What are the basic *functions and/or tasks* to be performed or managed?
- What are the *key results* expected in each functional area or task?
- To achieve these results, what are the *principal problems* that must be solved and *specific challenges* that must be met?
- What *specific knowledge and/or skills* are needed to successfully address these problems and challenges and meet expected results?
- What are the *strategic, longer-term challenges* facing the position?

- What are the *major changes and/or improvements* expected of the position?
- What are the *major problems and/or challenges* that must be faced in order to successfully implement this longer-term strategy?
- What *specific knowledge and/or skills* will be required to successfully address these future problems and challenges, and accomplish the longer-term strategy?

The purpose of this set of questions is to help you ferret out and define the technical dimensions of the job—in other words, the core knowledge and skills required for successful performance. You will need to get answers to these key questions during the course of your job interview, so that you have the information needed to make a good assessment of your "job fit."

After you have completed the job interview and collected the relevant information regarding core knowledge and skills required for successful job performance, record these requirements in the Job Profile circle that you previously drew. You are now ready to evaluate the second important dimension of job fit: "motivation to perform."

Motivation to Perform

Although you might have the knowledge and skills needed to perform the job, the question that remains is, "Will you be sufficiently motivated, by both the job and the work environment, to perform well?" Obviously, the "ability to perform" (skills and knowledge) and the "desire to perform" (motivation) are both required if you are to realize performance success and job satisfaction.

Motivation to perform is in part determined by the nature of the work itself. Certain aspects of the job you might enjoy doing, and therefore, you will do them well. Other job tasks and functions you might find boring, routine, or generally unpleasant to perform. You might not perform these with quite the same level of enthusiasm, or, in some cases, you might even avoid them entirely. Such lack of motivation or avoidance can eventually take a toll, from both a job-performance standpoint and a personal-satisfaction standpoint.

If you have completed exercise 1 in chapter 2, you have already identified those job-task elements that are essential to your personal motivation. If not, take a moment or two to look at this exercise. It will probably take you no more than a minute or two to complete it, and the learning that occurs will be well worth the time you invested. This exercise will help you pinpoint the types of work and work characteristics that you find motivational and that you require to ensure your job satisfaction and performance success.

Another approach to assessing your motivation to perform a job is to look at the nature of the work itself. Systematically look at each of the job or individual functions and tasks you will need to perform and, based on your experience in previous jobs, honestly ask yourself, "How much do I enjoy doing each of these job elements, and how often will I have to perform them in the new position?" The short exercise below will help you accomplish this assessment. Directions for completing this exercise follow:

- Using a copy of the job description (acquired from the employer), as well as information gathered during the interview, list all key functions and tasks you will need to perform in the new position.

- Now, as best you can, estimate the total percentage of work time needed to perform the given task or function. (When added together, these should add up to 100 percent, as shown in the % *Time* column.)

- Now drawing from past experience in performing the same or similar functions or tasks, record the appropriate symbol (+, −, or 0), depending on whether you enjoyed, felt neutral about, or disliked performing that particular function or task.

- Now, record the percent of time you previously assigned to that specific function or task in the same column, next to the symbol (+, 0, or −) that reflects your motivation or satisfaction level. Example: If the first task on your list is "making formal presentations" and you dislike this, you would first put a − symbol in the *Minus* column next to this task. Assuming the new job would require you to spend 25 percent of your time making formal presentations, you would put this 25% in two places:

  1. In the % *Time* column next to the task
  2. In the *Minus* column, on the same line as the task

This now shows that the new job would require you to spend 25 percent of your time doing something you don't care to do very much (make formal presentations).

Job Motivation Assessment				
Key Job Tasks and Functions	**% Time**	**Motivation/Satisfaction Level:**		
		Plus	**Neutral**	**Minus**

(continued)

(continued)

Key Job Tasks and Functions	% Time	Motivation/Satisfaction Level:		
		Plus	Neutral	Minus
Total	**100%**	**%**	**%**	**%**

When you have finished filling in all information for each respective function and task, add each of the three columns to get a total percentage of time for each separate column. When you add the total percentage of time for each of the three columns, they should add up to 100 percent.

You can now readily see what percentage of time you would spend doing things you enjoy and that motivate you, and what percentage of your total time you would spend performing tasks or carrying out functions you dislike. This is a simplistic way of quickly assessing whether this would be a job you would find motivating and satisfying, or one you would find boring and dissatisfying.

In making your final assessment, I would recommend one further step. On the same exercise sheet, circle each function or task you would judge to be "key" or "critical" to successful performance of the position. Are any of these functions or tasks you dislike performing? If so, what percentage of the time would be spent doing this part of the job? Also, putting aside your dislike for this function for the moment, are you able to perform this task or function on a satisfactory level? You might dislike doing this work, but you could also be good at it.

If you find that you would be spending a large percentage of your time performing work you dislike, you might want to think seriously about continuing your job search, even if you can do that work well. Certainly accepting such a position is not going to be an ideal solution for you, and you are likely to find yourself unhappy and again looking to change jobs within three to six months of accepting the new position.

As I have already mentioned, how well you are motivated to do the work is also greatly affected by the environment in which the work must be performed. You might enjoy performing the various functions and tasks of the job, and be generally happy with the job itself, but might not enjoy the culture or work environment in which you must perform this work. This can drag you down emotionally and eventually cause you to lose your enthusiasm and motivation to perform at your highest level.

So, when assessing a new employment opportunity, you need to assess the culture and work environment as well, instead of focusing solely on the tasks you will need to perform.

Compatibility with Organizational Culture

As previously stated, how well you fit into the culture of an organization can have an enormous impact on your success and overall happiness.

Case Study: John

At the risk of digressing a bit, I would like to share the following real-life story with you that really makes the point. For reasons of confidentiality, I have changed the names of both my client and the companies involved in the case.

A few years back, while doing quite a bit of career-transition consulting for a number of large companies, I was contacted by the director of human resources of a major British-owned company (hereafter referred to as "BritCo"), who told me they would be letting John (not his real name) go, and needed my services. John, at the time, was serving as general manager of a small $13 million division of this $3 billion company.

When I asked what the problem was, the director replied as follows:

> *"John has such poor interpersonal skills that we considered taking him behind the plant and shooting him!"*

I thought this a bit extreme, but asked if I could meet with John's boss, Harry (not his real name), to better understand, more specifically, the nature and extent of the problem I would be dealing with. A meeting was arranged for me with Harry.

When probing the matter further with Harry, I was told that he, and the rest of the group, found John to be "very aggressive and hostile." I was told that John was a person who was constantly challenging everyone and everything. He was seen as being "argumentative, bull-headed, opinionated, and generally obnoxious" (plus a few other adjectives I am reluctant to include here).

Up to this point, John, by all reasonable standards, had been hugely successful. He had been an outstanding student who earned an engineering degree (with honors) from one of the top engineering schools, followed by an MBA from the Wharton School, where he also excelled as a student.

Following graduation from Wharton, John accepted employment with a world-renowned international corporation, UCo (not the real company name). During his 12 years at UCo, John continued to excel, advancing through several positions, and was finally named director of operations for one of UCo's smaller divisions. It was at this time that he was contacted by an executive search firm, who convinced John to accept the position of division vice president with BritCo, which John accepted. John was with BritCo for only about six months when the bottom fell out and I received the phone call.

John's former employer, UCo, has a reputation as a bit of a "rough-and-tumble" company, one that practices what insiders like to call "in-your-face management." That is to say that the culture is one that values confrontation and aggressive behavior, and, in fact, even rewards it! (Witness—John!) They support the notion of continuously challenging the status quo as the basis for bringing about change and improvement. UCo prides itself on being unusually innovative and the technological leader in its field. Aggressiveness, forcefulness, and confrontation are valued behaviors at UCo.

Nevertheless, John fit in rather nicely. He was always at the forefront of leading change and improvement at UCo, and he was rewarded by a string of promotions and salary increases, and encouraged to continue his assertive behavior. It was just what the company wanted!

Now enter BritCo. BritCo, as you will recall, was a British-owned company that exemplified the best of British culture. People treated one another with respect, sensitivity, and proper decorum. If you disagreed with someone, or wished to challenge his or her viewpoint, you were expected to do so in a proper and dignified way. And, if you wanted to really argue your point, you did not do so in public, but rather in the privacy of a closed-door office.

If you haven't guessed by now, I am talking about an extreme difference in cultures here. John, who had been highly successful for 12 years and continuously rewarded for "in-your-face" behavior, suddenly found himself in a culture that valued just the opposite. He was a fish out of water, and it quickly took its toll.

Now, here is the point of my telling you this true story. There was John, an enormous success in the first culture and a colossal failure in the second! There was John, the same guy with the same education; the same level of motivation, drive, and energy; the same traits, characteristics, and behaviors—a booming success at UCo and a complete disaster at BritCo. No difference in the man—but a huge difference in the *culture*!

So, as you can see from this tale, the culture of an organization can play a significant role in job and career success. The problem, however, is that too often the candidate and the company are so focused on the core skills and competencies required by the position (in other words, the "technical aspects") that they neglect to look at compatibility with the culture of the organization (in other words, fit with the organization's values, beliefs, and behaviors). John is a great case in point.

Different Companies Have Different Values, Beliefs, and Preferred Behavior

Behavioral scientists have long recognized the strong connection between a person's value/belief system and his or her behavior. What a person values and believes, in their hearts and minds, will determine how they behave. The two are connected and virtually inseparable. Sure, a person can change his or her behavior for a short period of time, but sooner or later, they will revert back to what makes them feel comfortable and "at home" with themselves.

Companies are much the same way. Much like BritCo and UCo, they have an over-riding value and belief system that drives and reinforces certain types of behavior. This is reflected in every facet of the organization's life: how they make decisions, their management style, how they relate to their employees, and how employees relate to one another within the company.

For example, one company might believe that success is dependent on employee involvement. They favor working in teams, creating an environment that encour-ages full employee participation, joint decision-making, and group reward. They favor managers who are participative, who enjoy team building, and who believe in the power of the group over the power of the individual. Such a company rewards managers for managerial behavior that is supportive of the principles of employee involvement.

Another company, on the other hand, might believe in autocracy: management by a small group of talented and powerful executives who make all key decisions and have employees execute them in accordance with their plans. For the most part, employee opinion matters little, and managers are expected to be smart, tough, and demanding of their employees.

As you can see, these are two different worlds—two very different cultures with very different value systems. A person can be extremely knowledgeable, talented, and skilled in their area of professional expertise, and still fail if they don't fit the overall culture of the organization. When one doesn't align well with organiza-tional culture, doesn't support the values and beliefs of the organization, and doesn't exhibit the preferred behaviors, sooner or later they are doomed to job fail-ure and social isolation. They are seen as "misfits," "people who don't understand the big picture," "argumentative," "not a team player," "disruptive," "lacking a sense of focus and priority," and any other of a number of unflattering adjectives intending to categorize their lack of overall compatibility with the workgroup and the organization as a whole. Such individuals are often denied success. They are seen as outcasts, people whose ideas are not worth listening to or supporting. Without management support for their ideas, and the needed resources to carry them out, they are essentially denied the opportunity to succeed. They may be bril-liant, but, if they are working in the wrong organizational culture, they will become a "brilliant failure." Such is the power of organizational culture!

Profiling Organizational Culture

On page 261, you will find an exercise you can use to profile the culture of any com-pany with which you interview. This exercise consists of a group of key questions, to which you will need to get answers if you are to get a complete picture of the com-pany's culture—its values, beliefs, and preferred behaviors. Many of these questions cannot be answered until the actual job interview, but they will fully prepare you with an excellent framework for compiling a fairly accurate and insightful picture of the company's culture during the course of job interview discussions.

Before moving on to this exercise, however, be prepared to incorporate the information you gather as part of the overall "organizational profile" you are creating. So, at this point, draw a large circle on a second sheet of paper, which you will label *"Organizational Culture."* Once you have concluded your job interview and are in a position to answer the questions posed in the exercise, record these answers as descriptive "bullet statements" in the circle that you have just drawn.

As you will see, some of these questions are best answered by the hiring manager, but others are better answered by your future peers, who report to this manager. If possible, you will want to request some one-on-one time with these peers as part of the interview day.

> **Tip:** Most potential peers will be reasonably candid if you begin the discussion by stating that you would appreciate their candor and will treat the information provided as confidential. Then be sure that you do.

The questions posed in this exercise should enable you to develop considerable information about a company's culture. And, by cross-referencing the answers you get from various individuals with whom you interview, you will see some clear patterns emerge that should provide a fairly thorough and accurate picture of the organization's culture, from which it should be relatively easy to measure your own compatibility (or lack thereof). This will include such factors as the following:

- Organizational values and beliefs
- Preferred employee behaviors and personal characteristics
- Management style and behaviors
- Freedom to make decisions
- Freedom to act
- Opportunity to have personal impact on strategy and planning
- Degree of employee involvement
- Team involvement vs. independent freedom
- Characteristics of high performers (values and behaviors)
- Characteristics of poor performers (values and behaviors)

If you previously completed the Career Mapping exercise (exercise 6) in chapter 2, you are already a few steps ahead at this point. If you have not, I would suggest that this would be a good exercise for you to complete because it provides a great opportunity for you to define the organizational characteristics and attributes that are so important to your own motivation and career satisfaction. By comparing these two profiles (yours and the company's), you then have an excellent basis for making an intelligent and informed career choice.

Had John had the benefit of this self-knowledge, combined with an understanding of the BritCo culture, I am sure he would have avoided a great deal of anxiety and unhappiness. I am sure you would like to avoid this kind of pain and anxiety, too. The power to do so is in your hands, and you need to take full advantage of this opportunity to be sure that you join a company that appreciates you as an individual and shares the same values and beliefs for which you stand.

Profiling Organizational Culture
Questions for the Hiring Manager

- How would you describe the culture at X Company? How is it different from other organizations for which you have worked?
- What do you like most about this culture? Why?
- What aspects of the culture or work environment here at X, in your judgment, could be improved?
- What two or three things do you feel are most important to employee success here at X Company?
- Please tell me a little bit about your management philosophy.
- How would you describe your management style?
- How do you like to manage those who report to you? How do you go about planning and managing their work?
- What do you consider to be your top two or three priorities?
- When you think of strong performers in your group, what do you feel are the traits and characteristics that set them apart?
- How about people who have done less well in this group—what principal qualities or work characteristics do you feel they lack?
- What do you feel will be most important for success in this job?

Questions for Peers

- How would you describe the culture here at X Company?
- How does it compare with other cultures in which you have worked?
- What do you like most about working here?
- What do you like least about working here?
- How would you characterize the work environment in this department?
- What traits and characteristics do you feel are required for success in this group?
- What is it like to work for Jane (boss's name)?
- How would you describe Jane's management style?
- To what degree does Jane involve you and others in planning and decision-making?
- What kinds of planning and decision-making does Jane reserve for herself?
- What is the process for setting individual job goals and priorities in this department?
- How is performance managed, and what kind of feedback do you get?

- What are the two or three things the department needs more of to be successful?
- What do you believe are the two or three biggest barriers to individual and group success in this department?

Boss Compatibility

Using the preceding exercise as the basis for profiling organizational culture, you have also already learned quite a bit about the profile of the new boss. Specifically, you have uncovered such important information as the following:

- Management philosophy (what he or she believes about how a manager should behave)
- Management style (how the boss manages subordinates)
- Management behavior (how the boss actually manages subordinates)
- The work environment created by the boss's style of management
- The boss's key priorities (what he or she is most focused on and will emphasize)
- The freedom the boss grants to subordinates in the areas of planning and decision-making
- The traits, characteristics, and behaviors the boss values most in subordinates
- Those employee traits, characteristics, and behaviors that the boss values least
- How the boss views the general overall culture of the company itself
- Performance expectations for the new position

Clearly, the traits and characteristics of a boss can have a significant impact on your motivation and attitude toward the job. If the two of you align well philosophically, and your styles are compatible, there will normally be a great deal of harmony, and you will thoroughly enjoy your working relationship. Conversely, if your values/belief systems and styles are very different, chances are there will be constant friction and a good deal of stress in your life.

Although the preceding exercise, combined with the answers you receive during the job interview, will give you a good picture of your future boss's profile, you need to compare this to your own profile in order to arrive at an intelligent employment decision. If you have only the future boss's profile, you have only "half a loaf."

If you have not already done so, let me suggest you complete the "Best Boss" Profiling exercise (exercise 7 in chapter 2). This will enable you to better understand yourself, in addition to the specific characteristics and attributes you need in a boss in order to enjoy this important relationship and fully thrive in the new environment.

In order to complete the full assessment process and arrive at a well-founded employment decision, you will want to prepare one more sheet of paper, on which you will draw a third circle. Label this circle *"Boss Profile."* Following completion of your employment interview, and while the information is still fresh in your mind, record your observations about the future boss's profile as descriptive "bullet statements" in this circle.

Making the Final Decision

You now have all the ingredients needed to make an intelligent, well-informed employment decision based on the three main areas of focus (Job Fit, Organizational Compatibility, and Boss Compatibility). The overall organizational profile you have created (the three circles) now contains the following components:

1. Job Profile
   a. Core Knowledge and Skills Summary
   b. Motivation to Perform Summary
2. Organizational Culture Profile
   a. Core Values and Beliefs Summary
   b. Overall Company Culture Summary
   c. Preferred Employee Traits, Characteristics, and Behaviors
   d. Department Values and Beliefs Summary
   e. Department Work Environment Descriptors
3. Boss Profile
   a. Boss's Management Philosophy
   b. Boss's Management Style
   c. Boss's Management Practices
   d. High Performer Traits and Characteristics
   e. Poor Performer Traits and Characteristics
   f. Boss's Priorities and Key Focus Areas

You now have a very complete profile of the target organization and all of the key elements that are critical from both a job performance and compatibility standpoint. The "organizational model" you have just developed now becomes the target against which you can compare the "ideal job model" you developed back in chapter 2. So, at this point, pull out that "Ultimate Job" Profile and begin the comparison process.

By laying these two profiles side by side and comparing one against the other, you will readily see whether the target job, which you are evaluating, will be a good match for you. Specifically, you will want to make the following match between the two:

Organizational Profile	Your "Ultimate Job" Profile
Job Profile	Job task management
	Self-management
	Interpersonal relationship management
Organizational culture profile	Ideal work environment
Boss's profile	"Best Boss" Profile

Of course, no job will ever be a 100 percent match for your personal profile. It would be unrealistic to expect that to be the case. You will need to decide where you are willing to compromise. Such compromises, however, should be relatively minor and have little effect on your overall level of job satisfaction, performance success, and general career and personal happiness.

You are now well equipped to make an objective and intelligent career decision.

Chapter Summary

The goal of *The Ultimate Job Search* is not just to find a job, but to find the "right" job—one that will provide a high level of personal satisfaction and greatly enhance the potential for career success. This important choice cannot be left to chance. When selecting the right job and employer, key points to keep in mind are the following:

- Picking the right job requires a good match in three critical areas: job content, organizational culture, and boss compatibility.

- Too often, employment decisions are made on the basis of job content alone. This can be a fatal mistake, leading to discontent and much unhappiness.

- When gauging "job fit," you must consider both your ability to perform the job (your knowledge and skills) as well as personal motivation to perform the type of work being offered.

- Gauging your fit with a company's culture (in other words, "cultural fit") requires you to evaluate the compatibility of your own personal values and beliefs with the values and beliefs of the organization as a whole, as well as the organizational unit in which you will be working.

- The traits and characteristics of your future boss can also have a significant impact on your motivation to perform the work as well as your overall attitude toward the job. Understanding which boss traits and characteristics motivate or demotivate you is essential to selecting the right job for you.

By asking the right questions of your potential new boss and peers during the job interview, you can systematically collect the information you need to create a reliable "organizational profile." Comparison of this "organizational profile" with your "Ultimate Job Profile" (see chapter 2) provides an excellent basis for selecting the "right job," one that will prove both rewarding and personally satisfying.

CHAPTER 15

Negotiating the Job Offer: Strategies for Getting What You Want

To bring your job search to a successful conclusion, you will need to be a skillful negotiator. Well-honed negotiating skills at this phase of the job search are critical. If you fail to capitalize on the opportunity, all of your hard work up to this point will have been for nothing.

The danger of failure is twofold. First, you could end up with a job offer that is completely unacceptable. Or, second, you might scare away an employer by presenting them with unreasonable demands that they are not prepared to meet. This is a delicate balance that you must manage carefully.

This chapter will introduce you to some strategy and techniques to help you plan and execute effective negotiations. It will provide you with the basis for determining a fair and reasonable compensation package as well as equip you with various techniques for best positioning your requirements with an employer. Likewise, it will help you view your compensation requirements from the employer's perspective and provide you with insight on how employers typically think, and the principal concerns they commonly share when formulating a job offer. Moreover, it will suggest alternative ways to structure an offer that might help alleviate employer concerns and still satisfy your own needs as well.

Determining the Employer's Compensation Limits

When preparing to negotiate a reasonable compensation package that both you and the employer can live with, the first priority is for you, as best you can, to determine the compensation parameters within which the employer must operate. All employers have their absolute limits, beyond which they cannot go (with apparently the exception of professional sports!). You need to establish what that limit is.

Most employers prefer not to make a job offer at or near the top of the salary range for a given position. And, if they do, you should have some concern. Occasionally, if pushed, some employers, if they want to hire the person badly enough, might feel compelled to make an unusually high offer at or near the salary range maximum, with the idea that they will use conservative salary treatment in the future (for example, giving no increase or meager increases), until such time as the new hire's salary falls comfortably in range. This is, of course, a strategy they are not likely to share with you at the time they make the offer.

If You Are Working with a Search Firm or Employment Agency

If you are dealing with a third party (a search firm or employment agency), the job of finding out the salary range is usually much easier. Although the agency might not know the full salary range, they are likely to know the maximum salary offer the employer is prepared to make. Most, if they know the salary range, will confidentially share this information with you if you ask.

Highly reputable executive search firms that are under contract retainer with the employer, however, might be loathe to share this information with employment candidates for fear of compromising their client company's negotiating strategy and financial leverage. For example, if the salary range for the position is $110,000 to $130,000 and you are currently making only $90,000 per year, knowing the range maximum might encourage you to ask for considerably more than you would have otherwise.

The fact that some of these firms might be unwilling to provide you with salary range information should not stop you from asking. Because this information is vital to your negotiation strategy, you shouldn't hesitate to ask. In many cases you will find these firms, in the interest of putting the deal together, quite willing to share what they know. This is particularly true if they are a "contingency" firm, which doesn't get paid unless and until the deal is done. In such cases, you might find they are even willing to provide you with a bit of coaching, encouraging you to ask for a higher amount than you were planning to ask for. This is especially true if their fee is based on your total compensation package and they will be paid a higher amount based on your higher compensation package.

Tip: In the event that you ask for salary range information from a third-party recruiter and they don't have this information to share with you, ask them to find out and get back to you. Most have ways of getting this information if you really want it. In some cases, however, they will try but might be unable to deliver. In such cases, you are on your own.

Ask the Employer

If there is no third-party employment agency involved in the process, or if the agency is uncomfortable sharing this information with you, you could go directly to the employer with your request for information. Policies vary by company. Some are quite open with salary ranges and will disclose these ranges if asked. Others are very secretive and will not disclose such information at all. But it's certainly worth trying.

If an employer is reluctant to provide salary range information with you, here is an approach you might try with the company's recruiter or human resources manager:

> *"Jane, I can understand your reluctance to share salary range information with me, and I certainly don't want to make you uncomfortable in any way with my question. However, I am sure you can understand my predicament. I am certainly looking for a fair and reasonable offer, but I want to make sure what I am asking is not unreasonable. You already know what I am making. I will, of course, be looking for some reasonable financial incentive to make the move worthwhile. Can you at least give me some rough idea of the range you have in mind for this position?"*

This seems like a reasonable request, especially the way it is couched. The subtle message here, which won't go unnoticed by the employer, is that you feel the employer has a unfair advantage and you are simply saying you do not want to be taken advantage of. Most employers, with a request of this type, will feel compelled to respond in a reasonable way, or potentially risk alienating the job seeker. Some will simply open up and disclose the entire salary range for the position, or at least provide some pretty strong clues.

If this first attempt fails, you might try the following tactic, although it's somewhat risky:

> *"Jane, I can completely appreciate your reluctance to provide me with salary range information, and, again, I don't in any way want to make you feel uncomfortable. But let me share my principal concern with you. If I decide to make a move from my current job at ABC Company and leave behind a successful career, I don't want to suddenly discover I have salary issues because I was hired too high in the salary range. When this happens, sometimes, despite outstanding performance, employees are passed over for salary increases due to salary range compression. I would certainly not want to see this happen. Can you at least give me some idea where my current salary falls in your overall salary range?"*

Put yourself in the employer's shoes. What would you do? I am sure you could see the wisdom of at least sharing some perspective on salary range with the candidate, especially with this explanation for making the request. I think, if you were the employer, you would be very hard-pressed not to provide at least some reasonable idea of range.

This is a very reasonable request, and by using this tactic you have provided the employer with a legitimate reason for requesting the information. Considering the circumstances and the way the request was framed, it would be difficult for the employer not to respond in some meaningful way without appearing rude or insensitive and potentially alienating you as an employment candidate. Most employers will not take that chance, assuming the candidate has reasonable qualifications for the position they are attempting to fill.

> **Tip:** You will also want to ask the employer about incentive compensation plans. Do they have such programs? If so, how do they work? Additionally, you will want to ask, assuming good performance, what has been the typical payout for this position. Perhaps the employer can at least provide you with a "ballpark range" for these bonus payments.

Beginning to Formulate Your Compensation Strategy

Once you are armed with at least some feel for the job's salary range, you are now in a position to begin to formulate your compensation strategy for salary-negotiation purposes. Also, by asking questions, you have put the employer on notice that compensation is an important consideration, and they will need to make a reasonably competitive offer if they are to attract you.

When formulating your compensation strategy, it is important to know that most employers prefer to make job offers at, or below, their salary range midpoint. In doing so, they can provide the new employee with ample opportunity for salary growth and reasonable salary treatment. Experience has also taught them that being able to provide for reasonable salary treatment is a good deterrent to employee turnover. So, they don't want to hire too high in the salary range, provide below-average salary increases, and then have to fill the same position again a year or so later. This becomes an expensive proposition.

Aiming for a salary offer at the higher end of the employer's salary range, in some cases, might not be nearly as great an issue for the employer as you might initially think. This is especially true if you are well qualified for the position and there is an identifiable promotional opportunity for you in the near term.

In cases where there is a line of progression providing stepped job grades, salary compression might not be a problem. For example, many scientific jobs have a promotional line of progression or promotional ladder where a new hire can enter as a Scientist, advance to Senior Scientist, then be promoted to Chief Scientist, and finally be promoted to Scientific Fellow. In such cases, if the job seeker is hired at one of the lower-level positions in the chain, salary compression is not as much of an issue. The employer knows that if the new hire is a strong performer, and his or her salary is at or near the range maximum, the problem can be remedied quickly by simply promoting the person to the next higher job in the ladder, where the salary range can easily accommodate the employee's new salary level.

Another example where being hired at or near range maximum is not a problem is when the candidate is seen as a future replacement for his or her new boss, who will be leaving in the short term and will need to be replaced. There are many times when a candidate is specifically hired for this very reason. When the employer sees the candidate as "heir apparent," there is likely to be less concern about salary-compression issues.

Putting these few exceptions aside, however, if your current salary is already high in comparison with the employer's salary range, you will need to be particularly sensitive to this fact. In such cases, if you demand too large an increase, you could well price yourself out of the market and walk away empty-handed. In such cases, you will want to shave your expectations a bit and ask for something that will make the employer comfortable from the compensation standpoint. Perhaps there are some things you can negotiate for, other than compensation, that will help off-set the lower compensation level. (See the section "Benefits Differential," later in this chapter, for more details on these optional areas.)

If you are at or below the midpoint of the employer's salary range, this can be an entirely different matter. In this case, you have considerably more leverage and can ask for a more generous salary increase over what you have been making. How much you can command will be determined by a number of factors, which I address momentarily. Suffice it to say that if you are an exceptionally well-qualified candidate working in a high-demand occupation, where qualified candidates are scarce, you have considerably more leverage than if you are a person with average qualifications in a field overcrowded with unemployed talent.

So, you will need to not only look at salary range position, but you must also consider the state of the labor market and the supply-demand balance in your particular occupational field.

Compensation: The Employer's Perspective

Any good negotiator knows, to be effective at negotiations, you must have a thorough understanding of your opponent's reasoning, motivations, and any barriers or limitations that constrain them. It is virtually impossible to formulate a good negotiation strategy without having full understanding of the opposition. What are the various factors, other than salary range, that will influence or impact what salary level an employer is willing and able to offer? Here are the major factors:

- Internal salary equity
- Difficulty filling the position
- Interest in the candidate
- Candidate's interest in the position

- Candidate promotability
- Critical nature of the position

Internal Salary Equity

The term "salary equity" refers to the comparison an employer makes between the salary they are considering as their offer and the earnings of other employees with similar credentials now working in the same group. Employers are reluctant to hire outsiders at considerably higher compensation levels than the pay levels of existing employees in the same group. This is particularly true if the group has a number of high performers whom the employer can't afford to lose.

Employers are normally willing to risk creating internal salary inequities only if they feel they can justify the salary difference based on a difference in the overall qualifications and experience level of the new hire. Thus, for example, it would be difficult to hire a Ph.D. with four years of experience for $110,000 a year if other solid-performing Ph.D.s now working in the group have an average of six years of experience and are making only $95,000. This could lead to mutiny and several valuable employees jumping ship.

On the other hand, if the circumstances were reversed, it would be an entirely different ballgame. In this case, a Ph.D. with six years of experience and a salary of only $95,000 being hired into a group of Ph.D.s averaging only four years of experience and paid an average of $110,000 is simply not going to create a salary equity problem. In this case, the employer can afford a far more generous offer without upsetting the internal apple cart.

Difficulty Filling the Position

If the employer has been having difficulty filling the position, and it has been open for quite some time, there might be a lot more flexibility in what they are willing to offer a qualified candidate. This is especially true if it is important to get the job filled and there are no other qualified candidates in sight. This means that there is a lot more negotiating room for you to ask for a much higher salary.

Conversely, you might want to pull in your horns a bit if the position the employer is attempting to fill has been open only a short time and there is a long list of well-qualified candidates already scheduled for interviews right behind yours. In this case, you probably don't have much bargaining room at all.

So, when formulating your negotiating strategy, plan to gather some basic market intelligence during the interview. To do this, here are some of the questions to ask:

- How long has this position been open?
- Have you interviewed many candidates for this job?
- What is the status of this position; when do you expect to be filling it?
- Are you anticipating filling this job shortly?

Questions of this type, asked directly of the employer or of a third-party employment agency representing the employer, should get you all the answers you need to understand what degree of negotiating leverage you will have if offered the position.

Interest in the Candidate

How interested is this employer in hiring you? Have they told you they are interested? Have they said they are *"very interested"*? Have you heard statements like the following:

> *"Mary we are extremely interested in you and plan to be making an offer to you by sometime tomorrow!"*

> *"John we are really looking forward to having you join our team. I have told our human resources manager to get an offer together by the end of the day if possible. We think you would be a great addition to our group!"*

> *"Linda, what is your current job status? Do you have other offers that you need to give an answer to? If so, can you tell me what they are? We would like to make you a job offer by tomorrow and want to make sure we are competitive."*

Well what do you think? Do these employers have strong interest? Do you believe they will be willing to make a fairly generous offer? You can bet on it! Of course they are interested and are prepared to make a competitive offer.

Now consider the following employer statements at the end of the interview day:

> *"Fred, we appreciated your coming in and spending the time with us today. I'd like to let you know we have some initial interest and feel you have some fine qualifications. We have a few more candidates to interview, but will plan to get back to you in a week or two."*

> *"Barbara, we appreciated the time to get to know you today. Thanks for joining us. We are still fairly early in our search for this job, and will be interviewing other candidates in the next few weeks. We will plan to get back to you then. In the meantime, should your status change, please let us know."*

It is certainly apparent that the interest in these candidates is not nearly as strong as in the prior examples. Obviously, there is some modest interest in the candidates; however, it is apparent that the employer is not in a hurry to make a job offer. This suggests the employer is perfectly willing to lose these candidates and wait until a better candidate comes along. It also means the candidate was not seen as an ideal fit for the job, and it is likely that he or she is missing some aspect of qualification the employer considers as desirable, but probably not critical to success in the position.

In cases, such as these, if the employer comes back in a week or two and expresses interest in making a job offer, you probably don't have a lot of negotiating leverage. Under these circumstances, as a candidate, you are probably best advised to be conservative in your salary demands; otherwise, the employer is likely to move on in search of that ideal candidate who also has that one qualification that you were lacking.

Candidate's Interest in the Position

If you are interested in the job, make sure you express your interest—but not too strongly! If a candidate is clearly excited about the position and shows this excitement, the employer will probably shave compensation a bit when formulating the job offer. In this case, the employer knows it's a "sure thing" and will normally not hesitate to come in at a lower salary level than if there were more uncertainty about the candidate's level of interest.

On the other hand, where the job seeker has expressed interest in the position, but implied that there were other interesting opportunities in the wings, the employer is bound to be less sure of himself. In such a case, the employer is bound to come in with a much higher offer in order to cement the deal.

As part of your negotiation strategy, therefore, you will want to "keep your powder dry." Express interest in the position, but don't telegraph your excitement if you want to get the employer's higher offer. And, you will want to drop some subtle hints that you are seriously looking and have some other "chickens in the pot." The thought of competition is usually sufficient to nudge a job offer a little higher than what it otherwise might have been.

On the other hand, if the competition for the position is stiff and you have a strong interest in the position, by all means express your excitement and enthusiasm about the job. In this case, getting a little lower salary offer is a small price to pay for getting a job you can love. As a former employment manager of a major corporation, I have seen more than one offer go out to a candidate who showed genuine enthusiasm for the position when compared to another candidate whose interest level seemed to be moderate at best.

Candidate Promotability

Promotability is another factor an employer will consider when determining the level of the salary offer. If you appear to have good potential for promotion beyond the current job, and should promotional opportunities be readily identifiable, the employer will usually be a little more generous about compensation. In such cases, the employer is likely to be far less concerned about making an offer that is high in the salary range.

However, if you have excellent potential for promotion to the next job level, but there is no appropriate opportunity available in the foreseeable future, the employer is less likely to consider making a job offer that would fall high in the salary range. In such cases, the employer is likely to shave the offer a bit, coming in at a lower level. Moreover, if the candidate demonstrates below-average abilities and does not appear to be promotable beyond the current job level, the employer is bound to make a much lower offer in order to forestall future salary administration problems. In these cases, the employer is concerned about having enough room in the salary range to keep the new hire satisfied for a fairly long period of time.

Critical Nature of the Position

How important is it that that the employer fill the position quickly? Is it a key position that needs to be filled on an immediate basis? Have they just lost the key project manager on a major capital expansion project that will have serious financial repercussions if the position is not filled quickly? Did they lose their director of sales just as they landed that new $20 million customer, the biggest order they ever had?

If certain positions are not filled quickly, it can have serious financial implications for the company. In such cases the company is anxious to fill the position as quickly as possible. If you are lucky enough to be the one and only qualified candidate at the time, you are likely to have considerable bargaining power, and can expect an offer that is quite generous. They are not about to risk losing you as a potential employee if the financial stakes are high. If such is the case, you are definitely in the driver's seat from a salary negotiations standpoint.

What They Will Pay: Putting It Together

So, as you can see, there are a number of factors that will impact just how much an employer is willing to pay you. Your job, of course, is to gather as much of this information as possible, in advance of receiving a job offer, so that you can intelligently plan your negotiating strategy and determine what your "asking price" is going to be.

You can get some of this information from the employment agency, if one is involved, some from the company's human resources representative, and some directly from the hiring manager. Suffice it to say, you need to pin down a number of these variables (what the status of the job is, how long it has been open, how many other candidates there are, and just how interested the company is in you) before you can gauge the bargaining power you wield and the amount of leverage you will have when it comes time to negotiate for that higher salary amount.

How Low Will You Go?

Now, on one hand, you have gauged what you are likely to be able to command on the high side of the salary spectrum. But now, how about the other end of the scale? How low will you go? This is obviously a question you need to answer in your own mind before you begin the negotiating process.

Depending on the nature of the specific job and the longer-term opportunities presented by the position, under rare circumstances you might even be willing to take a reduction in salary to have the "job of your dreams." This might especially be the case if the job is located in a geographical area that has substantially lower living costs than the area where you are now living. For example, if the position requires moving from New York City or Los Angeles to Jackson, Mississippi, you might be able to accept a substantial cut in pay and still sustain a lifestyle equivalent to the lifestyle you previously enjoyed in either of these more expensive locations.

> **Note:** An increase in gross income does not always translate into an increase in net disposable income or buying power. Depending on area living costs, in some cases, even a sizeable increase in salary can sometimes translate to less spendable money in your pocket. If, for example, you have to carry a much larger mortgage, pay a great deal more in taxes, spend more for food and clothing, pay higher insurance costs, and so on, you could actually have less money to spend on discretionary items such as entertainment, nice vacations, and the like.

To determine how low you will go, you need to take a much broader view of the overall financial picture, not just the gross income you will be paid. Essentially, you need to do a cost-of-living analysis, which enables you to compare the cost of living in your current location to that of the area in which the job is located. You can do this either manually or by using some of the convenient tools available to you through the Internet.

Cost-of-Living Comparison

If you have an Internet connection and a computer available to you, when attempting to calculate and compare living costs between two or more locations, check out the Internet site www.homefair.com. On this Web site you will find a "Salary Calculator" feature that will instantly do all the work for you.

After you select the city or town in which you currently reside and the location of the new job, this site will tell you what you need to make in the new location in order to have the equivalent net disposable or discretionary income that you now enjoy. For example, I recently moved from West Chester, Pennsylvania, to the Ocean City, Maryland area. Although Ocean City was not listed, I was able to choose Salisbury, Maryland, which is close by. By inputting both locations into the appropriate boxes, the calculator told me that if I made $100,000 in West Chester, Pennsylvania, I would have to make $103,540 in Salisbury, Maryland, in order to maintain the same standard of living.

This told me that I would need to start at a initial base of $103,540, in order to essentially break even. If I were looking for at least a 10 percent increase in salary, therefore, I would actually need a minimum salary offer of $113,894 ($103,540 + 10 percent) rather than $110,000 ($100,000 + 10 percent). So, you can begin to see what effect cost-of-living differential can actually have on either increasing or decreasing your net discretionary income. This might also significantly impact what you are likely to accept as your "rock bottom" asking price during salary negotiations.

The Cost of Moving

Another important item you will want to factor into your compensation request is the cost of physically moving you from the old location to the new location. If the employer is unwilling to reimburse this cost, you might want to take it into consideration when determining the salary you would be willing to accept.

How much does a physical move actually cost? Obviously, this cost can vary greatly depending on the distance required by the move as well as the size of your house or apartment and the weight of the load. Here again, the Web site www.homefair.com can be a very useful source for acquiring moving cost information. The site also has a "Moving Calculator," which can save you a lot of time and legwork. By inputting "to and from destinations" or mileage between the two, as well as information concerning the size of your household, you can get a quick estimate of both the low and high range of moving costs. In my case, by putting in a move of approximately 150 miles and a four-bedroom house, the high estimate for shipping my household goods was about $7,500. If the employer were not going to pick up the cost of this move, I would want to factor this cost into my negotiations, as justification for requesting a higher salary amount.

Manual Comparison: Cost of Living

If you don't trust the accuracy of a Web site to calculate cost-of-living differential for you, or you don't have access to an Internet connection, you might want to do a manual cost-of living calculation. You can use the following form in making this calculation. If the cost of living in the new location is less than your current cost of living, you might want to scale your salary demands down a bit. On the other hand, if it's going to cost you more to live in the new location, you will want to scale your salary requirements up a bit to make up the difference.

When applying the formula in these worksheets, there are a few subtleties to keep in mind:

- Both state and local income taxes are deductible from federal income. The number used for federal income tax in this formula must therefore be adjusted accordingly.

- Mortgage interest, real estate tax, and personal property tax may also be deductible for federal tax purposes. Check with you tax advisor and adjust the amount you use for federal income tax based on your tax advisor's advice.

- In order to reflect an accurate housing comparison, you need to do an "apples-to-apples" comparison. In making this comparison, therefore, you will want to compare your house to a house in the new location that is of comparable size. Thus, if you are now living in a 2,500-square-foot house, you will want to use a 2,500-square-foot house in the new location as the basis for this comparison.

Net Disposable Income Comparison
(Old Location)

Gross Income (Salary, Bonus, Other): $ _____

      Less: <u>Income Taxes</u>:
          Federal $ _____
          State   _____
          Local   _____
               Total $ _____

      Less: <u>Housing Costs</u>:
          Mortgage Interest $ _____
          Real Estate Taxes   _____
          Homeowners' Ins.   _____
          Heat   _____
          Water   _____
          Electricity   _____
               Total $ _____

      Less: <u>Cost of Co. Benefits</u>:
          Life Insurance $ _____
          Heath Insurance   _____
          Disability Insurance   _____
          Dental Insurance   _____
          Eye Care Insurance   _____
          Retirement Plan   _____
          Other Benefits   _____
               Total $ _____

      Less: <u>Misc. Expenses</u>
          Personal Prop. Tax $ _____
          State Excise Tax   _____
          State Sales Tax Est.   _____
          Commuting Costs   _____
          Auto Insurance   _____
          Other   _____
               Total $ _____

      Less: Total Expenses   _____

Net Disposable Income (Old Location) $ _____

Figure 15.1: Net disposable income (old location).

Net Disposable Income Comparison
(New Location)

Gross Income (Salary, Bonus, Other): $ _____

    Less: <u>Income Taxes</u>:
        Federal $ _____
        State   _____
        Local   _____
           Total $ _____

    Less: <u>Housing Costs</u>:
        Mortgage Interest $ _____
        Real Estate Taxes   _____
        Homeowners' Ins.   _____
        Heat   _____
        Water   _____
        Electricity   _____
           Total $ _____

    Less: <u>Cost of Co. Benefits</u>:
        Life Insurance $ _____
        Heath Insurance   _____
        Disability Insurance   _____
        Dental Insurance   _____
        Eye Care Insurance   _____
        Retirement Plan   _____
        Other Benefits   _____
           Total $ _____

    Less: <u>Misc. Expenses</u>
        Personal Prop. Tax $ _____
        State Excise Tax   _____
        State Sales Tax Est.   _____
        Commuting Costs   _____
        Auto Insurance   _____
        Other   _____
           Total $ _____

    Less: Total Expenses   _____

Net Disposable Income (New Location) $ _____

Figure 15.2: Net disposable income (new location).

- Realtors in your new location are an excellent source of this kind of information, and they will be more than happy to be of assistance. After all, you are a potential client for them, and they would certainly love to sell you a house once you have accepted your job offer. I would recommend calling two to three Realtors and then averaging the amounts they give you for each item of cost you are attempting to estimate.

Note: Your new employer should not be expected to help you finance the cost of a larger house. All calculations should therefore be made based on a house of comparable size in both locations.

By experimenting with different gross income figures, it should be possible to calculate the cost of living differential between the two locations and to adjust your current base salary accordingly. This places you on a level playing field, so that you are basing all salary calculations on a new location gross income that, after adjustment for cost-of-living differential, is the equivalent of what you are currently making.

Competitive Compensation Levels: New Location

Before you finalize your salary-negotiation strategy, there is one more piece of information you will need. You need to know what the pay levels are for people who hold comparable positions in the area where the job is located. As you know, what an employer is willing to pay is often dictated by the local labor market, as well as what an employer would need to pay someone with comparable skills who is hired locally. There are a couple of ways to get this information.

Salary.com is a website that provides information to users concerning local salary ranges for given jobs and occupational areas. The site contains a "salary wizard," which you can use to make this determination. It also provides information regarding the average cost or value of certain employee benefits when these benefits are provided by the employer as part of the total offer package. All of this information is quite useful from a negotiations standpoint.

By selecting a specific job title and location, the salary wizard generates a bell-shaped curve reflecting the range of salaries paid for the same position in the local or regional labor market in which the position is located. This curve shows you the entire spectrum of the salaries paid, from low to high, for that type of position in the local market you have selected. It also shows the 25th percentile, median, and 75th percentile salary values for your target position as well.

Moreover, Salary.com's salary wizard also provides information concerning bonuses paid for the target position as well. In this case, the salary wizard feature generates a similar bell-shaped curve, reflecting total compensation (base salary plus bonus) paid to people who hold your target position and work in the local market. Thus, the information supplied by this site allows you to compare the total compensation package offered by the new employer to what is being paid to others in the same job market. This is great information for you to have in your back pocket as ammunition for later negotiations, should you need it.

If you are unable to find salary data on Salary.com for the specific area in which you are interested, or if you do not have Internet access, you might want to check with your professional association to see whether they publish an annual salary survey that covers your target area. Today, many professional societies conduct annual salary surveys reflecting pay rates for their profession on a national scale. If they do publish such surveys, chances are the data is also broken down by region, type of industry, and employer size as well. This is again some convincing data for use during salary negotiations, should you need it. This information also serves as a good check for determining whether your salary expectations are realistic and in line with what the market will bear.

Benefits Differential

When looking at the total offer, job seekers often overlook the benefits area. Many times, job seekers consider this an area of secondary concern that requires little scrutiny. From an economic perspective, this could be a huge mistake. This is especially true in light of today's rapidly escalating benefit costs—especially health insurance. In addition to health-care insurance cost differences, there can also be big differences in insurance coverage as well. Should you or a member of your family develop a serious health issue and need to count on this coverage, you could be in for an unpleasant surprise when you discover that your coverage is inadequate and you are faced with thousands of dollars in bills.

So, in order to adequately prepare for negotiations, you need to get answers to the following questions:

- What benefits does the new employer provide?
- How do these compare with the benefits you now have?
- What new benefits will you gain?
- What benefits will you forfeit? Are they essential? If so, what will it cost to replace them?
- Is there a difference in benefits cost? How much additional will you need to pay out of pocket?
- How comprehensive is the health-care insurance coverage versus the health-care coverage you now have?
- Will you need to replace some health coverage? If so, what will it cost you to do so?

The firm's human resources manager can answer many of these questions. At the time of your job interview, therefore, you might want to ask for a summary of benefits that also provides cost breakout between what the company pays and what the employee is expected to pay. This information is normally readily available and can be provided quickly.

It is strongly recommended that you not request this information prior to the interview, as you might be seen as presumptuous or as someone who is principally interested in the benefits the company has to offer, rather than the job. This is not the kind of impression you will want to create. So wait until the interview to request a benefits summary.

The Negotiation

By now you are "loaded for bear." You have a ton of good information at your disposal and your arsenal is well equipped to do some friendly battle. This information includes the following:

- Employer's salary range (or approximate range)
- Local market salary range (from Salary.com)
- Regional market salary range (from your professional society)
- Cost-of-living differential (your location versus the employer's location)
- Household goods moving costs
- Benefits differential (if any)
- Benefits cost differential (what you will need to pay versus what you now pay)
- Urgency to fill job (how long it's been open; desire to fill it quickly)
- Employer's level of interest in you (as expressed by the employer)

Obviously, these are all variables to factor in when formulating your overall negotiating strategy and the level of compensation you will require. If you have done your preliminary research well, by now you probably have an excellent idea of where to peg your compensation requirements when the employer asks or makes an offer. You completely understand the absolute compensation level you require (in other words, your bottom line) and have a reasonably good idea of the employer's salary parameters as well. At the very least, you are now prepared to wade in and test the waters.

Name Your Price

Once the employer has decided they want to make a job offer, they will typically ask you for a range of salary you would consider acceptable. They will probably say something like this:

> "Michelle, we are very interested in making you a job offer, but I need to get some further information from you at this point. Can you give me some idea of what you might be looking for in the way of compensation?"

Of course, if the employer is working through an employment agency or executive search consultant, at this stage of negotiations, they are likely to want to keep you at arm's length. However, you are likely to get pretty much the same question from the consultant.

The best strategy, when answering the "name your price" question, is to cite a compensation range that, in your best judgment (considering the data you have already gathered), is higher than the employer will probably want to pay. However, don't be ridiculous in the amount you ask for. For example, if you feel the employer will probably not go beyond $90,000, you might say you are looking for something in the range of $92,000 to $94,000. The idea is to get the employer to stretch their thinking a bit. In a case such as this, the employer is likely to balk. The negotiations have now moved into stage two ("The Price Is Too High").

The Price Is Too High

If the range you have proposed is too high, you are bound to get an immediate response similar to the following:

> *"Mike, quite frankly, that's a little higher than we were thinking."*

You now need to further qualify the employer's thinking and get a clearer understanding of what the employer considers to be an acceptable range. So in response, you might say

> *"I see. Well, Joan, can you give me a better idea of what you are thinking?"*

The employer's response is likely to be

> *"Well, Mike, we were thinking somewhere in the neighborhood of $85,000 to $90,000. $92,000 is a bit higher than we are thinking."*

You will now want to qualify the employer's range further and get absolute confirmation on their willingness to make an offer at the highest number they provided in their counter-proposal. So here is what you would say:

> *"So, you would be willing to make an offer of $90,000, then?"*

The employer is likely to feel somewhat uncomfortable at this point, but will probably feel even more uncomfortable if they were to back off of a number they had put on the table as a valid consideration. So, their response is likely to be something like this:

> *"Well, Mike, that is a bit on the high end of what we really wanted to go, but I suppose we could live with it."*

You have now nailed down a specific number at the high end of what the employer had wanted to pay, so there is probably not much more you can do to get the base salary any higher. However, there are some other creative ways to negotiate for some additional compensation that are outside of base salary.

At this point, you might want to use some of the negotiations ammunition you have stored from your prior research, such as cost-of-living differential or local salary survey data, as leverage for requesting added revenue. Here is how you might accomplish this.

> *"Well, Joan, we seem to be about $2,000 or so apart. Let me share one of my concerns with you and see if it is possible to work something out. Joan, I did some cost-of-living research using some authoritative sources and found that there is about a 12 percent cost-of-living differential between Pittsburgh and Washington, D.C. Based on my current income, it will cost me about $6,000 a year more to live in Washington than it does now in Pittsburgh. I would be happy to show you the data if that would be helpful."*

> *"I know we are on the high end of your salary range at $90,000, and I don't want to make you uncomfortable since I am very interested in the job, but is there some creative way we can address this cost-of-living issue completely aside from base salary? For example, could consideration be given to a one-time signing bonus? This would at least provide some partial relief from this cost-of-living difference for the next year or so, until my salary has had a chance to catch up. I would be appreciative if the company might take this into consideration."*

When using this tactic and citing a reasonable and legitimate reason for requesting more compensation, most employers, if they are able to do so and are truly interested in hiring you, will attempt to do something to address this issue. They realize you are not being outright greedy, and that you do have a sincere interest in the job, but you are simply trying to address what is a financial inequity and economic penalty you will pay if you accept the job and move to the higher-cost area.

Another negotiating tactic you can use under these same circumstances is to request an early salary review—say, at six months into the job rather than the normal one-year anniversary review. Here is how you might use this approach with the employer:

> *"Joan, it appears we are about $2,000 lower than I had hoped to be. I know you have indicated that $90,000 is probably as high as you can go from a salary standpoint. I want you to know, I am certainly interested in the job, and would consider an offer at $90,000; however, there is another financial concern with which I am wrestling. My research shows there is about a 12 percent cost-of-living difference between Pittsburgh and the Washington area. Based on my current salary, that cost difference amounts to about $6,000 a year. That means it will cost me about $6,000 more a year to live in Washington. Joan, I'm sure you can appreciate that this is not a small amount. Is there some creative way we can address this issue? Would you consider, for example, providing me with a six-month salary review during my first year, rather than the normal one-year anniversary review? This would*

meet me part way and remove at least some of the burden of making this move until my salary has had a chance to make up this cost difference."

Again, this is a very reasonable request. In using this approach you have provided a legitimate reason for your request and have asked the employer whether they can help you address the issue. It also shows that you are willing to make some temporary sacrifice in the interest of accepting the job, but would like to ask the employer to share some of the financial burden.

Unless the employer absolutely cannot do so, there is a good possibility that they will see this as a reasonable request and grant the earlier salary review date. By then, salary ranges are likely to have increased, and the employer will feel a bit more comfortable with giving you the extra $2,000.

Get It in Writing

Don't ever accept an employment offer without getting the full details of the offer in writing. Sometimes memories are short and the details get lost in the shuffle. Getting the details in writing will provide you with the protection and assurance you need to accept the offer and know that the employer will abide by the terms to which the two parties have agreed.

Their Offer Is Too Low

You have already seen how a signing bonus or early salary review might serve to offset a low salary offer. Putting these techniques aside, however, what else can be done to address this problem?

One way is to be assertive and hit the issue head-on. You need to know that there are some risks involved when using some of the tactics suggested in this section. So, should you elect to use them, you need to be prepared for the possibility that the employer will walk away from the bargaining table and withdraw their offer completely. In other words, you might need to be prepared to either lose the job offer or walk away from the bargaining table yourself if you can't get the employer to budge on compensation.

Here is a more forceful, direct approach to negotiating salary. The following scenario will give you a feel for how this approach is likely to play out:

"Mike, I am very pleased to make you an offer, and we look forward to your joining our team. We would like to offer you a base salary of $90,000 a year. You would also be entitled to our excellent employee benefits package as well as participation in our annual bonus program. We are excited about the possibility of your joining our company and look forward to welcoming you aboard."

Now, we will assume the same scenarios as before. You were hoping for an offer in the $92,000 to $95,000 range; so this offer is too low for you to accept. Here is what you might say:

> *"Joan, I really appreciate the offer, and would very much like to join the team at ABC Company. I must admit, however, that I am somewhat disappointed with the offer. Is there any flexibility here?"*

Obviously, in employing this tactic, you are being very direct, and have clearly signaled to the employer that you are prepared to walk away if necessary. Quite frankly, there is either flexibility or there is not. You are about to find out. It is likely you will get one of two responses to your statement and your question concerning whether there is any flexibility. Let's examine both possible scenarios:

Scenario 1: Possible Flexibility

> *"Mike, I am sorry you are disappointed; we had thought this would be a reasonable and competitive offer. Let me go back to the drawing board and see if there is anything further we can do."*

In most cases, if you get this kind of response, the employer already knows they will be willing to do something. It might be to meet your requirements; to meet you partway; possibly offer a signing bonus, or, perhaps, an early/out-of-phase salary review. Although highly unlikely, the employer might return to the bargaining table to say that they need to stick with their original offer. At that point, you will need to make a decision based on what is presented.

Scenario 2: No Flexibility

In the event the employer feels they have made you their best offer, this is likely what they will say:

> *"Mike, we have considered all the possibilities here, and feel we have made you the best offer we can. I am sorry you are disappointed, but hope you can appreciate we have done the best we are able to do. We hope you will reconsider. We would certainly love to have you join the ABC Company."*

Well, at this point the ballgame is over. You have done your best to move the employer to a higher number, and there is nothing more to be had. It is either time to accept the offer or move on to the next opportunity.

Real Estate and Related Costs

When negotiating with the employer, an area sometimes overlooked by the inexperienced job seeker is the cost associated with buying and selling a house (i.e., real estate closing costs), and other miscellaneous expenses typically associated with a physical relocation. If the position will require you to relocate, sell your existing house, and purchase a new one, this is a consideration you will not want to ignore.

The costs associated with selling and buying real estate alone can be considerable and can prove financially devastating if they are not at least in part paid by the employer. Real estate commission (generally 7 percent) on a $250,000 house, for example, can cost $17,500. Depending on the size of the house and the distance of the move, the cost of shipping your household goods could easily add another $6,000 to $10,000. Add to that the cost of temporary living expenses in the new location while waiting to move into your new residence, and the cost of the entire move could easily be $25,000 to $30,000 or better.

So that you are not caught by surprise, here is a list of real estate and related moving expense items, the cost of which you might want to negotiate with the employer:

- House-hunting trip to the new location
- Shipment of household goods (and temporary storage, if necessary)
- Temporary living expenses (while waiting to move into new quarters)
- Double housing expense (if you need to carry two mortgages and incur other duplicate expenses on two homes while waiting for the old-location house to be sold)
- Third-party home-buying expense (if you anticipate difficulty in selling your old-location house)
- Sale closing costs (the closing costs incurred in connection with the sale of your old-location house)
- Purchase closing costs (closing costs incurred in buying a house in the new location and in securing a mortgage loan on the new property)
- Lease penalty fee or forfeited rent (if you need to end a house or apartment lease early)
- Tax gross-up for all moving expense reimbursement items recognized as taxable income by the IRS

As this list illustrates, the out-of-pocket expenses associated with moving go well beyond simple shipment of household goods, and can be substantial! It is important, therefore, that you take time to estimate them in advance so that you know what the price tag will be. This estimate will enable you to be more definitive when entering into discussions with the employer in regard to this matter.

It is difficult to suggest a specific strategy for negotiating reimbursement of many of these listed expenses because this is normally governed by company policy, which can vary considerably from employer to employer. Even within the same company, when transferring employees from one location to another, there can be a great deal of variance in reimbursement based on job level within the organization. I strongly recommend that you thoroughly investigate this topic during the interview or at the time of job-offer negotiations so that you fully understand the employer's position and can negotiate accordingly.

Here are some general questions you might use to explore this area:

- What is your policy regarding moving expense reimbursement?
- What specific items will the company reimburse?
- What moving expense items will the company not reimburse?
- Does the company gross-up reimbursed expenses for income tax purposes?

Answers to these questions will enable you to better understand the company's position and provide you with the information you need to intelligently negotiate for additional expense reimbursement, should this be necessary.

Chapter Summary

The key to effective job offer negotiations is effective planning and the use of specific strategy to get what you want. Key points to remember when preparing your negotiating strategy:

- Determine the financial parameters of the job (i.e., salary range and potential bonus payout).
- Research and understand what you are worth in today's marketplace (nationally, regionally, and within the local market in which the employer is situated).
- Assess the competitive environment in which you are competing (i.e., the number of other qualified candidates the company is interviewing).
- Determine the employer's urgency to fill the position.
- Use interview feedback to determine the employer's level of interest in hiring you.
- Consider cost-of-living differential (new vs. old location), and calculate a break-even salary (based on your current compensation level).
- Consider all out-of-pocket moving expenses associated with your physical relocation (if relocation is required).
- Determine the employer's relocation expense reimbursement policy to understand which costs are reimbursable by the company and which are not.
- Compare benefits coverage and costs to determine the extent of the employer's coverage and any additional out-of-pocket costs to you.
- Formulate and plan your offer strategy to include all financial parameters (compensation and expense reimbursement).
- Learn and practice the negotiating tactics and techniques in this chapter for getting the most out of your employment offer.

CHAPTER 16

A Formula for Success in Your New Job

Well, the job search is now behind you, and it's "Day One" of your new job. You've been assigned your desk, been introduced to your co-workers, and have just settled into your new digs. You're the new kid on the block, and feeling a bit awkward and somewhat alone.

The surroundings are all new, and you don't even know where the cafeteria or restroom is. Everybody seems cordial and friendly enough, but you really don't know any of them. You are wondering whether you're going to like them, and whether they will like you. There is some mail on the desk, but you're not sure where anything is, let alone where to start.

You have a 10:00 a.m. meeting with the new boss. That's almost an hour away, but you wish it were now. You feel useless and awkward just sitting there.

But there's also the bright side. You are excited about the new job and the new opportunity. The job sounded exciting during the interviews, and you are looking forward to digging into the challenges you had discussed. You feel confident you can make some positive contributions and have a real impact. You are glad to have left your old boss behind. The two of you were like oil and water and you felt a great deal of stress while working there.

Sharon Green, your new boss, seems to be a breath of fresh air. She's smart, knowledgeable, and very personable. She has a lot of energy and is enthusiastic about some of the new direction and improvements they are bringing about in the department. You can't wait to meet with her, but hope you'll still feel the same way six months from now. Who knows!

The First Day

Welcome to the first day of your new job. This wide range of emotions and mood swings is not uncommon for any new employee. Everyone goes through the same thing, no matter how competent and experienced they are. The first day is always an awkward time. You are dealing with a lot of change, a lot of unfamiliarity—new job, new colleagues, new environment, and new procedures. Nothing is familiar, and the learning curve is straight up. Amid all this turmoil, it's quite normal to feel a bit anxious and unsure of yourself. It will take time to make all the adjustments and acclimate to it all.

For most new employees the typical "honeymoon period" spans about five to six months, give or take a month or two. Although new employees can begin to make substantive contributions much sooner than this, it normally takes this long to reach the point where they feel their contributions are noticed and they are finally beginning to feel comfortable with the new job and work environment.

At the very beginning, things will seem a bit out of control. There is a lot of uncertainty. You are attempting to get some initial direction and focus, and start to "mesh" with the operations of the department. Despite these initial feelings of helplessness, you need to jump in, seize the initiative, and begin moving things in a positive direction. You need to move quickly to "size up" the situation and get a toehold as fast as you can.

There are a number of things you can do to get through this awkward stage rapidly and begin to establish a positive reputation as a solid contributor. The first step in this process is to get a sense of focus—to set some firm goals and a plan to get you there. This all begins with that first meeting with your new boss.

Meeting with the New Boss

In going into this initial meeting with the new boss, it's a good idea to have an overall plan as well as some concrete objectives. The key to short-term job success is very simple: "You need to please your boss." So, the overlying objective of this meeting needs to be understanding what kinds of accomplishments will cause your new boss to be extremely pleased with your performance and generate good feelings about his or her decision to hire you.

So, in this initial meeting, there are a number of items you will need to get "nailed down" before you can begin to formulate a plan for job success. Here is a list of these important items:

- What are the boss's overall expectations of you in the job?
- What are the key things that need to be accomplished?
- What improvements would the boss like to see in the way the job is performed?
- What are the key problems or issues that need to be addressed, and what results would the boss like to see in these areas?

- From a business-strategy perspective, what changes or improvements need to be made to support any new or emerging business needs and initiatives?
- Considering all of the preceding topics, what are the main priorities—those things the boss would most like to see accomplished?
- What process does the boss like to use in monitoring and tracking job performance?
- What is the boss's process for providing both short- and longer-term performance feedback?
- Is there a formal performance evaluation process? If so, how often is evaluation carried out, and how does the process work?

Based on the preceding list of questions, it should be clear that there is much you need to know before you can begin to formulate a plan for job success.

One of the biggest mistakes new employees make when starting a new job is not establishing a clear understanding of the new boss's expectations and priorities, right from the beginning. Instead of achieving a clear understanding of these critical factors at the start, the new hire may simply dig in and begin working, only to find out six months later, despite working very hard, that the boss is not impressed with what has been accomplished. Instead, the employee is told the boss has concerns about the need to improve performance in specific areas and to focus more attention on other needs and priorities on which the employee has not been working.

This is not the kind of feedback you will want to receive six months into a new job! If you fail to establish firm expectations and priorities at the onset, you can end up disappointed and with one foot in the ditch. Just working hard alone does not guarantee job success. You need to be working on the "right" things and delivering the "right" results—results that your boss will value. Unless you are clear, right from the start, and have aligned your work plan and priorities with the needs and priorities of your new boss, you are shooting in the dark and may be headed for some disappointment.

Contracting with the Boss

Once you have gotten answers to the important questions in the preceding section and you feel you understand the new boss's expectations and priorities, you need to get confirmation of this during a second meeting. You will want to set the stage for such a meeting during this initial session. In order to do so, you might say something like this:

> *"Thanks for the overview, Barbara. This has been helpful. If it's okay with you, what I would like to do now is go back to my office and take some time to digest what we just discussed. I would like to summarize what I believe I heard and then establish some basic priorities. Could we meet either later today or tomorrow morning to take a look at my list? I would appreciate your input. I want to make sure I am focusing on those things you feel are most important and are the priority issues you need me to address."*

In almost all cases, your boss will be more than happy to accommodate your request for a second meeting. During this second meeting, you will want to hand a copy of your priority list to your boss and, after discussion, arrive at agreement on the order of these priorities as well as the desired results for each.

Formulating Your Success Plan

Now that you are clear on the priorities and results your new boss expects of you, you need to formulate a performance plan that will all but guarantee success in your new job. Since you need to begin to establish an effective working relationship with your new boss, you will want to take advantage of this natural opportunity to get him or her involved in some of the planning process. Moreover, you will want to be sure, no matter what plan you have developed, that the new boss is in full agreement and will be fully supportive of the actions you are planning to take.

The Planning Process

Any good performance plan is based on the need for improvement in certain aspects of the job. Having met with your new boss and finalized your list of priorities, you already know which aspects of the job need to be improved. Additionally, based on this discussion, you should also have a pretty clear understanding of the type or degree of improvement the boss would most like to see in each of these improvement areas.

At this stage, you have already established some specific objectives or "end states" you will want to achieve. The next step in formulating your success plan is to perform an *end-state analysis* for each of the targeted improvement areas.

Performing an End-State Analysis

The process of end-state analysis begins by describing, as best you can, the end state or final result needed for each of your objectives. To measure progress against your goal and know when the goal has been achieved, you need to define the parameters by which success will be measured. Wherever possible, these should be defined using measurable, quantitative criteria.

The following are examples of end-state goals or objectives:

- Reduce operating costs by 10 percent.
- Reduce hiring cycle time by 20 percent.
- Reduce inventory investment by 15 percent.

The next step in end-state analysis is to define the *current state* of each of the targeted improvement areas. Using the preceding examples, you will want to know the following:

- Current operating costs
- Current hiring cycle times
- Current inventory investment

Having established both the desired end state and the current state for each targeted improvement area, the next step is to determine the *performance gap*. The performance gap is the difference between the end state and the current state. It is the degree of improvement that must be realized if you are to achieve your desired performance objective or end-state goal.

Barrier Analysis

Now that you know what areas need improvement (the priorities), what the objectives are (the performance goals or desired end state), and how much improvement is needed (the performance gap), you need to determine what specific actions you need to take in order to close these performance gaps and achieve the goals you have set. This combination of stated goals, plus action steps to be taken, then comprises your entire job success plan.

In order to complete this last step in the planning process, you need to perform some basic *barrier analysis*. This simply means you need to take a look at the obstacles or barriers standing in the way (those that are preventing the goal from being achieved) and plan some specific actions to address and remove these barriers.

Here are some basic questions to help stimulate your thinking:

- What key barriers stand in the way of achieving these goals?
- Which are the principal barriers (those having greatest impact)?
- Why do these barriers exist?
- What are the variables that affect these barriers?
  - People?
  - Practices?
  - Things?
- Which of these variables can be controlled?
  - By you?
  - By others?
- Which of these variables cannot be controlled?
- Who needs to be involved in making the necessary changes?
- What specific actions or steps do you need to take in order to remove these barriers and achieve the principal performance goals you have set?

Sample Job Success Plan

The following example of a partial job success plan for an employment manager illustrates what a final plan might look like.

Goal:

Reduce employment-agency fee expense by 20 percent ($90,000).

Action Steps

- Increase use of niche boards to identify qualified candidates.
- Increase use of major Internet job boards to advertise jobs.
- Train the administrative assistant in basic candidate research techniques.
- Take a course in using Web crawlers to identify passive candidates.
- Establish a basic infrastructure to support the "direct sourcing" process.
- Begin using "direct sourcing" to identify candidates for more senior positions.
- Negotiate fee reduction with principal agencies from 20 percent to 15 percent.

The following example illustrates a partial job success plan for a production manager working in a manufacturing plant.

Goal:

Reduce product-manufacturing costs by 10 percent (from $2.00 to $1.80 per unit).

Action Steps

- Reduce raw materials inventory.
- Implement just-in-time raw material delivery.
- Reduce spare parts inventory.
- Implement just-in-time spare parts delivery.
- Work with Purchasing to negotiate raw materials contract price reductions.
- Search for new raw material suppliers.
- Work with plant engineering to identify and eliminate production bottlenecks.
- Track down and eliminate principal sources of waste.
- Initiate predicative maintenance program to reduce unscheduled downtime.
- Form and lead cost-reduction team (get employees involved).

Getting the New Boss's "Buy-In"

If you have taken your performance/success plan to the level just shown, you are on the right track. You now have goals and specific action steps well established. You now need to get your new boss's "buy-in" on your plan.

Because you are new to the department, you may lack sufficient knowledge about the operation and its people to know whether your plan is practical and achievable. Additionally, there may be some history that suggests that some of your ideas have already been tried and will absolutely not work in the new environment. So, before going to your new boss for his or her input and final plan approval, it might be a good move to discuss your proposed plan with others in the organization who can give you some historical insight as well as additional ideas for improving it.

Once you have incorporated any last-minute changes and ideas into the plan, you are ready to meet with your new boss for his or her thoughts and final blessing. In meeting with your boss during this second session, you will want to present him or her with a copy of your performance plan, including both the goals you have set as well as the action steps you have planned. Tell the boss that you would like to start by reaffirming that the goals and priorities you have established are completely aligned with his or her thinking. Also indicate that you would like to jointly review your planned action steps for any ideas or suggestions he or she may have as well.

Once you have jointly reviewed and finalized your performance plan, tell your new boss that you would like to meet from time to time to update him or her on progress toward your goals. Suggest monthly meetings or whatever time frame seems reasonable based on the specifics of your plan and the goals you have set.

You are now in great shape to move ahead with your plan. You have put in place what is needed to ensure your success, and you are now fully aligned with your new boss's needs and priorities. The only thing that remains to be accomplished is for you to carry out your plan and to achieve the goals on which your new boss and you have agreed.

Emulating Success

Beyond establishing a performance plan, there are other steps that you can take to ensure job success. One of these is to be a good observer. As you become acclimated to your new environment and begin to implement your performance plan, take a good look around. It doesn't take very long to realize that certain employees are considered to be "high flyers." They are easy to spot. These are the employees to whom management seems to listen. These are the ones whose careers are on the rise. They are the ones who are frequently promoted and who are given the juicier assignments. It is clear that management holds them in high regard and values their thoughts and ideas. In the company cafeteria, these are the handful of employees who more senior executives seem to search out, sit down with, and enjoy talking to.

Especially have a good look around your own business function. Whether you are in accounting, operations, human resources, law, or another business area, see whether you can spot these individuals early in your career and make a conscious effort to built relationships with them. Observe them closely, and ask yourself the following questions:

- What is unique or different about these individuals?
- How are they different from others in the organization?

- What skills, traits, abilities, and characteristics seem to account for their success?
- When they are in a meeting, how do they behave?
- What do they say, or how do they present their ideas that seems to win management's support?
- Who do they associate with, and what is the nature of this relationship?

You should make it your mission to discover the pattern that seems to account for their widespread acceptance and obvious management support. They must be doing something different from the rest. What is it?

If you are a good observer and student, you might be able to pick up some helpful clues on ways you can modify your own behavior to emulate this success pattern. For example, it might cause you to change who you go to see for approvals and support or how you might change your presentation style or approach to win support for your plans and ideas.

Learn what you can, always looking for ways to be better at what you do and how you do it. Observe the behaviors, values, and beliefs that seem so important to success in this new company environment. And, without compromising your own values and beliefs, consciously modify some of your own behaviors to better align with those behaviors that the organization seems to value and reward.

And, finally, remember the old adage, "You are judged by the company you keep." So, make sure you are in the very best of company. Some of the "halo effect" definitely rubs off.

Aligning with Sources of Power

Obviously, the most significant source of power is your own boss. I have already discussed in some detail how to best align yourself with this person. However, you need to look more broadly than this.

Who are the real power brokers in the organization? Who are the ones, further up in the organizational ladder, who appear to be the real decision-makers? And, of these individuals, who are the ones most likely to have the greatest impact on your career? This could be your boss's boss or other executives within your business function who are in a position to observe you and will have a major say in your career. Or, they could be managers or executives in other business functions to whom you provide service. Think broadly about who these important people are and make a short list of their names.

Although pleasing your boss should be your number-one priority, you will also want to cultivate relationships with these other important individuals, whom you need to get to know. Look for frequent opportunities to deal with them so that they have the opportunity to get to know you.

Meet Your "Clients"

This is especially easy to do if you are in a function that provides a support service to another business function (your client). As a new employee, you have the perfect opportunity to get this relationship off to an excellent start, and to impress your client with your concern for their welfare. Within the first few days in your new job, call to arrange a meeting with each of your key "clients." Tell them you would like to meet them, but are also interested in getting some general feedback as well as their ideas on how your function could improve overall service to their organization or group.

When meeting with your new client, here are some questions that should help you open up meaningful dialogue:

- "How do you generally feel about the overall service you have been getting from our function?"

- "From your viewpoint, what has been going well as far as the service you have been getting?"

- "In what areas would you like to see improvement? Can you be specific? What kind of improvement would you like to see?"

- "Which of these is most important to you?"

- "What ideas do you have on how we could improve in these areas?"

Certainly these kinds of questions are going to be impressive and create a very positive reaction. However, they will also create a certain level of expectation as well. So, you will want to deliver!

Take Action on What You Have Learned

To reinforce the initial positive impression you have created with the client, you will want to initiate some immediate steps to demonstrate your commitment to improving service in those areas identified as improvement opportunities. Because you have asked the client to designate which of these improvement areas is most important, you should focus on these areas first.

Perhaps, if your client has periodic staff meetings, you might ask to join them. In this way, you can stay abreast of what is happening in their world and formulate additional actions you can take to support their overall efforts. In addition to the visibility this creates, it provides a perfect opportunity to demonstrate your sense of urgency and responsiveness to any of the client's issues or new needs, thus establishing a strong positive relationship. Moreover, you will begin to be seen as a valuable member of their team, rather than an outsider.

There is a saying among service organizations, "When the client is happy, everyone is happy!" If you are going to experience a high level of job success, you will want to be highly attentive and responsive to the needs of your clients.

Impressing the Power Sources Within Your Own Function

When it comes to aligning with power sources in your own business function, the best way to accomplish this is to simply perform well. You should not only shoot to meet the goals to which you and your boss have agreed, but you will also want to exceed these goals. If you want your career to really take off quickly, you should willingly take on additional work and goals beyond what is expected.

It won't take long for you to be recognized by those who are above you. You will find there will be opportunities to make presentations to them, highlighting major accomplishments or planned improvement initiatives. As you continue to consistently deliver results and exceed expectations, you will be looked at as the "go-to" person. You are someone they can consistently depend upon to "get it done." And, when it comes time to fill a key vacancy on their staff, who do you think they are going to think of? You, of course!

Chapter Summary

There is much you can do to guarantee success in your new job and in your career. When starting a new job, you need to seize the opportunity immediately. Here are some key pointers to ensure success:

- Get clear on your new boss's key needs and priorities.
- Establish concrete goals that will satisfy these needs.
- Prepare an action plan to accomplish these goals.
- Get your new boss's "buy in" and support of your plan.
- Set up periodic "progress review meetings" with your boss to report on progress against your goals and get periodic performance feedback.
- Meet and, wherever possible, exceed all plan goals.
- Form close working relationships with your clients.
- Get clear on clients' needs and priorities, right from the beginning.
- Take immediate action to demonstrate your commitment to satisfying client needs and priorities.
- Emulate success—study and emulate others who are "known successes" and are treated favorably by senior management.
- Identify and cultivate relationships with those in power, and who will directly impact your career.

INDEX

K–L

M

X–Z

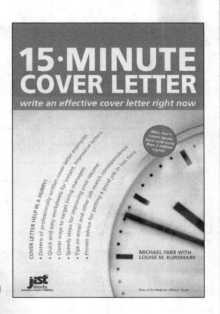

JIST Order and Catalog Request Form

Purchase Order #: _____
(Required by some organizations)

Billing Information

Organization Name: _____
Accounting Contact: _____
Street Address: _____
_____
_____
City, State, ZIP: _____
Phone Number: ( ) _____

Please copy this form if you need more lines for your order.

Phone: 1-800-648-JIST
Fax: 1-800-JIST-FAX
World Wide Web Address:
www.jist.com

Shipping Information with Street Address
(If Different from Above)

Organization Name: _____
Contact: _____
Street Address: (We *cannot* ship to P.O. boxes) _____
_____
_____
City, State, ZIP: _____
Phone Number: ( ) _____

Credit Card Purchases:
VISA_____ MC_____ AMEX_____
Card Number: _____
Exp. Date: _____
Name As on Card: _____
Signature: _____

Quantity	Order Code	Product Title	Unit Price	Total

jist ®
Publishing
8902 Otis Avenue
Indianapolis, IN 46216

Shipping Fees

In the continental U.S. add 7% of subtotal:
• Minimum amount charged = $5.00
• FREE shipping and handling on any prepaid orders over $50.00
Above pricing is for regular ground shipment only. For rush or special delivery, call JIST Customer Service at 1-800-648-JIST for the correct shipping fee.

Outside the continental U.S. call JIST Customer Service at 1-800-648-JIST for an estimate of these fees.

Payment in U.S. funds only!

Subtotal	
+Shipping (See left)	
+6% Sales Tax *Indiana Residents*	
TOTAL	

JIST thanks you for your order!